D1017193

Georgette
Mosbache

Feminine
FORCE

*Release
the Power
Within to
Create the Life
You Deserve*

Simon & Schuster
New York   London   Toronto   Sydney   Tokyo   Singapore

SIMON & SCHUSTER
Simon & Schuster Building
Rockefeller Center
1230 Avenue of the Americas
New York, New York 10020

Copyright © 1993 by Georgette Mosbacher

All rights reserved
including the right of reproduction
in whole or in part in any form.

SIMON & SCHUSTER and colophon are registered trademarks
of Simon & Schuster Inc.

Designed by Levavi & Levavi
Manufactured in the United States of America

10 9 8 7 6 5 4 3 2 1

Library of Congress Cataloging-in-Publication Data
Mosbacher, Georgette, date.
    Feminine force : release the power within to create the life you
deserve / by Georgette Mosbacher.
       p.   cm.
    1. Mosbacher, Georgette, date.   2. Women—United States—
Biography.   3. Women—Psychology.   4. Success.   I. Title.
HQ1413.M67A3   1993
305.42'092—dc20
    [B]   93-25315
                                                                          CIP

ISBN: 0-671-79896-0

Acknowledgments

I'd like to gratefully acknowledge the contribution of my collaborator, Deborah Bergman. With her insight and patience she helped me choose the right words.

My sister Lyn Paulsin worked tirelessly, going through photographs, working on details, and reading draft after draft. I thank her for loyalty and constant support. My brother George was generous to allow me to tell the story of his alcoholism. And I must acknowledge my sister Melody for her example. She's a woman who really is doing it all.

Thanks to Kathy Banks for her astute judgment and helping hand. Thanks to Gila Sand and Rebecca Presley for listening to and transcribing hours and hours of tape, to Gabriela Schwartz, who graciously assisted beyond the call of duty, and to Barney Stein and Jane Fleming, who were there in a pinch.

A special thank you to Horst for all the beautiful photographs he so generously let me use, and to Pat Harrison who was there in the very beginning and encouraged me to tell my story. Ron Greenberg and Marty Michael were ever present to guide me through. And many thanks to Vlad Gastevich who held my hand through that very first meeting with Simon & Schuster.

If it were not for the tenacity and Feminine Force my editor Judith Regan brought to this project, there would be no book. She was the one who convinced me I should do it. She was the one who believed in my story and supported me the whole way.

And thanks to all those other women I've met along my journey who have not only enhanced the ride but have gifted me with an even greater knowledge of our collective Feminine Force.

Last but by no means least:

A loving thank you to my husband Robert Mosbacher for his belief in me and his assistance in helping me to heal the wounds of the past.

*For the Feminine Forces in my life: my mother,
Dorothy Paulsin, my grandmother, Mary Bell, and
my great-grandmother, Pauline Navlan*

Contents

I Love Being a Woman

"Nothing in life is to be feared. It is only to be understood."

—M<small>ARIE</small> C<small>URIE</small>

T he day I decided to write this book was a day like many others. I spent it on the road for La Prairie—the skin care company I owned before I formed my current company, Exclusives by Georgette Mosbacher.

On this particular day my sister Lyn and I had gotten up at five forty-five A.M. in Los Angeles to travel to Tucson to make an in-store appearance at around ten A.M. After spending the day in the department store, we prepared to move on to an evening in New Orleans, where I would give two talks to women's groups.

Lyn often traveled with me. She organized all my business appearances for the company—coordinating with our reps, prepping the department store staff, setting up media interviews. In the most hectic, high-pressure situations, she was amazing. She had become my right arm at work. For a year she'd been traveling and working from her home base near Chicago. Now she was about to make a move. She had separated from her husband, and was coming to New York to work out of the main office. Lyn had made herself indispensable at La Prairie, and had grown to love the business. She was ready to take the next step up the career ladder.

The flight to New Orleans that evening was the first and only opportunity we would have that day to catch our breath. So after take-off, as we settled back with cups of tea, Lyn began to confide in me about her pending divorce. The two of us began to talk about love, and then the subject turned to the inevitable sadness and anxiety you go through with a divorce. Lyn's was proving to be very amicable as divorces go. But, of course, there were still going to be changes and regrets.

I knew what that was like. I'd been there. For a while the terrain we traveled was bittersweet, but familiar. And then my sister shocked me.

"Sometimes," Lyn confided, "I just feel totally overwhelmed. Here I am getting a divorce. I'm in my thirties. I never went to college. I don't really have a professional background. Everyone around me seems smarter and more sophisticated than I am. I don't think I'll *ever* find someone to love me. Why should anyone? What have I got to offer? I don't really *deserve* it. *I don't feel I really deserve to be loved.*"

Nothing could have prepared me for *this.* I was stung. How could my sister's image of herself be so far from the truth? How could I be hearing this from this truly spectacular woman—a woman I'd watched skillfully handle a hundred and one problems in the past twenty-four hours alone? The same beautiful and competent woman who'd worked so effectively with me in so many, many high-pressure situations? My eyes welled up with tears.

I was dumbfounded. Lyn was so close to me, and yet I'd blissfully gone along thinking she was sure of herself and aware of her own inner resources. That she had them was obvious to anyone who met her. I'd assumed she knew how to gather her strength and focus herself. I relied on Lyn. Didn't she know what she had to offer?

I had to do something. Lyn was a grown woman, but I still felt like a big sister, and I felt as if I'd failed her. We worked together every day. How was it possible that I hadn't sensed what she was going through? *How was it possible she could think such a thing about herself?*

But I knew the answer to that. It was as possible for her as it was for all the other women I talked to around the country as I made those in-store appearances and gave those speeches. So many of them came up to the counter and said, "You know, I've been through a rough time. I need help." And as the technicians sat them down and we began to make them over, they'd tell us their stories. Many of those stories were no different from the one I was hearing right now. Or from my own personal history. So yes, it was possible for Lyn to feel this way about herself as it had been for me to think those things about myself at many points in my own life.

But that didn't mean that I didn't have to do something about it.

So I turned to Lyn in my narrow plane seat, took her by the shoulders, and looked her straight in the eyes. Then I told her that the time had come to start acknowledging what a terrific, competent, deserving, and lovable woman she actually was—and always had been. The time had come for her to acknowledge that she *herself* was all she needed to create that life she deserved, and that her innate inner resources were more than ample to do the job.

"Lyn," I said, "I've been there. Boy, have I been there. And let me share a little something that worked for me. Every night before you go to bed, you must stop, review your day, and identify at least one thing you did that you feel good about. At least one thing, and hopefully more. It doesn't matter how small your achievement may seem or how hard you have to work to find it. Do NOT go to bed until you have identified it and written it down. And in the morning when you get up, you are going to look in the mirror while you read that accomplishment out loud and tell yourself how terrific it is, no matter how small or insignificant it might seem."

I told Lyn that if she made that list every night and congratulated herself every morning, it would become easier and easier for her to recognize exactly how much she *did* accomplish and just how valuable a person she was. Sure, she had room for improvement here and there. None of us is perfect. But it was time to concentrate on her strengths. It was time for her to acknowledge what a powerful, feminine, and lovable woman she really was.

At first she was skeptical. She thought this was a little simplistic. But she tried it anyway.

And it worked. Lyn's nightly list of achievements started to grow longer and longer. And as it did, she began to put her defeats into their proper perspective.

It was her first step in discovering what I call her Feminine Force.

The Feminine Force is my way of describing the intangible but indelible powers or energies that all women are born with but that many of us lose somewhere along life's way. The Feminine Force operates according to its own principles and moves uniquely through each of us. Yet once any part of the Feminine Force is unleashed, it can map the way for all women through the uncharted and unfamiliar terrain of our own possibilities.

Today women are at what I call the "what is" point in our lives. But what interests me more than "what is" is the possibility, the potential, the *"what can be."* And the Feminine Force is what turns "what is" into "what can be."

What happened in the plane between Tucson and New Orleans that night convinced me that I wanted to share what I've learned, to show other women the possibilities of their own lives, to convey my deep belief in leaving behind any negativism in our lives and creating the beautiful and fulfilling lives we deserve.

Reflecting on both the bitter and the sweet in my life, I realize that I have lived in some ways an extraordinary life, even though I am *not in any way* an extraordinary woman.

Some people look at me and say: "Oh, it was easy for her. She's good-looking. She's sexy. She married three successful men. She has money. She could never relate to *my* life."

Well, wait until you hear my story.

First, I wasn't born beautiful. I just learned how to *make* myself as beautiful as I can be. Believe me! Just look at the back cover of this book.

Second, I was not born to privilege—far from it. But I was privileged to be born into a family whose values gave me the strength and the tools I needed to face the challenges that would come my way.

Furthermore, I wasn't a whiz kid who took the high road from an Ivy League college to an executive position in business. I was a *very* average student who worked my way through school, doing ironing and waiting on tables. And believe me, I learned many of my lessons the hard way.

Yes, I'm now married to a wonderful, generous man, and I enjoy a very comfortable life with him. But I'm proud to say that my financial security is something I don't depend on my husband to give me. I've won my own financial independence. I've owned and run one successful business, and I've embarked upon a second that I'm building from scratch.

But as happy and as comfortable as I am now, there are still days that I get scared. Days that I'm scared for myself and my employees and my family. Days that I wonder if I'm doing the right thing. In fact, not a day goes by that I don't have to talk myself through the rough spots.

Even though I've had my share of difficulties in life, mine is not a book about being victimized. This book is a celebration. It celebrates the Feminine Force that got me through and helped me live a remarkably rewarding life. I LOVE being a woman. I've never wanted to be anything *but* a woman. That's why I'm dismayed when I see women focus on the idea that as women, we are victims.

As I searched my soul to write this book, I kept coming back to the turning point of my growing from being a girl to being a woman, the moment I realized that "life isn't fair" and that I was going to have to take care of myself. That is the moment when every woman has to call on her innate power—to transform her life in ways she may never have imagined.

For me, it happened after I experienced a family tragedy at the age of seven. It may have happened to you much later in life or when you discovered that there is still an "old boys' club" that you don't belong to. Or it may hit you when, after buying into the fairy tale that a man will take care of you, you discover that you have naively entrusted your emotional and financial security to someone else.

But however that moment comes, and *come it does,* once the initial shock subsides, we only have two choices. We can throw up our hands and surrender to life's cruel ways and become victims. Or we can shake off the terror, stand a bit taller, and say to ourselves: "Life isn't fair? So what? I have what it takes to fight my battles, and with hard work and dedication, I can create the life I choose. By myself. I don't need to lean on others. I have everything I need right here inside."

That is the moment of discovering your Feminine Force.

The Feminine Force is a sense of mastery, the feeling that you've jumped a hurdle. By leaping over one of the most negative roadblocks life can throw at you, you've discovered one of the most positive and inspirational secrets life can yield.

When you tap your Feminine Force, you've learned that to create the life you deserve, you need no one but yourself and no one's approval but your own. You've found, inside yourself, something uniquely female and uniquely liberating that can help you achieve something, and I mean *anything,* in life.

Once unleashed, the Feminine Force doesn't just show you how to triumph over adversity. It comes in handy in good times too. It *creates* good times. Yes, my Feminine Force empowered me to leave an abusive marriage. But it also showed me how to experience joy. It reminded me that life is a candy store. It allowed me to create happiness and abundance and delight. It propelled me right into the arms of a man who cherishes me. And it has given me the ultimate freedom and happiness of personal financial independence, an achievement that allows me to nurture myself and others in my life without worry or limitation.

The Force is certainly not mine alone. Women everywhere, from all walks of life, are already out there, tapping into the Force to achieve their goals. Perhaps you recall a story from the front page of *The New York Times* about a woman named Ladeeta Gaynell Smith, an eighteen-year-old from Bedford-Stuyvesant in Brooklyn whose mother and father both died recently, one from AIDS, the other from alcoholism. Ladeeta's story is inspirational because she is not wallowing in self-pity and she is not looking to blame someone else for her situation. Rather, she takes care of her brothers and sisters as well as attending to her grades so she can go to college in the fall. As the story read: "Ladeeta has survived almost every plague of adolescence in neighborhoods defined by hopeless girls with babies and angry boys with guns." Ladeeta has made her plans and she is working with what *is* today to accomplish what *can be* tomorrow. She will soon leave her crack-ridden neighborhood and enter college.

How did Ladeeta do it? She called on her Feminine Force to accomplish her goals. As she told the *Times* reporter: "I know Mommy would want me to go on, she would not want me to sit around and cry. If I get down and start doing poorly, who knows how long it would take me to get back up?"

And then there is the story of Judy Resnick, a woman who ten years ago was destitute with two teenage daughters to feed, no money, no husband, and no family. Judy's story was published recently in *Forbes* magazine. A native of Los Angeles, Judy had grown up in an affluent family and her father had always taken care of her. When she got into an abusive marriage, she walked out and leaned on her dad. Then, he died suddenly and a few months later she lost her sister and her mother in a plane crash. She found herself unexpectedly penniless with two girls to raise, having never worked a day in her life.

Instead of being undone by this string of tragedies, Judy summoned up her Feminine Force and elbowed her way into the brokerage business. She took control of her own life and relied on herself for the strength and tools to achieve her goals. She knew she couldn't be a winner and a whiner at the same time. Merrill Lynch wouldn't even interview her and Shearson offered her a secretarial job. Undaunted, she kept plugging away. Finally, she was hired by Drexel Burnham to be a stockbroker trainee. Now, just ten years later, she co-owns her own brokerage firm in Los Angeles that manages hundreds of millions of dollars for clients.

Judy and Ladeeta are not victims. They don't view themselves as victims and won't allow others to view them as victims. I don't know them personally, but I recognize their Feminine Force.

Blaming is very dangerous. When you blame other people, you hand to them control and power over your own life. The victim state eats away at your dignity and self-respect and undermines your ability to tap into your Feminine Force.

Your Feminine Force is the key to a fulfilled and successful future. If Ladeeta Smith, Judy Resnick, and I could do it—then you can *certainly* do it, too.

This book will show you how—based on my hard-won life experience—to tap the Force within your own life and to create the results that *you* want to create. This book offers no theories, no hypotheses, and no statistics. Just one woman's hard-won wisdom, and a realization born one night, on a plane from Tucson to New Orleans, that there was something I urgently needed to share with my sister.

Now I want to share it with you.

Chapter **1**

And I Was Supposed to Be the Strong One

"What does not kill me makes me stronger."

—ALBERT CAMUS

It was a warm night in New York, but the room was as cold as ice.

"I almost forget how stupid you truly are," the man on the couch was saying. "But then you remind me." Or maybe he was saying, "I thought you said these curtains were peach. They're not peach, they're pink. Can't get too far in the cosmetics business if you're color blind." Then again it could have been, "Your presentation today was the worst I've ever seen."

It didn't really matter what he said. He may have said all of it, or he may have said something else entirely. What really mattered was that he was on his sixth or seventh vodka, I was numb and terrified, and this scene was playing out not for the first, or even the tenth, but probably the hundredth time.

It all blended together now in one long emotional spasm: the bullying, the berating, the rage, the drunkenness. I was married to a powerful man who abused alcohol and people. I was living inside a cage of solitary misery. When we went out to dinner it was to a restaurant where the staff would fawn over him because he paid them to. Anyone who joined us belonged to a coterie of those beholden to him. No one

19

who didn't need him would fawn over the legendary George Barrie, or G.B., as I called him. He was just too mean. I never felt so lonely in my life as I did when I was surrounded with his entourage of yes men. Of course, G.B. could be charming and even seem attentive to me, as he told his stories or played the piano or a saxophone that was almost as tall as he was. My husband's love for music was his one attractive feature. But I never felt valued by G.B. or respected by his friends. I always knew that if I remarked how white the tablecloth was, and G.B. replied, "No, Georgette, it's pitch black," everyone in our group would agree with him unconditionally.

As soon as he was out of earshot, the same people would warn me to get away while I could, because G.B. was abusive to me. They'd tell me how he surrounded himself with vulnerable people, people he knew he could control. My husband traveled in a private plane and was not only powerful but a true Renaissance man who had composed the Oscar-nominated music for the film *A Touch of Class*. He also produced the movie. But no one who didn't need him would tolerate him.

Unfortunately, a lot of people needed G.B. because he was a king-maker. He was the CEO of Fabergé, and despite his unremarkable appearance and speech, he was a powerful, brilliant man. When I'd met him in Los Angeles at the end of my first marriage, Fabergé also owned Brut, a film production company. G.B. had the clout to make you a corporate mogul or a star.

I needed him the way everyone else needed him. I wanted glamour, and I wanted power. I was riding high then, and I'd indulged myself in thinking I was different than the rest. I'd been very lucky, very young and very quickly. I had only been in California one week at the age of twenty-three when I met my first husband, a caring, generous, and wealthy man. I was a working-class girl from Indiana. I'd practically raised my three younger siblings, and after a brief stop in Detroit I'd come to Los Angeles to make a better life for myself. I'd always dreamed of being able to provide for my family, and suddenly I could. Living in a beautiful home, being able to afford a housekeeper, wearing beautiful clothes that didn't come from the Salvation Army—these things were suddenly mine. I was so sure that conquering the entertainment business with someone like G.B. at my side would be just as easy. All I had to do was attach myself to him and watch my career soar. Was I ever naive. And shallow to think there was such a thing as an easy way.

And I was so wrong, so disastrously wrong to ignore all the warnings. I foolishly believed I was the one who would tame G.B. I rued the day I decided he was a man who could make my dreams come true. I rued the day I decided that I was invincible.

But I had, and now we were married. Things had gone bad long before we made it legal. By the time we said our vows, our relationship was very destructive. I knew I'd been totally, utterly wrong about him and about me. I wasn't invincible; I was vanquished. Choosing to be with G.B. had been a terrible mistake, and I was sure I'd used up all my chances to be lucky. The first marriage I'd decided to leave because I thought it stifled me now seemed like heaven. Strange as it may seem, I think I married G.B. as a way to end the relationship with him. "Georgette," I said to myself, "you're going to have to marry the guy to divorce him." And now the time had come. I wanted desperately to get out but didn't know how.

My desperation must have showed that night, because G.B. was berating me even more severely than usual. A bully always knows when he has you cornered. Those are the moments he lives for, when he knows he can move in for the kill. So he kept talking. I shot back, contradicting him. The liquor flowed, and the words became sharper and meaner.

And then he leaned forward. I flinched, half hoping he'd fall over in a stupor. It wouldn't be the first time. But instead he reached out and punched me hard in the face.

I reeled back, gasping. Pain burst through my nose and cheek. In my entire life, no one had ever struck me. Sobbing, terrified, furious, I grabbed my purse and ran out into the night. I hailed a cab, and told the cabby to take me to the hospital. I could feel my nose swelling and I prayed it wasn't broken.

Not at all concerned, G.B. didn't follow me.

I quivered with relief as the doctor told me my nose wasn't broken. But even as my body was attended to, fear after fear passed through me: Where was I going to go next? How was I going to sever the ties to this man who controlled so much of my life? I worked for G.B. now, and both my career and my salary were very important to me. Was I going to go to work in the morning? How could I *not* go to work? My husband was wealthy, but I wasn't. I needed my income; it was all I had of my own, and not only that, I was my grandmother's sole financial support. This man I had built a life around was perfectly capable of undercutting my financial security and that of my family.

If I wasn't going to go home, where was I going to go? How much security would a hotel room buy me anyway? How had I, the oldest child who had practically raised her three younger siblings, the one everyone *else* counted on for good advice, gotten into this situation? Who could I tell? What could I do? I was so disoriented, so lost. I had no idea where I was in life, and I had no idea where I was going.

As I left the hospital my instincts walked me straight to a pay phone. But as I raised the quarter to the slot, I froze.

Who on earth could I call? I was the one in my family who always solved all the problems. My mother and grandmother and sisters and brother all came to me—I didn't go to them. I wasn't supposed to be vulnerable and needy. I began to think of friends. But there weren't any friends in New York who were my friends—they were all *his* friends. I had foolishly sacrificed my own life in so many ways and attached myself almost exclusively to his world. I had no one to blame but myself. I had allowed this to happen.

I put the quarter back in my wallet. The moment had come to look reality square in the face. I'd spent the last four years isolating myself from everyone who cared about me. G.B. had helped, of course—an abuser always tries to separate you from the ones you love. But the onus was on me. As G.B. insidiously undermined my self-esteem, I loathed myself more and more for letting him. As the private planes soared and champagne bubbles flowed, my sense of self plummeted and crashed. As my life got more and more divorced from my values, I started to hide everything from those who loved me. I simply didn't want them to know how lost and numb I was, how far I had gone from the person they had known. There was no one left in my corner but me. I was the only person who could get myself out of this.

I'd tried to leave him before, but fear of being worthless without him had brought me back every time. In a city where I knew no one else the structure of the life we had together was the only structure I knew, and I needed structure. I felt my only chance was to try to make what I had work. I hadn't had enough life experience to know that being rich and successful and married to a powerful man didn't guarantee you personal fulfillment and self-respect. I hadn't realized that in some cases sacrificing your sense of self was the price you paid.

But I learned. For months when he'd called me in his drunken rages, I'd actually held the phone away from my ear until he stopped screaming. I'd left early in the morning or pretended to be asleep when he came home. I'd tried everything. But none of it was enough.

Now everything was clear: I might not like myself any more, but I was going to have to be my own best friend to get myself out of this. And if I didn't do it now, however hard and painful it was going to be, I knew that my life would be at stake. Being with him was worse than being dead. I felt totally unproductive, I felt totally worthless. First to myself and then to the world. But I had to deal with the grim reality of the situation to *change* that reality. I had to stare the darkness down. I couldn't flinch, or he'd get me, or I'd get myself. Fear is insidious. Low self-esteem is insidious. Self-pity is insidious. They can erode you like acid.

"Take a deep breath, Georgette," I reminded myself. "And then think through your options clearly. Going to a hotel is an option. But what is that going to get you?"

The reality was that it was going to buy me a few days at most. I couldn't stay there indefinitely.

Once summoned, that calm, strong, forgotten part of myself took over. Now that I'd let it in, it went on talking and making sense, serenely sidestepping all the fear, the shame, and the pain.

"You know he'll apologize to you in the morning," it said. "So when he does, go back to that apartment and face the fact that you're living with someone who has a serious problem with alcohol. The difference is that it's not your problem anymore. You're going to go back there, go to work, and not do anything precipitate. You're not going to cut off your nose to spite your face. However, you *are* going to start to get yourself out of that relationship."

It wasn't easy to confront myself. And I knew it wasn't going to be easy to do what I needed to do. But a real change had taken place. I knew that however long it took and whatever strength it might require, I was going to start building another life for myself. Suddenly, all the courage I'd lost over four years of emotional cruelty, bullying, and abuse came flooding back to me.

I had allowed all this to happen to me, but I wasn't allowing it anymore. I was taking control of *my* life. Step by step I was uncovering and recovering my strength.

In the morning I went home, and for the first time I stood up to my husband: I told him to move out. Slowly, small step by small step, I started to make arrangements to extricate myself from the marriage. I began by identifying and then taking advantage of those resources I already had at my disposal. That was the first big step. Once you start looking, you can always find some small advantages to build on. I happened to know that some friends were about to go to the South of France. I realized this was an opportunity, so I called and asked if I could go along. Step two. They said sure, and, suddenly, for the first time in years, I found myself having fun. I was with friends watching the Bastille Day fireworks on the terrace of the Hotel Carleton in the South of France and having a wonderful time. Step three.

Through my traveling companions, I met a man who took me out to dinner and dancing. He was courteous and considerate. And in the course of the evening I realized I'd forgotten what it was like to laugh and be happy. That led to a bigger step. It was becoming clear that life didn't have to be the way it had been. All I had to do was decide to change it. I could end this marriage and not ruin my entire life. Even if G.B. fired me, I would eventually find another job. I could see that I had merit and value of my own. There was going to be a future for me.

When I got back from the vacation G.B. wanted to move back in again, but I wouldn't let him. My guts, intuition, and strength were back on track. I wasn't going to ignore them again as I had done for far too many years. I was never going to get back in that box of pain, self-flagellation, and fear. I was never going to doubt my ability to flourish and survive.

I'd had to hit bottom, to feel completely worthless, before Feminine Force rose up against G.B. and for myself. Out of necessity I tested my friendships, by asking for help. To my surprise, I discovered that my husband's power wasn't absolute. It didn't corrupt everyone.

Not only wasn't I completely worthless, I wasn't completely alone, either. Some of my friendships had actually withstood the test. Someone in New York aside from me actually cared about me. And that realization was another small step leading me forward into the light. It all began with having the *courage* to take the first step. After that, each one illuminated the way to the next. Buoyed by the strength of support from unexpected places, I gained new courage with every step I took. With each one, I felt more self-worth and pride and strength. And each time the certainty of who I really was and what I was really capable of swelled inside of me, and I became stronger and stronger.

I was going to continue to use my guts and my smarts and my ability to nurture to release this new but familiar power inside of myself. It wasn't going to be pretty. But no matter what, I was going to stand up to him.

The era of living my life by Feminine Force had begun.

Chapter 2

The Navlan, Bell, and Paulsin Women of East Chicago and Highland, Indiana

"Character, self-discipline, determination, attitude and service are the substance of life."

—MARIAN WRIGHT EDELMAN, *THE MEASURE OF OUR SUCCESS*

For bestowing on me the power of Feminine Force, I have the Navlan, Bell, and Paulsin women of East Chicago and Highland, Indiana, to thank.

Most of what I know about Feminine Force I learned by watching how my mother, my grandmother, and my great-grandmother dealt with the full spectrum—and I mean the *full* spectrum—of life's challenges and joys. Call it fate or coincidence, the women of my mother's family have always had to go it alone.

Out of necessity, we've always had to nurture others, bring home the bacon, and follow the voice of our intuition and guts. We learned how as life took the men out of our lives, and left us to fill every role. As far as I knew, there wasn't any difference between men's work and women's work—there was just *work*. As far as I knew, there was no earthly reason why I couldn't be a CEO, a warm and nurturing wife, *and* iron perfect shirts. There was no reason I couldn't accomplish anything I wanted to accomplish or be anyone I wanted to be.

My first role models ran boarding houses, switched trains, demonstrated products at local grocery stores. They were sisters, mothers, widows, amateur dancers, bakers, and community theater buffs. They raised their families on shoestring budgets, and bought their most beautiful possessions secondhand. They are among the most creative women I have ever met, and they taught me just about everything I know.

I grew up in a little town. Highland, Indiana, just south of Chicago, was a steel belt town my family had lived in for a couple of generations. My great-grandmother Pauline Navlan, whom we called Baba, emigrated there from Austria. She never learned to read or write English, but she could count. She came from a generation that believed men were the breadwinners, and women were dependent on them. Her husband, a trained violinist who had immigrated before her, worked in a pipe factory. Together they raised their five children on a factory worker's salary. Even though their means were slender, after a few years Baba and my great-grandfather managed to save enough money to build a large house across the street from where he worked.

It wasn't fancy but it was roomy, with a big tree out back and a porch across the front. In their spare time, Baba and my great-grandfather added on more rooms, which Baba rented out to other newly arrived immigrants. The place grew as they added on, and became a well-established boarding house with Baba at the helm. Even though Baba was running a business *and* raising five kids, still she never missed making my great-grandfather his lunch. In this two-career family, she saw opportunities to advance his career at the factory, and she'd pack brown bags and baskets with more and more good things from her kitchen so my great-grandfather could share his lunch with friends. The day the shift supervisor joined great-grandfather's group, Baba started making home-baked pies.

She also had a soft spot for people in need, though she preferred not to advertise the fact. When an out-of-luck tenant confessed he couldn't cover his rent one month, she let it slide—an arrangement she kept just between the two of them, even when one month stretched into three and four.

The account books told the tale, though, and when great-grandfather finally caught up with Baba's secret, he hit the ceiling. He gave Baba a lecture about her lack of business sense, and then went down the hall to collect the money himself. His daughter Mary, my grandmother, who was ten at the time, tagged along.

A very confused and angry confrontation ensued, and the boarder, who eventually wound up in a mental hospital, pulled out a gun. Aiming no doubt at my great-grandfather, he fired a shot that hit Mary in the leg. His second round found its mark, and hit my great-grandfather point blank, in the chest. My great-grandfather died on the spot, in his wounded daughter's arms.

It was a tragedy that stunned everyone in the community, and left Baba with a family of five to support on her own.

The week after her husband's funeral, Baba crossed the street to the factory, pulled my great-grandfather's time card, punched in, and took his place on the line.

No one said a word. Baba must have scared those men a little. But she didn't waste any time telling herself they'd never let a woman, and an untrained one at that, take the job; she simply decided to take her husband's place and deal with whatever came down that line. It wasn't long before she was pulling her own weight, and then some, along with all the men.

Here was a woman who couldn't read or write, who didn't waste a minute dwelling on what she couldn't do. She pulled all of her resources together and boldly took control of her life.

Baba was the essence of Feminine Force.

My great-grandmother didn't just survive; eventually she thrived in her triple role as factory worker, boarding house landlady, and mother of five. But to be blunt, she worked like a dog. Given her long hours, it's to her credit that Baba found time to encourage her daughter Mary to be the free spirit she was and is.

In fact Baba worried that she'd encouraged her daughter a little too far in that direction. Mary was a gorgeous redhead who started attracting suitors at the age of fourteen. It was the era of the flapper, and my grandmother had a particular talent for dancing—entering and winning what, by all accounts, was a marathon series of Charleston competitions that drew hundreds of contestants to one of the big auditoriums in Chicago. For several years during her teens, Mary Navlan only wanted to dance. She was passionate about it. Oh, she worked—in fact she had to drop out of school in the seventh grade to take a full-time job at a local bakery, in order to help support the family. She was so diligent at that bakery that the owners wanted to adopt her! But in her spare time, in the evenings and on weekends,

Mary played as if there were no tomorrow, and Baba began to worry about what would happen to her once Baba herself wasn't around to keep the business of living in proper perspective. It was difficult to see how being a great dancer was going to help my grandmother survive life's twists and turns, which Baba knew all too well could be surprising and hard.

It wasn't many years before Grandma had to prove her mettle. She met and married a dashing Irishman called Bill "Red" Bell, a handsome redhead my mother remembers as wonderfully affectionate and caring. He owned real estate, including a big building in Chicago, but when the crash of 1929 came he lost that and all of his holdings. He never fully recovered. He was a World War I veteran, and family lore has it that between the war and the crash he was so devastated he never again was able to motivate himself to reenter the work force.

It was a rocky marriage after that. My grandparents would quarrel; he'd go off, then come back, they'd make up, then he'd go off again. From time to time he'd take the grocery or rent money or any other household money he could find and go off on a gambling jaunt, leaving Grandma and his children alone for days, without so much as two sticks to rub together. After one such trip, he brought back a beautiful gold lamé evening dress for his wife, a dress that became immortalized in our family's history as the "gossamer gown." He announced his return from this particular gambling binge by hanging the gown from the little chandelier in their parlor.

At that point, his wife had pretty much had it. Here was this extravagant dress: could she use it to pay the rent? Could she feed it to her family?

She tore it down and ripped it into pieces.

My grandparents made up that time, but it was one of their last fights. The "gossamer gown"—which would reappear later in a new form—outlasted their marriage. My grandmother and grandfather divorced by the time my mother was six, and like her mother before her, Grandma was suddenly left to support her family on her own.

It was a gutsy, dramatic move for a woman of her generation. My grandmother had—and has—great dignity. In her era, divorce was barely considered respectable, but she found her husband's behavior totally unacceptable for her family, and she had the *self-respect* to do something about it. With no more than a seventh-grade education, she took on the responsibility of raising her two small children alone, and she did it in the face of society's disapproval of divorce.

She and her children went to live with Baba for a while, and my grandmother and Baba both did whatever work was available. They'd clean other people's houses from time to time, making up little games and amusements for themselves to make the work interesting, such as deciding how they would redecorate if one or the other was the lady of the house.

Mary the dancer soon showed what her high spirits were made of. She was a popular young woman. She was beautiful—she's *still* a gorgeous redhead—and had a lot of suitors in her youth. Because she was convivial and caring, many of them turned into lifelong friends. Once, when part of her crowd came to the house for a visit, one of the men mentioned that the Baltimore and Ohio Railroad needed a night switcher.

In those days, the signal crossing wasn't automatic; it was operated by a system of levers that had to be cranked or pumped by hand. Raising and lowering those heavy gates was manual labor—definitely *not* considered "women's work." But that was a minor detail, as far as my grandmother was concerned. What mattered to her was that the rail yards were only a few blocks away—important because she never did learn to drive a car. More important was the fact that it was a night job, so that she could be with her children during the day. Though Baba was around to keep an eye on things, Grandma was still a single parent. This job struck her as the perfect solution to the dilemma of having to be both breadwinner *and* nurturing mother to her family.

Grandma's friend knew the foreman at the railroad, and put in a character reference for her. Being a switcher was considered to be the lowest, most degrading, and worst-paid job on the railroad, as far as the insiders were concerned. But Mary didn't care what other people thought. None of the men around there would touch that job with a stick, so when my grandmother applied for it, Baltimore and Ohio hired her on the spot.

My grandmother's best instincts told her this was work that would allow her to achieve her goals, to live the kind of life she wanted. She listened to her own head and heart, and tackled her new job with the same strength and stamina and grace that made her such a standout on the dance floor. It turned out to be a great job for her. She continued to switch trains right up until the day she retired, at sixty-five. And she did it wearing the clothes she loved, the clothes that made her feel feminine—skirts and stockings and heels! In fact, Grandma's now in her eighties and she *still* wears heels and tight skirts—and she's *still* got a great figure.

Her daughter, Dorothy, my mother, was the third generation of women in my family who had to go it alone. But she had a lot of special encouragement when she was growing up. One of my mother's earliest memories is that when she was very, very young, before her parents divorced, her father would leave a little treat every morning that she'd find when she woke up—an apple under the bed, a dime in her shoe, a cookie on the dresser. And whenever she looked sad, he would say to her, "Oh, Dorothy, you look a little unhappy. Come sit on my lap and let's talk. Between your brain and my brain, we can conquer *anything*." Sadly, he seemed unable to take his own advice, but what he told his daughter at that young age became an important factor in her life.

Baba and Grandma were just as attentive to my mother as Grandfather had been, and that didn't stop when harder times came. Even when money was scarce, they found a way to give my mother dancing and music lessons and other things that were important to her. In fact it was my mother who ended up with the "gossamer gown." A few days after my grandmother tore it up, she took the pieces of that ruined dress and made a recital costume for my mother out of it. Mother was only five years old, but that costume became an emblem of the resourcefulness of the women in my family. It was an important lesson in how to turn a negative into a positive, and my mother has kept that costume to this day—a tiny short dress with matching panties preserved in a plexiglass frame.

After my grandparents' divorce, when things were very tight, Baba and Grandmother continued to pay attention to the things that mattered to my mother. When Dorothy got to high school, and wanted to fit in with the popular kids who were all wearing cashmere sweaters, they made sure she had a cashmere sweater, too. They could only afford one, and they saved up until they could get it for her.

Of course, these two women gave my mother other less tangible but more important gifts. In Baba and Grandma, my mother had two strong models of women who did what they had to do to survive and thrive. And neither Baba nor Grandma ever took anyone else's word for what it was they had to do: they determined that for themselves. Just as important, both of them approached work with great gusto. They *enjoyed* it. They were very creative in their solutions to problems, and it was a creativity they encouraged in my mother.

My mother says that despite the family's outer circumstances, from an early age she felt a powerful sense of freedom and self-determination inside. She believed she could do whatever she set out to do. As she was growing up, whenever she announced what she wanted to do or be, she was praised for her ambitions and assured that her dreams were wonderful. Baba and my grandmother may not have read any books on psychology, but they cherished my mother, and seemed to understand, intuitively, that rewarding Dorothy's independence and decision-making would reinforce her ability to make the next decision, and the next, up through the most important choices of her life. Because of her models, Mother always felt she had the freedom to follow her own inner voice.

She had another role model a little farther from home—her Aunt Virginia, who was childless, who also took a hand in educating my mother. She made sure she had riding lessons and tennis lessons and was exposed to the sorts of activities that make a young person well-rounded. By the time my mother was old enough to marry, she was as accomplished in the social skills as any expensive finishing school graduate.

My mother likes to say that because of these gifts, she always expected miracles in her life. And that is why, in one way or another, those miracles usually happened.

When she married, it was to a man as full of love and charm as any woman could hope for. When she is asked to describe him, my mother says George Paulsin looked like Clark Gable without the moustache—and without the big ears. In his pictures he's very handsome, but what I remember was his warm, deep voice, and his affection. Whenever my father came home, no matter what the day had been like, everything seemed to turn out all right.

My mother always felt that my father took care of her, too. He had the same kind of nurturing, demonstrative nature that my grandfather had. It was a similarity my mother no doubt sensed, and it's probably one of the reasons she married him. My father came from a big family, and wanted a lot of children of his own. He knew how to make a big family work. Sometimes he cooked the meals, and when friends came over he was the one taking the coats, seating the guests, serving the drinks. He was often the one who made the family—and whoever else was in the house—feel comfortable. My mother, who felt very much loved by him, likes to say that he gave everybody their moment in the sun. Caring for a brood of four did nothing to dampen her own high spirits. She continued to be playful and affectionate. She married my father when she was only a teenager, and in a lot of ways she was still something of a kid.

She was only twenty-seven when the police came to the door one rainy afternoon to tell her that my father had been killed in an automobile accident.

My mother spent a period of time in shock. She had grown up expecting miracles, and up until that moment those expectations always seemed to be fulfilled. Now she was terrified. She feared she didn't know enough about raising children to do it on her own, and worried that she could not support the family financially. Four children. For a while, Mother says, she couldn't even feel she wanted us, so frightened was she, so angry at being abandoned by this man she loved so dearly.

She began looking into different religions to try to find an acceptable answer to the question she kept asking herself: why did this terrible thing happen? She talked with priests, ministers, rabbis. No one came up with a satisfactory explanation, but that didn't lead her to reject religion. Instead, she began to pay attention to her spiritual life, and began to investigate non-traditional kinds of religious experience. She joined the Spiritualists, a church organized near the turn of the century to explore esoteric phenomena and ideas.

Her desire to develop and better herself included other ways of seeking knowledge, and before we knew it, Mother was taking all kinds of educational courses, looking for ways to improve her life and ours.

She regained her emotional strength and clarity very quickly. She focused on the job she had to do: the job of raising a family by herself. She approached that day-to-day challenge with great pragmatism, discipline, and imagination.

My father's family had moved out to California shortly before he was killed. None of us kids ever really knew our father's side of the family. They'd never been a big part of our lives, and after his funeral they went back home and dropped out of our lives entirely. They had some money, but they saw no reason to help us out.

For a while Mother augmented her meager Social Security income by taking whatever jobs she could find. It wasn't easy for her, but it was *very* important to her to prove she could provide for her children without the Paulsins' help.

And Mother didn't stop with that. She was determined that no matter what our financial circumstances were, we would live well. We would appreciate what was fine in life. We would take care of ourselves and our appearance. We might not have money, but by golly we would have *style*.

She taught us—not so much in words as by her example—that even when resources are limited, there is a lot of pleasure to be had in life if you learn to think creatively about what you *can* do with what you *do* have. It was a matter of ingenuity, effort, and desire, and she showed her Feminine Force in small ways as well as large ones.

Mother's lifelong quest for personal growth helped to fuel the entrepreneurial schemes that kept her family going. But it wouldn't have been possible for Mother to do all that she did in those years without teamwork from the family. Her grandmother and mother had worked hard all their lives, and no one questioned that all of us would do the same.

One of the things I marvel at now is that I never, *ever* heard any of the women in my family complain about hard work. I never got the sense, when I was with any of them, that any job was a hardship or shameful or embarrassing. Each job had its own meaning. The most menial labor was no more or less than a piece of a larger, more important task—an essential piece.

My earliest recollections of Baba are of the practical, spirited way she went about running her boarding house. Even after she became a great-grandmother several times over, Baba kept two houses—one to live in, one for boarders. I remember watching her sitting at her kitchen table carefully counting the rent money, but she never fretted about the loss of income when a tenant moved out. As soon as he or she left, she assaulted that vacant room with mops and brushes and paint. It was as simple and straightforward as showing up for work at the pipe factory: when a boarder moved out, his old room was immediately cleaned, painted, and fixed up for the next tenant.

And we kids were enlisted to help. We were all expected to do our part, and not only did we do it, we *loved* it. I *loved* the moment Baba put a paintbrush in my hand. Getting ready for that next tenant was a family affair, and scrubbing and painting and fixing up together was fun for all of us.

It was easy to pick up the spirit of running a business from Baba. As far as Baba was concerned, as soon as you closed one deal, as soon as one job ended, you got ready for the next. You moved from A to B. Running a business was as straightforward as baking an apple pie. It also took the same care, and gave the same kind of satisfaction.

I still enjoy that kind of work. Though I have plenty of household help, I still scrub the carpets at home. I prefer to do it myself. It's actually a means of relaxation for me—instant gratification and an escape from the kind of work I do every day.

I call scrubbing and painting and fixing up fun. It all comes down to your frame of reference in life.

What I learned from all my mentors was to approach work as an *adventure*. When I was little, going to work at the switching yard with Grandma Mary was a big treat. She took only one of us along at a time. By the time her children were grown, she was working at a site farther from home, but it was still the night shift. Going with her meant we got to stay up late. We'd leave our house around ten P.M. and take a bus that traveled for what seemed like hours and hours before it finally let us off way out in the middle of nowhere. I knew when we were getting close, because Standard Oil had built giant storage tanks there with bright red lights that blinked on and off in the darkness.

Her post wasn't much more than a shack. The only sign of habitation, for miles around, was a little workers' bar at the crossroads. We'd stop there first and she'd buy me treats.

Here was an attractive woman entering a working-class bar with only a child in tow, and I never once remember a remark or a whistle or any kind of unseemly suggestion made to or about her. She had a presence and a dignity that quelled any horseplay. She simply overpowered them.

Grandma would buy me potato chips, peanuts, and Coke. It was an indulgence my mother didn't often allow. Then we'd go up to the switcher's shanty, a building maybe five by six feet that was raised up on stilts so that the switcher could see the train coming from a distance.

Below it was a little padlocked shed, where Grandma stored blankets and a pillow, all wrapped up in plastic. We'd unlock the shed, gather the blankets, and then go up the stairs where I'd help her spread the blankets out on the floor. If it was winter, we'd fill and light the coal stove, an old black pot-bellied thing. When I got tired of looking out over the tracks, hoping for a train, I'd sit in front of the stove and stuff myself with potato chips and soda until the warmth of the stove made me drowsy. I always stirred briefly when Grandma covered me with a blanket, and I'd make her promise she'd wake me when the first train came. There was nothing like the moment when the signal lights started going and we had to jump up and close the gates. She'd work some switches and levers and then I'd help her pump the long lever that operated the hydraulic lift, and the gate would slowly lower at the crossing. Once the train was safely past, we'd pump again to lift the gate back up, and by the time we were done we were both huffing and puffing. Then I'd climb back under the blanket and gratefully fall asleep again. At dawn, we'd descend the stairs and gather coal along the tracks to fill the bucket for the next shift, before we caught the bus for home.

There was always that sense of *can do* in our family, and it was handed down from one generation to the next. It was handed down to my mother. And it was handed down to me.

I was seven years old when I first said the words "I'll find a way." It was the day I lost my father. As I walked home from elementary school that rainy, cold afternoon, I couldn't wait to get into the warm house. I knew that my little sisters and brother would already be snug inside, playing. If I was lucky, I thought, my father would be home early. He always made home feel like something special. But when I rounded the corner I could see that our house was surrounded by cars. There were a lot of people milling around in the house, which had lights on everywhere. Suddenly I felt very cold. I knew something was wrong, and a *terrible* small voice inside me said *Daddy*.

Inside, the crowded living room felt hot and stuffy, and all the people sitting and standing around seemed like strangers. They were talking and some of them were crying, and for a moment they didn't seem to notice me. I didn't see Baba or Grandma or Mother anywhere. Finally someone saw me, and I was led to the sofa, sat down, and told that my father had been killed in a car accident. By then I was looking wildly around for my mother, who was nowhere to be seen. Finally someone said, "Mommy isn't feeling well," and led me past her bedroom, where I caught a quick glimpse of her lying in bed. The worst part, among all the solemn condolences and strangers urging me to be brave, was hearing someone across the room say ". . . hope they don't have to split up the kids."

Hope they don't have to split up the kids. It took a painful moment for that to sink in, but as soon as it did an urgent voice inside me said *I have to keep us together.* It was as if all the hubbub around me suddenly went silent, and that's all that I heard, a voice inside me saying *I have to keep us together.*

Suddenly I felt very calm, very determined. I picked my way through the groups of grownups, and went to gather up my two-year-old sister Lyn, who seemed to have been forgotten in her crib. I found my four-and-a-half-year-old brother George, named after my father, and my six-year-old sister Melody, and marshaled them into the bedroom Melody and I shared. George climbed shakily up onto the top bunk, while Melody sat close to me and I held Lyn. None of the adults paid much attention to any of us.

I looked at the stricken, frightened faces around me, and took a deep breath.

"We're staying together," I started slowly. "We don't have a father any more, but we're still a family. Mother isn't feeling very well, but don't worry—*I'll* take care of you. I'll protect us."

Something in George and Melody's faces seemed to relax, at least a little, and it gave me strength to know that I could comfort them.

"We'll all have to be strong," I said solemnly, "and stick together. But we can do it. I'll protect us."

Right then and there I became convinced that no one would ever be able to break us up. At the age of seven I became convinced that *I* had the power to keep the family together. I was furious at whoever it was in that room who even suggested we might be split up. It frightened me, but it made me angry and determined, too. *Let them come and try to break us apart. Let them just try it.* If they did, I'd fight them with all my might, and I'd win.

It was later that evening before my mother gathered herself together enough to come in and speak to us. Her eyes looked red and tired. Her whole body seemed to have changed.

She didn't say a word to me about the huge event that had just changed all our lives forever, but clearly she was peering down what must have looked, at the moment, like a very long, dark tunnel. "Georgette," she said, looking square into my eyes, "I can't stay at home any more and take care of you kids. I have to go out and get work. You have to take care of things at home, now. You're in charge."

I nodded my head. Though I didn't know what to say, I felt calm and clear-headed. At the age of seven, I understood what she was saying to me, and why. I didn't know that it was my Feminine Force that was directing me, but it was. If we were going to stay together as a family, a lot depended on me. I didn't know exactly what lay in store for us, but whatever it was, I was ready.

Chapter 3

Finding Your Role Models

"I think it's the end of progress if you stand still and think of what you've done in the past. I keep on."

—LESLIE CARON

Ilove business, but taking risks still frightens me. No matter how successful I become, part of me will always be the little girl who's afraid she will fail and not be able to keep her family together. I love going up against powerful men and the media and breaking the mold, but not a day goes by that I don't have to talk myself through the rough spots. In moments like those, I turn to my role models.

The Navlan, Bell, and Paulsin women weren't the only women I looked up to when I was growing up. I absorbed a lot from many role models, usually without even thinking about it. And some of them were straight out of fiction.

When I was a child, I loved Nancy Drew. I read all of those mysteries. She was a girl with a mind of her own, always going where she wasn't supposed to go, always putting herself at risk and bucking the odds. She stood up to everyone who told her she shouldn't be doing this or that because it was dangerous, because girls weren't supposed to, because she was just a kid and what could she know? But she always prevailed. She went out and did what she wanted to do, and created an exciting life for herself.

I especially loved Maureen O'Hara in the roles she used to play.

There aren't many female stars now who portray the kind of strong but feminine women she played in movies like *The Quiet Man* or *At Sword's Point*. In *The Quiet Man* she was a passionate, fiery redhead who's herding sheep the first time you see her in the movie, and the second time she's in the kitchen, cooking and waiting on her brother. But no one made the mistake of thinking she was meek or obedient. She had enormous energy and dignity and a very strong, clearly defined sense of what was *hers*, and she let everyone know it in no uncertain terms. Though she might have been head over heels in love with John Wayne, she was determined to control her own destiny, and because of that, she was an absolute match for him. The male leads would carry on about her temper and her willfulness in those movies, but they always *adored* her—and so did her audiences. Katharine Hepburn was another great role model who was her own woman in her films. Both of them were glamorous. Both of them were ladies, in the true sense of the word. But both were opinionated. Both of them stood their ground. They were *fighters*, and I loved them.

I was lucky enough to *live* among women who saw no contradiction in looking and behaving like a woman and being strong. I took something essential from watching my grandmother fix her hair and put on her lipstick before she went out to work on the Baltimore and Ohio Railroad. Being feminine didn't mean you couldn't do a man's work. Being feminine had nothing to do with whether you had the strength to pump a hydraulic lift or manage a business—or herd sheep, for that matter.

At the age of eighty-five, not only does my grandmother still wear lipstick and heels, she still colors her hair. In our family, being powerful means you never, ever apologize for being a woman.

FINDING NEW ROLE MODELS

The collective wisdom of all those women, their Feminine Force, became the cornerstone of everything I've achieved in my life. But there are times that the terrific women I see around me now serve me in more immediate ways, simply because they prove it's possible to do what I want to do now—because it *has* been done—by them.

I admire Linda Wachner, the CEO of Warnaco, for being the only woman in the country heading a Fortune 500 company. I admire Margaret Thatcher for her firmness, for how she made her own way in a man's world, and by her own rules. I admire Barbara Walters. She started out from a position of privilege in life, and could easily have settled back and enjoyed the ride. But she didn't. She took the opportunities life offered her, and blazed a trail for all women in broadcasting. She's been called the "Chuck Yeager of female broadcasters," and she's been very supportive of female correspondents as they struggle over the terrain she traversed earlier in her career. I consider her a personal role model.

Oprah Winfrey is another pioneer and another of my role models. Not only did she come up from the most difficult childhood and make herself a star, but she produces and owns her own show—a situation that's practically unheard of. I had the honor of being seated with her when she was given a Women of the World award by Childhelp USA, a cause I've devoted some time to. This remarkable woman worked her way up from the most oppressive circumstances, but she's no victim. And she used her visibility and her talent on behalf of other women as well as children.

The first step in taking charge of your destiny and carving out your life is locating your inner voice. That's a step you have to take alone. But once you do, the process of stretching yourself and coming out of your cocoon is magnetic. The process itself will attract the people and the opportunities that will give you the help and inspiration you need.

NEGATIVE ROLE MODELS

Finding and cultivating your inner voice means getting past the fears, hesitations, and bad baggage you may have accumulated in your life. You probably have some negative role models in your life—most people do. Don't allow yourself to be victimized by them. If you find yourself being stopped in your tracks because their voices are still in your head, this is the time to weed them out. This is the time to identify what part of "no" they play in your life. If the voice of an aunt who always worried about what other people would think is something you carry around in your head, put her down on a list. That is a voice of fear. It is your aunt's voice, not yours. If the voice of a teacher who was fiercely critical of your work is a voice you still carry around in your head, put him down on your list. That is your teacher's voice, not yours. If your mother constantly told you you'd never amount to anything, that's your mother's voice, not yours.

Those negative voices are part of the noise that can sometimes drown out your own inner voice. Label them. Write them down. Fix in your mind whose voice it is when a negative idea gets in your way. Then tear that list up and throw it in the trash. Burn it in the fireplace. Flush it down the toilet. And focus your attention on your *positive* role models.

Good role models don't have to be people you want to *be* like. They may simply be people whose wisdom or bravery or grace under pressure has made a lasting impression on you. They don't have to be limited to people you know personally; they can include public figures and even fictional characters. Think about the particular principles they embody, or the particular ways you find them inspiring. Make a list in your head, or write it down. When you really need allies, you may be surprised to discover what strong allies these can be.

BE YOUR OWN ROLE MODEL

Don't leave yourself out of the loop as you gather this chorus of good voices in your head. Even if your childhood was miserable, and even if good role models were in short supply, there are bound to be some powerful experiences in your past that you can rediscover and use—experiences that are part of the proverbial bootstraps by which you can pull yourself up.

Warnaco's Linda Wachner is a perfect example of what I mean. When she was eleven she was put in a full body cast and spent a year and a half in bed because of a spinal disorder. Then she spent more years in various casts and braces. Today this CEO of a Fortune 500 company still cannot stand on her feet for long periods of time. But whenever she needs strength, she looks back to the long months she spent in that body cast. "When I wasn't able to walk," she says, "I used to make these little vows to myself: 'Oh, if I could walk, I know I would never get tired. I know I could do more.' "

And she did do more. She walked, and then she flew, going from a position as merchandise clerk at the age of twenty to chief executive officer at the age of forty. It was her *own* childhood experience that she tapped to find the reserves of energy and drive she needed to pursue her goals. She reminded herself of the vow she made from a hospital bed, and drew new courage and strength from the courage she had found as an eleven-year-old.

Think back to those moments in your childhood when you realized something important about life, about yourself, or about your values. Along with your other role models, give that child a voice. She may know something you've forgotten.

To a large extent, the process of tapping your Feminine Force is a matter of drawing on your own history and experience to discover who you are emotionally and spiritually. It's a process that will uncover the wellsprings of your own happiness and emotional well-being. It's a process that frees you from emotional dependency on others. And it goes beyond that.

Too often, women are socialized to "resign themselves" to circumstances, while their brothers and husbands and friends are taught to reach, grow, and win. Their brothers and husbands are taught to find their own versions of the American Dream, and they expect nothing less.

It's true that the sheer ability to *endure* has been a trait attributed to strong women since the beginning of history. Many of the women we most admire are those who survived wars, natural disasters, or great personal tragedies because they were able to bend but not break, like a tree in a storm. It's an enormous strength, the kind of strength my great-grandmother had in spades. But the trouble is, most women don't stop to notice how much courage, how much imagination, just what kinds of fancy footwork it takes—mentally, spiritually, physically—just to hold the line in their lives. They draw on enormous reserves of resiliency and tenacity just holding on to what they have.

They run faster and faster, as the Red Queen said to Alice, just to stay in the same place.

What too many women fail to do is to look *beyond* that place, and to understand that *all along* they've been developing the skills to conquer new territories beyond the ones they're familiar with. They're afraid of what lies beyond, even though where they are *now* may be a pretty painful place to be.

Tapping your Feminine Force means understanding *and accepting* that you will achieve and experience things that lie well beyond what you've taken as boundaries—the restricted orbit that your family, your background, your time and place and culture seem to dictate. I'm not talking about the tired subject of sexual politics. I'm talking about your ability to stretch your mind and embrace possibilities that go beyond the limits you yourself have come to accept.

You must change your hopes into expectations.

Life's hardships have taught me and many other women that come what may, there is always, and I mean *always*, something worthwhile, something better waiting around the corner. The trick lies simply in getting to that corner.

Success, joy, fulfillment, achieving the American Dream—no matter what your circumstances are today, no matter how far away your goal may seem, achieving what you want is little more than putting one foot in front of the other, come hell or high water, until you get there.

Chapter 4

If You Get Good Grades, You Can Go to the Circus

"As God is my witness, I'll never be hungry again."

—SCARLETT O'HARA, IN THE FILM VERSION OF *GONE WITH THE WIND*

W hen my father died, my family's financial security died with him. His Social Security payments were nowhere near enough to support the five of us. So my mother pounded the pavement like her own mother and grandmother before her, to ferret out whatever work a woman in her late twenties with no experience or degree could get in the early 1950s. Mother demonstrated products in grocery stores. She evaluated hotels for the travel industry by traveling alone and staying the night. Not that many women traveled alone in the fifties.

It wasn't easy. And it didn't get any easier.

But that didn't mean we didn't figure out how to make it work. We didn't have many toys. The ones we did have were things all four of us could use. That left out dolls, which were of no use to my brother George. But it did include the family bicycle, the Monopoly game that we could all play together, and the marbles that Lyn would eventually use to double and triple her stash by beating all the boys in the neighborhood.

Personally, I had no time for toys. I was too busy taking care of the other kids, budgeting, shopping, and doing the laundry. My primary interest in toys lay in the way they regularly ended up all over the floor, because it was my job to figure out how to get my brother and sisters to straighten them up again.

Recently Lyn asked my mother, "When she was little did Georgette ever climb a tree or beat up on a boy?" And Mother said no. She even said that there was always something a little sad about me. And she was absolutely right. From that young age I always had my eye on the big picture. Play and games just didn't interest me. I didn't have time for them. It never occurred to me to go outside and play, although I was always telling my sister Lyn to. There were too many, so much more important things to think about. You can't climb a tree while you're figuring out how to run a household. You can't roller skate while you're making dinner.

Do I regret it? No. My success has as much to do with what I *didn't* have as what I did. I also believe there's no point looking back on life. Your power to make a difference always resides in the present and in the future.

The fact that Mother wasn't around full time didn't mean she was an absent parent. Far from it. Mother faced up to the fact that she had challenging and rewarding work to do—raising four young children. Mother's personal tastes were expansive and sophisticated. Her exotic friends were always wandering in and out of the house quoting poetry. Our home was like some artistic *salon*. Mother was a natural-born seeker, a free spirit. In addition to her work and her family, she plunged headlong into a local little theater group. The theater was a bright spot in Mother's life. There she found the safety valve she needed to be free to dream about what could be, and about what might have been. That was how she got the heart and the courage to do the rest of what she had to do, and by golly, it was worth it for that reason alone!

We *all* need moments of pure pleasure in our lives—no matter how logistically impossible they may seem. In fact, the more our busy schedules and heavy responsibilities seem to crowd out the experience of joy, the more we benefit from making time for it.

Fortunately, there is a method to enjoying life. It has four parts. First, you have to identify those things that give you great satisfaction. Second, DON'T FEEL GUILTY about reserving special moments for yourself. Third, make a conscious, determined effort to make time for those moments or activities—even and especially when it looks like there is no time for them. And fourth, make a commitment to steps one, two, and three. Women all too often sacrifice themselves and put off celebrating the joys of life. DON'T DO THAT!!! It's too easy *not* to do for yourself, but you *must*. You and everyone around you will reap the results.

We certainly benefited from Mother's venture into the theater. There was a new gaiety and freedom around us, as soon the theatrical friends joined the spiritualists at Mother's gatherings. Nevertheless, as far as we kids were concerned, there was nothing permissive about our Mother. She ruled the roost with an iron fist. Our circumstances and roles may have been untraditional, and they certainly required creative thinking. But Mother's ideas about parents and children were very traditional. She expressed them bluntly and made no excuses for them. And they worked.

Every Saturday night we would have a family meeting, where we'd all get to share our feelings about the way things were going. Although we'd all participate, she was the one who was in charge. If one of us kids wanted a brand-new outfit, she'd firmly explain that new carpeting would benefit all of us, including her, and not just one of us. So all of us would be best served by putting that money in the bank. If we wanted to stay up later at night, she'd explain why our bedtime was just fine the way it was, because even though we had extra responsibilities in our family, we were still kids.

"This is not a democracy," Mother would remind us. "I'm the mother, and I'm the one who's supporting you. So you can contribute, and we'll all pitch in. But I'm in charge."

I started to follow her example by getting even more creative and resourceful about how I was doing my part in bringing up the younger kids. Instead of just disciplining them, I started to teach them the way Mother had taught me. Before I got out of grade school, I'd learned the value of money, and I wanted them to learn, too. Not a week went by that I didn't calculate how much it would take to buy the food, keep our clothes clean, and make the house comfortable. As they got older, I knew the other kids were going to have to understand that, too, and I urgently needed them to understand it—not only for their own good, but for mine.

At some point you have to be willing to be in charge of your own life, regardless of whether there is someone in your life who can take care of you—even and especially your husband. This is one lesson we just happened to learn early in our house, and the way I see it, this was an advantage.

The truth was that every time Mother walked out that door, the pit of my stomach dropped. I never told a soul but I was terrified that she wouldn't come back that night, just as our father hadn't come back, and that then I would somehow have to raise the kids on my own. What would we do for grocery money then? How would I convince the adults to let me be the parent? How could I possibly keep our family together if that happened?

For my comfort I'd go and give Baba a massage. It was the most comfort I knew. She'd lie down on her bed and I'd rub her shoulders and back with rubbing alcohol. Sometimes we'd talk, and sometimes we'd just be silent. It didn't really matter which. Everything else fell away in the soothing rhythm of the massage and the astringent smell of the alcohol. It was as if I could absorb Baba's serenity through my fingers and the very pores of my skin. That was safety; that was the protection that somehow only being with her or Grandma gave me.

Maybe it was knowing that Baba and Grandma had lived their own trials and were now at peace. Maybe it was the fact that their love for me and for the rest of our family was so accepting and unconditional. Or perhaps I just needed the intimacy. Whatever the reason, to this day the memory of massaging Baba makes my voice quaver and brings tears to my eyes. I think about the little girl that I was and the simple comfort and calm of the human touch. However fiercely I tried to be a small adult, I was still a child, and vulnerable.

Meanwhile, Mother continued—very consciously—to prepare her children for all of what life might hold for them. She might have been a dictator, but she was also a fairy godmother. Even while she laid down the law she was careful not to limit our expectations of life or our pleasure in it. Mother decided that lack of money didn't mean that we couldn't live in style, so we did. Soon, as we counted our pennies or did our accounts we drank from lead crystal and ate off bone china; it just happened to be crystal and china from other people's garages, and please throw out any piece with a chip right away.

By her example, she showed us never to limit our aspirations or the ability to experience pleasure no matter what we might be going through, or what our means might be. She was so, so right.

She also always made sure we looked great. Until my first marriage all my clothes came from thrift shops and the Salvation Army. But that didn't mean that they couldn't be beautifully cut and perfectly cleaned and pressed. It was vital to Mother that she could demonstrate to the world how she could still provide superbly for her children.

As she always reminded us, "If you don't take care of yourself physically, people will think you don't care about yourself. And if you don't, why should they?"

Mother always took us along to the garage sales. If she found an opportunity to impart wisdom, she didn't let it slip by, and in those garage sales she saw beauties.

"Children, just because we can't buy brand-new items now doesn't mean that you won't be able to some day," she'd assure us. "If you work hard enough, you can get whatever you desire. It might take you a little longer than some other people who started with more, but if you apply yourself, you'll get there just the same."

In our family it was important to take pride in yourself. That included the way you looked and the kind of home you made for yourself. Like some of her bohemian friends, Mother had a sense of style that now seems way ahead of its time. She'd look at labels and check seams when she went shopping for clothes, and much preferred to buy good designer labels at a used clothing store than to buy something new that was cheaply made.

At those garage sales, she'd point out the seams in poor-quality glassware and give the rim of a crystal goblet a little flick of her finger to make it ring. She'd turn over a china plate and show us the telltale signature of quality on the bottom.

"This is how you know whether a plate or cup is fine porcelain," she'd say. Or, "This is how you can tell whether a glass is mouthblown or molded." My mother never felt envy for what other people had; they were just symbols of what she could achieve.

She not only educated us in the fine points of the decorative arts, but expanded our expectations far beyond our current circumstances, even as she taught us also to accept our material reality. We couldn't change it without first accepting it.

Especially important, for me and my sisters, was the lesson that a woman could be her own provider and feather her own nest without having a man in the picture. That a woman's desire to have a nice home didn't have to be legitimized by the presence of a man, as if the only reason to acquire nice china and crystal and linens was to build yourself a dowry. It never occurred to me, later on, that I couldn't go out and select my own crystal and china and use it myself—as well as when I'd invited a man over for dinner.

I'll never forget her hauling us down to Maxwell Street in Chicago, the barter and discount neighborhood where everyone brought their cast-offs and horse-traded them for the building blocks of their dreams. In front of our eyes our worn-out vacuum cleaner would turn into a throw rug for the hall, and George's outgrown shoes would get traded in for exactly the sort of gilt mirror Mother had been visualizing on the empty wall of the bathroom for months. Mother knew how to get whatever she needed, and she wasn't going to let lack of money stop her.

She wasn't going to be shy, either, or let the professionals intimidate her. She was going to haggle right along with the best of them. She was going to learn to do whatever it took to turn her dross into gold. Every resource she had, no matter how insignificant, held the potential for transformation.

The fact that we didn't have much money to spend didn't stop us from celebrating the holidays in a big way, and some of my favorite memories come from those times. At Christmas, it was important to decorate the house just so, and we always started early. Mother would show us how to cut and glue shapes from colored paper so that they turned into beautiful lanterns. We'd spend hours threading popcorn and cranberries on string and looping them on the tree until she was satisfied that it looked perfect. If we were using foil icicles, there was no throwing them on in clumps! They had to be hung on the branches straight, one by one. We got our marching orders at Easter, too. Our Easter eggs couldn't be ordinary Easter eggs. We didn't just dye them, we trimmed them with sequins and paint and braid. The result of this kind of attention was that we always had the most festive and interesting gathering place for the holidays, and even though our circumstances were modest, our house was the place where all the aunts and uncles and cousins gathered.

To this day, round about the second week in December I blanket my own home with greenery, needlepoint Santas and stockings, and other things that have become traditions in our house and hold special memories. Not only does it make me and my loved ones happy, but it's a way of paying my own private Yuletide tribute to Mother's Feminine Force.

The idea that we had to work hard did not in any way limit my expectations in life. In fact, that need to work blasted away any limits on our expectations as forcefully as the blast of a freight train's whistle as it careered down the Indiana train tracks. Because my role models' *real* message was that as long as you work hard, you can have or get *whatever* it is you want. And I believe that all women everywhere deserve to have whatever they want.

It was by following her own inspiration that Mother eventually found the profession that worked the best for her. At a cast party at our house, Mother's friend took one look at my brother George, who was about seven at the time, and told my mother that George looked perfect for a part in a professional show she was working on. Mother took George to the Chicago theatrical agent her friend suggested, and soon George had a burgeoning career in commercials and television, with Mother as his manager.

It was the ideal solution for both of them. George loved the work and Mother could bank considerably more money for less time than she did demonstrating products at the grocery store. Through trial and error and resilience, Mother had found the best professional choice to support our lifestyle, and one that brought her closer to what made her happy.

Although it helped, George's new career didn't solve all our problems. While he worked often, residuals in those days were nothing compared to what they are today, certainly not enough to comfortably support a family of five. And while the train rides to Chicago theaters and casting agents gave Mother the perfect opportunity to read from her spiritual works to her captive son, their absence meant that the rest of us had even more chores and a greater need to pull together.

Luckily, I had learned how. The women in my family didn't merely show me the dignity of work; they showed me *how* to work. If you are going to decorate Easter eggs, don't stop with the dye, go for the sequins and paper lace. Don't just rerent that room—make it shining new first. And switching trains at the railroad yard wasn't low-level drudgery that had no place in a child's world. On the contrary. Going to work with Grandma was such a treat that each of us begged to know when we'd get to do it again.

Looking back, I can see that Grandma's job was a tough one. The physical work was hard, the winter nights were cold, and when one of us wasn't around, it was doubtless a lonely job. She couldn't have gotten enough sleep. Yet my overriding memory of the experience was one of fun, excitement, great dignity, and optimism. Independence, spirit, and the sense of can-do were part of Grandma's legacy to our family. In fact, she is still one of my greatest teachers. This prayer, part of which she wrote out in hand, is framed and hangs on my office wall today:

THINKING OF YOU
REMIND ME, GOD

Dear God, when I am lonely and
Perhaps I feel despair
Let not my ailing heart forget
That You hear every prayer.
Remind me that no matter what
I do or fail to do
There still is hope for me as long
As I have faith in you.
Let not my eyes be blinded by
Some folly I commit
But help me to regret my wrong
And to make up for it.
Inspire me to put my fears
Upon a hidden shelf
And in the future never to
Be sorry for myself.
Give me the restful sleep I need
Before another dawn
And bless me in the morning with
The courage to go on.
    Amen

Dear Georgette   I love you and miss you very much. My thoughts and prayers are with you always. God bless you.
Love,
Grandmother Mary

As the years went on, I was home with the kids more and between her work and the theater group, Mother was gone even more. She was realistic enough to see that as a single mother of four her personal dreams were only going to take her so far. She never said so out loud—she was too tough—but I think that at a certain point she realized that she was never going to buy her china brand-new, or pay for her own opening-night tickets in the front row.

"Georgette," Mother would say sternly to me out of the blue, "I expect you to do better than me. I know full well that you can and that you will." And then she'd talk about something else entirely.

She would come into our bedrooms at night after we had fallen asleep, shake us just enough to rouse us, and whisper, "You can be whatever you want."

And only after she'd successfully asked us to repeat what she'd said did she let us fall back to sleep again. That wasn't even the end of it, because then, just to make sure, she'd ask us to repeat it again. I repeat that every day to this day. Lyn has said that Mother did this partially to give us the strength and courage *she* needed to go on.

I suspect Lyn's theory may be true. But I also believe that this conviction of Mother's came from those core beliefs passed on to her by Grandma and Baba. They showed her that anything was possible. Immigrant mothers of five could become factory workers and landladies. Young mothers of two could switch trains in tight skirts and high heels. Despite the cruel twist life had dealt her, Mother still believed this wholeheartedly. If she couldn't have her heart's desire, then her children would.

"*The eyes are blind,*" Mother would say, quoting Antoine de Saint-Exupéry's *The Little Prince.* "*One must look with the heart.*"

If it wasn't Saint-Exupéry, it was her other source of strength, *The Prophet* by the inspirational poet Kahlil Gibran:

"*And is it not a dream which none of you remember having dreamt, that built your city and fashioned all there is in it? . . . Is it not your breath that has erected and hardened the structure of your bones?*"

And if that didn't work, there was always Black Oak.

We were still kids. So once in a while tempers would flare. Although we understood we couldn't be too disobedient or rebellious at home for our family to work, we weren't perfect, either. There were days I longed for a brand-new pink Shetland sweater I saw in the store window downtown and asked Mother repeatedly why I couldn't have it, especially when George was now in a show and I was working so hard. Or there was the inevitable day Melody sulked about having to wear my hand-me-down dress to church one time too many. Those were the days all four of us kids got piled into a car and driven to Black Oak. Black Oak was a tragically poor Highland neighborhood notorious for its shacks and garbage. Unlike us, the children who grew up there didn't have enough clothes to wear or food to eat.

Mother always took the long way around through Black Oak. The way she saw it, we required bitter medicine if the cure was going to last. And she'd make sure we saw every detail, from the broken windows to the sad, empty eyes.

"See?" Mother would say. "It's time to be grateful for what you have."

And no matter how often we'd been there, we fell instantly silent.

Even as my household responsibilities grew while Mother and George began to travel, she grew tougher in her demands. It was harder and harder to secure coveted privileges. I can remember one time in high school when I wanted to go out on a weekend for a special occasion. I knew that Mother was very strict about socializing. So I cleaned every inch of the house. I didn't need her to clue me in beforehand that this was what it would take to get her permission. After a careful inspection of my work she did say I could go.

I knew that my *actions spoke louder than words*, and that eloquent action was what it took. All four of us knew that if we wanted a special privilege, we would have to earn it first. But we also knew that achievement would be rewarded. If you got good grades, you went to the circus. If you didn't get good grades, you didn't go to the circus. If you didn't attend church on Sunday, you didn't go out Sunday afternoon. *Anything we wanted was achievable; the only variable was how much we wanted to give of ourselves to achieve it.*

That philosophy of Mother's endured. I still believe that you earn what you get in life, and in my experience that's better than trusting your life to luck. It's great to be lucky, but I don't want to base my life on it.

You earn what you get by working hard with what you've got. *But you also earn what you get by releasing the energy of your dreams. It is completely possible to visualize your dreams right into reality.*

That was another of my Mother's lessons, and one she taught in the most wonderful of ways.

Melody and I must have been twelve or thirteen when Mother decided it was time for us to go to the opera in Chicago. This was a major event. First, Mother had to save for it. Then she would get the libretto and record from the library so she could go through it with us before the big night. She wanted us to understand the story and the characters and the music when we got there. Nothing was good enough for Mother except opening night—even though we had seats in the top balcony. But we might as well have been crown princesses sitting in the royal box, we had such a good time. I'll never forget dressing up in our Sunday best and standing proudly on the curb to watch the glamorous procession of gowns and jewelry and tails float into the theater like sparkling clouds. Nothing but the best was good enough for us, no matter where our seats were. We had worked hard, and we deserved it.

Inside, Mother's focus was one hundred percent opera appreciation. Forget the slow, creaky elevators that took us up so high. They didn't even register on her. Opera was part of being educated, part of being cultured, and part of what we needed to know so that we would be prepared to have a better life. And Melody and I were dazzled by Mother's statement that soon *we* would be the ones sitting in the front row right next to the orchestra in our very own sparkling gowns. She'd even go so far as to point out our seats.

"Work hard," she'd say, "honor your dreams, and you'll get there."

I can remember first seeing Nureyev dance. Even though I didn't know who he was, I knew I was seeing greatness. I'll never forget how Mother held our hands as we watched and I realized she was feeling the same thrill we were. I could feel her hands transmit her excitement and vitality to ours. On these nights Mother was our fairy godmother waving her magic wand. As far as she was concerned, everything was possible. It was just a question of when. It was in that balcony of the Chicago Opera that I put my long afternoons of washing and ironing and cooking into a new perspective. Whatever lay in the future was going to be a great adventure.

Soon Mother found and financed her dream house.

The five of us had lived for years in a tiny two-bedroom white stucco house in a working-class neighborhood. Characteristically, Mother had done the best she possibly could with what she had to work with.

When we first got there, she called in a contractor to see if the wall between the dining room and living room could be torn down to make a larger space. He said it could, and he'd be happy to do it. She said she'd consider it. About as soon as he was safely out of earshot, she hauled out a sledgehammer and did it herself. The way she saw it, now that she'd been advised that the deed was possible, there was no reason on earth she shouldn't be able to do it herself. Next she tore the kitchen open to build a serving window above the sink, papered the walls with egg cartons to give them texture, and painted them yellow. She made the garage into a den for us kids.

Still, Mother longed for another house. She wanted her kids in a better school district. She wanted bedrooms for each of us. She envisioned a house where the extended family could get together more comfortably on holidays, and where she could entertain her theater group. She longed for a house in a neighborhood where many professionals lived. In short, she longed for the perfect home for all of us. As we got older, she started dreaming about that house. She could see it clearly: a charming Dutch colonial with a carved bench in front.

The house Mother saw in her mind's eye was clearly beyond our financial means. Still, she kept visualizing it. She began to practice visualizing it in full detail. She could even see all of us living in it. Then one day she drove down an unfamiliar Indiana street, and there it was—a charming Dutch colonial with a pretty carved bench at the front door, and a "for sale" sign on the lawn.

Mother started to tremble. She knew instantly this was the one. She stopped the car to take it all in, and as soon as she started driving again she began juggling numbers over and over in her head. That was when she panicked, because she couldn't make any configuration come out right. No matter how she added it up, there was no way she had enough money to make the down payment.

In the morning she went to see the realtors anyway, and asked them if they would lend her the key so she could take a look inside. It was a small town and Mother was well known, and they happily granted her request. Mother went home to pick up Grandma and Baba, and the three of them went to look at Mother's dream house. Baba looked over the furnace and the plumbing with her landlady's eagle eye and gave Mother her seal of approval.

Mother went out to sit on that perfect little bench to think. She was trembling again. She knew this was the house. She knew the structure was sound. She'd also confirmed the asking price, and knew she couldn't afford it. She had calculated that she might just have enough saved from my brother's earnings to almost make the down payment, but in no way, shape, or form could she cover the closing costs.

Baba came up from behind and sat down on the bench with her.

"You know what?" she said. "This is your home, darling. You gather up all the money you have. However much you have. And whatever you're lacking, I will cover for you."

Mother was flabbergasted, and told Baba so. After all, Baba was no longer a young woman and she was still working hard, renting out rooms and managing tenants and properties.

"Don't worry," Baba said. "I've got the cash. You get things going at the bank, and then you come to see me."

"You've got the cash?"

"I've got the cash."

Mother knew her Gran too well to doubt her, although she couldn't really understand how such a thing was possible. So Mother went to the bank, and to the real estate office. She brought along my brother and one of his residual checks.

"George," she said, "I don't know if I should be doing this or not, because maybe you wanted to have a savings account or something, but I want to get you into the best school system, I want you to be associated with the best people, and I've got to go for it. Everyone is saying I can't do this, but I'm going to. I'm going to find a way."

And then Mother went to Baba's.

"Gran, you mean to tell me you have cash in this house?" she asked as she barged in the front door.

And Baba said, "Don't worry. It's under the mattress. You know, darling, you always have to keep a little cash back. I do it, and you should, too. That way, if someone gets you into a corner and makes you uncomfortable, if you're miserable, you can just put your hand under the mattress, throw the money at him, and get out!"

And then Baba pulled the extra cash out from under her bed. That clinched it. My mother's vision turned into a reality.

But how could she make the mortgage payments?

All her friends told her she was out of her mind. The whole town knew full well that she had no money. They told her to forget it.

"Dee," they said, "you're gonna go broke. Do yourself a favor and go easy on yourself. Be prudent. Stay where you are. We're only telling you because we care about you. We don't want to see you and those kids in a bad way."

Well, luckily Mother didn't listen to those who meant well but underestimated her. She rented out our old house instead of selling it, following Baba's instructions. So she had both cash and an asset. And the bank had given her the mortgage.

She wasn't about to let her dream slip through her fingers.

It would be a cold day in hell before her Feminine Force let that happen. Mother and the rest of us lived quite happily in that house for years and years. Not only that, but we furnished the Ridgewood Avenue house, as we called it, exquisitely—from secondhand shops and Maxwell Street, naturally.

No one could figure out how we managed to make the interior so beautiful. But by then they'd thrown their hands up and stopped trying. It *was* a true dream house for Mother, who only sold it quite recently, when I was able to give her a condominium in Florida. The condo suits her lifestyle better these days. But she still talks wistfully about the old house she created from dreams. It is amazing what you can create from dreams.

I had dreams of my own. In high school my grades were respectable but unspectacular. I didn't worry about it. I kept my focus, and my focus was to graduate high school, have enough savings to go to college, and continue to take care of my "kids" at the same time.

At that point, no one in my family had ever gotten more than a high school diploma, but I didn't let that stop me and my family didn't try. In fact, Mother was forever drumming it into the four of us that to achieve what we wanted in life, we first needed that college degree. The fact that as an adult she had always struggled with night school and never finished—there just wasn't time—didn't color her expectations for the rest of us. No one ever told us that life was hard, or that going to college could be difficult when you had to finance it all yourself. Our ability to live our dreams was taken for granted, the way we took it for granted that the sun would rise every morning and Christmas would come on December 25.

As a result it never occurred to me that I couldn't put myself through state college, which was the only option with my grades and my budget, or that I was severely handicapped because someone else wasn't paying my way. I had been given every assurance that anything I wanted to do was achievable under my own steam. So I went about it by breaking that goal down into points A, B, C, and D like everything else.

While the other girls were dating and going to the dances at the country club, I was ironing linens at the country club. That was how I discovered what a darned good ironer I was, which, believe it or not, was profitable *and* satisfying. *Anything* that helped me go to college suited my purposes. If I could make money ironing, what other talents might I have that would help me achieve my goal?

That got me to thinking. What else did I like to do? Even then, I loved to read the glamour magazines and I had started to do my hair in the styles I saw there. I decided to offer to do my neighbors' hair to earn money, because that was a service I could perform on my own schedule, while I took care of the house. While I was at it, I also offered to babysit and take in ironing at home, too. Soon I had two or three jobs at a time, and all of them were work that I could do well and schedule around my domestic responsibilities.

Soon I was waking up in the morning with my savings account balance on the tip of my tongue, and from there I hit the ground not only running, but also planning and budgeting. Every day, I calculated how much I still needed to save for my college tuition and room and board. I wasn't a math whiz, and I wasn't going to major in accounting, but like Baba, I could count.

What I couldn't do very well was work my way through school *and* make straight A's at the same time. But I did the best I could. The reality was that I just didn't have the time to excel scholastically, or socially, either. I was determined that I was going to excel later in life, but I wouldn't be going to dances or getting on the honor roll in the meantime.

Mother had already taught me that making fantasy reality was much more satisfying than losing yourself in the safe sanctuary of endless daydreams. While other girls were imagining their prom dates and dresses, going to football games and graduation parties, I was constantly using Mother's visualization process to create the life I knew I would have when my moment came. Hadn't I seen her turn a pair of outgrown shoes into a gilt mirror, and even materialize a house on Ridgewood Avenue out of nothing but dreams and tenacity?

I was looking forward to the moment when I'd have everything I wanted in life. I was going to make sure that no one in our family ever had to worry again. I'd never again have that awful feeling in the pit of my stomach every time I saw Mother walk out the door.

I skipped my high school graduation festivities. I didn't feel I had the time or the money to spend on them. I was focused on my goals and what my life would be *after* I finished school.

When I left home that first time and hugged and kissed everyone goodbye, my tears didn't flow only from the sadness of leaving the brother and sisters and mother and grandparents whose laughter I'd shared and tears I'd dried. My tears were also tears of triumph. A college education was my first big goal. Achieving it, and having my family understand it was possible, was all the graduation ceremony any daughter could want. After that, the sky was the limit.

Chapter 5

Start in Your Head

*"The thing women have got to learn is that nobody
gives you power. You just take it."*

—ROSEANNE ARNOLD

I graduated from Indiana University the same way I graduated from high school: by working every step of the way. I had two or
three jobs at any one time, including store clerk, carhop, and switchboard operator. I also rebottled shampoo out of the huge bottles
Mother bought wholesale for the family and sold them to other girls at
school. I didn't worry about making the dean's list or pledging soror-
ities, because that wasn't part of my goal. My goal was to graduate,
period, and to do that I did whatever it took, including visualizing that
outcome daily, the way Mother taught me.

I still consciously use visualization almost every day. It still helps me
achieve major goals, helps me reenergize when I'm drained, and gives
me confidence when I'm feeling shaky. In fact, I use it to energize all
my major goals before I undertake them.

It takes just a few minutes. I start by connecting with my inner voice.
Then, in as much detail as I can muster, I imagine and see myself
performing the task I need to perform or feeling the way I need to feel.
Visualization always gives me new confidence in my instincts and my
ability. It also creates results. It turns dreams into goals.

There are many different techniques you can use for visualization.

I've always used my own method, which is no doubt based on everything Mother taught us, because that's what works the best for me.

I get very basic: If I am visualizing the successful outcome of a business meeting, I see myself in the room. I picture what I'm wearing, exactly where and how I'm standing or sitting, and exactly where and how others appear. I hear myself saying the words I plan to speak—the words, numbers, ideas, or even gestures that I produce to make my point most effectively—and projecting the exact attitude of confidence and energy I want to project. If I'll be bringing anyone else with me to the meeting, I might also visualize that person and the specific contribution she is going to make toward achieving the goal.

Finally, I picture the positive effect those words and gestures are having on the person I am meeting with. I see and hear the result I want—whether it's a verbal "yes" on the spot, a letter, or any other result. And then I visualize exactly how getting that "yes" will positively affect my business. Whatever that result is—be it a venture capital investment, or a distribution outlet for my product, or a magazine article that publicizes my business to the right market—I envision how it will positively influence my business in the short term and in the long term.

When I visualize, it often feels as if I'm making it up—and in a sense I *am* making it up: I'm literally using my Feminine Force to create part of my life before it happens. In this sense, "making it up" is the point.

Next I create my vision physically. It it's appropriate, I might tear out magazine articles that describe or illustrate my goal, or magazine pictures that stimulate my vision. Or I might create a little model or script. And by the way, I don't limit visualization to professional goals, I also use it to follow my dreams. And after all these years, I do it almost unconsciously. I dreamt of owning an apartment in New York, and after a number of years it came to pass.

I always remain open to the new information my inner voice may give me about my goal. If the name of a business contact I haven't talked to for a year suddenly comes to mind, I will pay attention to that information, act on it if appropriate, and use the results to continue to refine my vision.

I also ask for help: I call on my inner power, using the words that work for me. I allow for the possibility that my success may be even *greater* than what I've imagined. I always expand the horizons of a goal, the way Mother expanded the horizons of what was possible for us to achieve.

And then I let go. I know that my Feminine Force will now be continuously working in the background to create the reality I have chosen.

Chapter 6

I Wasn't Born a Redhead, But I Was Born to Be a Redhead

"A solitary fantasy can totally transform one million realities."

—Maya Angelou

When I graduated from Indiana University with a B.S. in Communications in 1969, I was just a girl with good role models and one immediate goal. I knew that Highland wasn't going to give me any opportunities to seriously pursue my interest. I knew I wasn't going to make a career in the steel industry. At twenty-one, I wasn't quite ready to raise another family. I wanted a career. I wanted to make my mark in the world. I knew I needed to be in a place that offered a more varied cultural life, richer resources, and wider fields of opportunity. I had achieved my first goal and gotten a college education. I had made it to point A. Now it was time to move to point B.

I was studying the job market long before I finished school, but after graduation I started sending out resumes in earnest. I probably mailed out a hundred before I was done. When I landed my first full-time job, it was with Grey Advertising in Detroit. Working on print, radio, and television advertising at Grey was good experience.

My brother George, in the meantime, had gotten a scholarship to UCLA. Going to school in Los Angeles made it possible for him to continue working as an actor, doing commercials and taking various roles in television productions to help pay his way.

1

2

3

At age one (above left); at 14 months with Mother (above right); ultra-feminine at three and a half (left); and at seven, the year my father died (below).

5

4

Baba and Grandma in the back yard of their boardinghouse (above); I'm in the front row, third from the right (below).

6

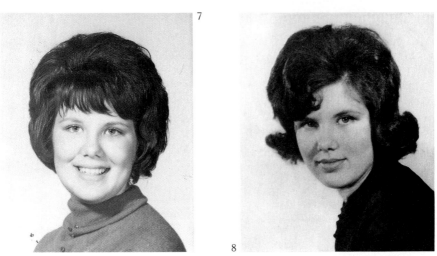

My ninth-grade class picture (left). If I look mature for my age, raising three siblings has that effect. At right is a school picture also taken during my early adolescence.

Our only complete family picture (below), taken just before my father died. Clockwise from upper left, Mother, me, Daddy, George, Melody, and Lyn.

HAMMOND 1967

10 That's me, first runner-up, second from the left. We found the dress at a secondhand store, and Lyn later wore it to her high school prom.

11  12

The start of my beauty experimentation. What's my excuse for that eyeliner (right)? I was nineteen and it was the sixties.

15

In California, with friend
Kenny Rogers and columnist
George Christie.

With my first husband,
Robert Muir (above); and
with my second husband,
George Barrie (below). With
G. B., it didn't matter that I
was smiling. I was completely
miserable.

16

My sister Lyn needed to
discover her Feminine
Force.... Now she's not
only beautiful, but she's
confident and in control
of her life.

14

17

19   Disneyworld, 1992: Five generations of the Paulsin family at our annual reunion, which I host. Clockwise left to right: my sister Melody, her son Bryan Dwyer, Mother, Melody's husband Mike Dwyer, and their sons Eric

and Todd, my brother George, Todd's wife Dawn, Grandma, me, my uncle Dick Bell, Eric's wife Lisa, Eric's son Derek, and my sister Lyn. In the middle with Mickey Mouse is Shaun, George's son.

With my movie-star-handsome husband, Robert. I visualized the perfect man and it worked!

What George had to say about Los Angeles only fueled my desire to go there. It was still a land of dreams to me, a place where people went to create and reinvent their lives.

After about a year of working in Detroit, I was getting ready to make a move myself. One weekend when I was home visiting my family in Highland, I decided to drive into Chicago to get my hair trimmed at a salon I liked, and when I looked into the mirror that day, the woman I saw there seemed to lack definition. For one thing, my hair was naturally brown, with tones of red in it. I had a strong sense of who I was on the inside, but what I saw on the outside didn't reflect that. My grandfather was a redhead, my grandmother was a *powerful* redhead. I decided to take the first step in reinventing myself. I walked out of that salon a flaming redhead. I looked into the mirror and thought, *I wasn't born a redhead, but I was born to be a redhead.* Somehow, taking that little step encouraged me to take a bigger one. I bought a plane ticket and moved to California.

Los Angeles offered the perfect opportunity for a kid with a degree in communications and big, unformed ambitions. I'd made a decision to move to point B, and Los Angeles was it. I'd helped take care of George when he was small, and I knew he would help me now, as I tried to get my feet on the ground in a new place. Family was important to both of us, and even though there were only two of us there, a long way from what we used to call home, we were family still.

George had his own apartment in L.A.—a pretty spartan place— and we had to double up for a while, with George graciously letting me have one side of what was, luckily, a king-sized bed.

George had friends, but I wanted my own. I also started urging him to broaden his circles, and we became something of a team. We couldn't afford a meal in places like The Polo Lounge, but we'd go there and order a soda apiece and nurse that one drink through the evening while we watched and listened and talked with the people around us. Pretty soon we were making friends, and getting invited to parties. It wasn't long before I became friendly with a woman who ran estate sales in Beverly Hills.

I thought George should fix his apartment up, and George seemed ready for that, so I set out to redo it for him. My new friend worked almost full time organizing what would be called yard sales in more modest neighborhoods. Around Hollywood, when people weren't changing their partners or careers and selling their homes, they were redecorating. Whenever one impulse or another had wealthy residents selling off their furnishings, my friend would tip me off to the address, and I'd get first pick. I was able to buy fabulous objects for George's place—antiques, pictures, furniture—for a song. I was still transplanting all I'd learned from my mother's ways of having a good life on a shoestring, and pretty soon George's place looked pretty darned good.

In the meantime, I was scouting jobs. I had some friends from college and from Grey Advertising who were working in L.A., and through them I immediately picked up some free-lance work as a production assistant on commercials and various radio and TV spots. George's contacts helped, too.

Although both of us were still scrambling, I remember that brief period as golden and very full. Everything was, in fact, to change within only a few weeks. But meanwhile, I was taking the first steps toward carving out a life in a new territory, and all of it felt like an adventure. I spent every second living it to the fullest. Besides soaking up the ambience at elegant restaurants, George and I cooked up other low-cost schemes to entertain ourselves. His car was an old 1939 Rolls-Royce that he loved—over the years he's developed a profitable hobby buying classic cars, fixing them up, and selling them—and one afternoon, after seeing an item in the paper, I talked him into joining the Rolls-Royce Club. It was hosting a kite-flying contest, not exactly the stuffy sort of thing George seemed to think a club like that would do. As George remembers it, I insisted that our homemade kite should be the best, most outlandish kite in the crowd. We took it and George's Rolls out to Newport Beach, where everybody seemed to be spending as much time gawking at the cars and the people as they were flying kites. But we had a great time.

There always were exciting, crazy things going on in Los Angeles, and as much as we could, George and I went to them. It was on one of our earliest adventures that I met the man I'd soon marry.

Sotheby's was running an auction for Twentieth Century Fox one weekend, to sell off some props, costumes, and different kinds of memorabilia from some of their productions. We didn't intend to buy a thing, but the sale was bound to be a treat for movie buffs, and seemed like a good way spend a Sunday afternoon.

It was one of those beautiful, sunny California days, and among other items, Fox had put up for sale the scale replicas of World War II ships they'd built and used in the filming of *Tora! Tora! Tora!* They were so enormous—fifteen and twenty feet long—that they had to be set up outdoors. And they were wonderfully detailed. George especially loved looking at them, but I couldn't imagine where you'd put one of those things if you *could* afford it. As it turned out, one bidder bought the whole lot.

The buyer caught my attention for more reasons than one. He was around forty and strikingly handsome—tall, with fair hair and intense blue eyes, very confident and prosperous-looking, but with a certain gentleness about him. I found myself glancing at him throughout the afternoon, and by the time George and I left, I realized I wasn't going to get this man out of my head anytime soon. What kind of man would be spending so much money in such an outrageously fanciful way? George and I were already out of the parking lot and headed toward home when I made a decision.

"George, please turn around and go back. Right now."

"Georgette, the auction's over. End of show. You want to go to the beach or something?"

"George, please, don't ask, just turn around and go."

Great guy that he is, George turned around.

I had to knock on the door, because by that time everyone was gone and the building had been locked up. When a woman finally answered, I asked her for the name of the man who bought the ships. Of course, she said she wasn't allowed to give out that kind of information.

I was only half-prepared for an answer like that, and I said the first thing that came into my head. "Well," I said, "I'm from *Time* magazine, and we're doing a story on Sotheby's."

I said some other things about needing profiles of Sotheby's bidders, that I had a deadline to meet, and so on, and somehow she bought it. Three minutes later I had the name I needed: Robert Muir.

I had to wait until Monday to get him at his office, and by then I'd had plenty of time to reconsider the whole idea.

I called him anyway.

And without even coming up with a better story.

"This is Georgette Paulsin from *Time* magazine," I told his secretary. "I'd like to come over and interview Mr. Muir about the ships he bought from Fox this weekend."

She said something like "*Time?* Oh! *Time,*" and told me she'd have to check with the boss. My heart was racing, but I pushed on. "Wait—first, I'd like to get a little background information from you." I got it in short order: He was a Mormon from Salt Lake City, the father of two, and he was . . . divorced. I managed to absorb all this, even though at this point my heart was really thumping, and when his secretary put me on hold I even jotted the information down as if I really were taking notes for an interview. Then she got back on the line and told me I could come on over.

As I pulled my best dress out of the closet, the nuttiness of this scheme sent my anxiety soaring. How was I going to get out of the big hole I'd just dug for myself with the *Time* story? Not only did I have to worry about the stunt I'd pulled, I'd had very little experience with men in general, and now I was going to meet an attractive stranger on no more than a chance sighting and, as my mother used to put it, *pure unadulterated gall.* My hands were shaking so badly I had a hard time buttoning my buttons.

When I drove to the address I was given and saw "Muir Medical Tower" blazoned across the top of the building, my knees started quaking as well. I had picked out a man who appeared to own a large building in downtown Los Angeles. A mover and shaker, although I was the one shaking in my boots.

But I had taken a considered look at my options. I knew I wanted to meet this man, and I certainly didn't know anyone who could make an introduction. If I was going to meet him, I had to swing it on my own. I repeated this to myself as I parked George's car, but it still took all my famous determination to march through the door and take the elevator to the top floor.

Robert Muir looked just as handsome the second time I saw him as the first. He had a warm handshake, great eye contact, and a radiant smile. He was gracious and charming. He suggested that we have lunch while we talked.

I don't remember much about the restaurant, except that it was in the building and the waiters clearly knew Mr. Muir. When we'd ordered he settled back and said, "Well, okay, shall we start the interview?" And I said no.

I took a deep breath and told him I wasn't going to interview him at all, because I wasn't working for *Time,* or for any other magazine. But

I had seen him buy those boats and had been fascinated. I was new in town and didn't know anybody, so I figured what the heck? What did I have to lose?

When I finished with this spiel, Robert Muir, bless him, threw back his head and laughed. When he was through laughing, he told me he thought I was very gutsy.

I was more than relieved, because after about five minutes with him, I was hooked.

We were married in August of 1972, after about a year of dating. And I had met him less than two weeks after I arrived in L.A.

A big, expensive church wedding was never one of my particular fantasies, so when Robert and I decided to get married we simply flew to Las Vegas and got married in a little chapel. My mother was delighted with the news: she'd been out to visit, and had been around Robert enough to know what a kind and generous man he was.

Although we signed a prenuptial agreement that protected Robert's heirs, from the first day of our marriage Robert Muir seemed to give me whatever my heart desired. When we met, he lived in an apartment. After we were married, he took me house hunting, and together we bought a huge house in Beverly Hills with one of the most fantastic views in the world. I thought this quiet, kind man could use a social life, so soon after we moved in I began throwing parties for people in the entertainment business. At the same time I took an active interest in his real estate developments, an interest he encouraged. My mother says that she'll never forget the day Robert invited the two of us to a board meeting he'd called, to go over plans for a new shopping center and hear proposals from two landscaping firms that were bidding on the job.

Right after the meeting, I piped up. "You know," I said, "I think both of those men are talented and astute, but I like the one with the shiny new wedding band. He looks like a newlywed; he probably needs a job—Robert, give it to him! Except don't let him put in crabapple trees. They look beautiful for a while, but when the crabapples start falling off the tree it's not a pretty sight at all. They attract wasps, they make a big slippery mess, and you might as well put a trail of banana peels for your customers to slip on if you don't have a crew out there cleaning them up every day."

Robert said, "Oh my God, Georgette, you're right."

And then, the way Mother remembers it, the conversation continued, with this very successful and well-established forty-year-old West
Coast real estate developer asking advice from a twenty-three-year-old
from a little town in Indiana.

In many ways, Robert was amazingly indulgent. One day, as we were
driving down Wilshire Boulevard, we passed a Rolls-Royce dealership.

"Aren't those beautiful?" I said.

Robert looked over and said, "The Rolls?" I answered that I used to
imagine riding around in a Rolls-Royce when I was a kid (and I wasn't
thinking about George's thirty-year-old model). It had been one of my
daydreams.

He said, "You dreamed about cars?" And I told him it was something that represented all the things I didn't have. I figured that if you
had a Rolls-Royce, you'd really made it.

Robert's response to this was to stop at the next light, make a U-turn,
and drive back to the dealership, where he wrote out a check for a royal
blue convertible—a Corniche. On the spot.

I could hardly believe it. I felt like a kid in a candy store. When we
got home I spent an hour in that Corniche just parked out in front of
the house, listening to the stereo. In those days a stereo was a big deal
and I was simply in awe. I just couldn't believe my good fortune. Soon
I was taking every opportunity I could to get into that car and drive
around town. I was quite a sight zooming around town with the top
down and my red hair flying out behind me.

Robert Muir was and is a fine man who was generous in more than
material ways. I'm the type that if you want to be with me, you get my
family as well, and Robert understood and fully supported that. He
and my brother became great friends. Even before Robert gave him a
job in his real estate business, George had begun to look up to him as
a mentor and even a father figure.

Hardly more than two years after I'd left Highland, I seemed to be
living the life I'd always dreamed of. I had a husband who seemed
ready to indulge me in every way. I was able to decorate our new house
just the way I wanted it. I had a swimming pool. I had a maid. It was as
if some fairy godmother had waved her wand and everything I had
visualized growing up had become a reality.

One day, when my mother was visiting us at home, I picked up a
box of Kleenex. "Look," I said, and started pulling tissue after tissue

out of the box. "Do you realize that in college I had to be careful how much Kleenex I used? And now, for the first time, I don't have to worry about little things like that."

Of course, my mother had always insisted that I'd find success and happiness in my life, but the truth is, I was thrilled. To be married to a wonderful man, to have a beautiful home, to be able to take care of my family—to have those dreams come true so quickly was pretty heady stuff. It was as if I'd been shot out a cannon and into my most glowing visions of what life could be.

Over twenty years later, I am now very clear about what two people need to do before they get married. One of the first things is to see whether or not they agree about certain fundamentals of marriage. To me, those include fidelity, children, and a shared set of goals and values. Well, if we had asked each other, Robert Muir and I would have agreed on numbers one and two. But as far as number three was concerned, we had little in common. And that would eventually be our downfall.

In 1971, however, I was delighted by my new life with this kind man, although in many ways Georgette Muir was still a Paulsin. You can take the girl out of Indiana, but you can't take Indiana out of the girl. I still did most of the cooking at home. I shopped at Sears. I had this beautiful blue Corniche with vanity plates on it that said "G Muir," and friends would recognize it parked around town and leave little notes for me on the windshield: "Georgette. Call me when you get home from Sears!" For the first time I could flip through magazines and walk through department stores and know that I could get anything that I wanted. And I did have beautiful things. But in some respects I remained pretty careful with money. For Kleenex and light bulbs and groceries and things like that I still shopped at Sears or Kmart.

And I still had dreams of doing great things.

It was only a few years into the marriage that I began to realize just how high my goals were. It was as if I had finally arrived at a vantage point where I could see where the real horizons of my life lay.

Chapter 7

Getting from Point A to Point B

"Knowledge must come through action."

—SOPHOCLES, *TRACHINIAE*

I was still very young when I left the Midwest for Los Angeles, and frankly, getting out of "Dodge City" and wearing nice
clothes was about as far ahead as I could see. But that was enough. It
was that simple, and, in retrospect, that powerful. What made that
modest dream powerful was acting on it. I simply took a step. And
deciding to take that step made all the difference in the world.

I had some ambitions about getting into the movie industry, but I
hadn't mapped them all out. I simply assumed that when I got to L.A.,
I'd figure out what my next step would be.

What I did was a good example of a Feminine Force technique I call
getting from point A to point B. If my mother hadn't gone and asked
for the key to her dream house, that house never would have become
hers. If Baba had sat home paralyzed with worry over her future, instead of simply showing up in Great-grandfather's place on the factory
line, her family would have been financially destroyed. If I hadn't made
the move to Los Angeles, I might still be ironing in Highland.

Acting on your goal is what counts. I never dreamed of marrying as
soon as I did. And I certainly never dreamed I'd eventually own a
cosmetics company or marry a cabinet officer and move in government

circles in Washington. Action always starts with one first small step—and you do not have to know precisely what your final goal is to start down the road.

It was a lesson I continued to learn throughout my life. Every large goal can be broken down into its component parts. That's how big goals are achieved. That's how you short-circuit the word "no." By breaking bigger goals down into a series of smaller goals you *know* you can accomplish, you can turn "no" into a "yes."

Unfortunately, action is the point at which many of us get stuck and block our own progress.

I've had friends say to me, "I want to be successful and to make a difference in the world. But I don't have any particular skills or resources. I feel like I'm starting from zero, and I don't see how anything I could do at this point would get me very far. I don't even know where to start!"

Well, here's a major Feminine Force News Bulletin for you:

Even the largest achievements start out with baby steps. Did you get that?

EVEN THE LARGEST ACHIEVEMENTS START OUT WITH BABY STEPS.

You do not have to take a big step to make big progress.

For many of us, getting from point A to B starts with building confidence in our own decisions. I know more than one woman who isn't sure she knows what she wants. And I'll never forget one friend, now forging a successful business career, who told me that real choice actually frightened her. She was always afraid that she would choose *wrong*.

I think people tend to spend far too much time trying to fathom the psychology of indecisiveness, and too many times I've heard men accuse women of indecision, as if it were a particular feminine weakness. Nonsense. Being decisive, discovering your goals and going after them, is a *process*. Decisions themselves are processes that can be broken down into steps.

I operated on instinct a lot when I was younger, but the more decisions I face, the more consciously I weigh the pros and cons of each decision I make. Janet Bailey suggested that you actually do it on paper in an article titled "Making Smart Decisions," published in *New Woman* magazine in November of 1992.

What follows is the gist of her suggestions. If the process sounds a little simple, that's the point.

First, write down the goal you're considering. Then list all the reasons why you want that goal, and why you deserve it. Third, list the positive things achieving that goal will bring you and your family. Then list the negatives—what you fear about the changes this move will make in your life. Next, weigh those pros and cons and see which come out ahead. Then discuss these with your family. And finally, make a decision based on what you've discovered. If the decision is to go for it, take the first step. Or, if the negatives win out, reformulate the goal and subject it to the same test.

A friend of mine who had both children and a career used this method when she was facing a decision about her next professional move. She worked in a high-profile, high-pressure public relations firm, and she wanted to take the next step up into senior management.

She listed that as her goal.

She felt she deserved it because she'd worked in the company for five years. She'd covered many different aspects of accounts, from drafting press releases to soothing clients to setting up publicity tours. She was a good communicator. And she knew that she'd work to make herself one of the best executives her company had ever seen—just because she wanted that job so much.

She was well aware of what she'd gain. She'd move into an area that really interested her. She'd get a lot more satisfaction out of her job, and make great contacts. And with an increase in salary, she calculated that within three years, when the family was really going to need more space for the kids, she and her husband would be able to buy a bigger house.

Then she listed her doubts. Could she really sell an account to a client? She thought she had the stomach for the corporate politics at her firm, but it was something she needed to consider carefully. And she wondered if her husband could give the kids dinner a few nights a week if she had to stay late at the office.

Then she weighed all the pros and cons. She felt she had good natural rapport with people, and she knew her family was supportive, so she felt reasonably sure she could deal with the high-pressure job situation. She also felt that buying a new house in a good school district would make an important difference in her children's lives as they got older, but she didn't much like the idea of working very late and being away from home in the evening.

When she discussed all this with her family, her husband said he couldn't guarantee he'd be home early every time she ran late, but he pointed out that no one would go hungry. Their daughter was nearly thirteen and perfectly capable of putting a simple meal on the table.

With all this in mind, my friend finally decided to find a better-paying job in a slightly smaller, less high-pressured environment—for the time being. For her own satisfaction, she wanted to spend her evenings with her family. It just wasn't worth it to her to miss important moments in her children's lives any more than she had to. This was a compromise that best served *all* her values—family and career alike. She had taken her original goal, and reformulated it slightly to fit the reality of her situation.

Putting complicated questions down in black and white, breaking them down like this and weighing the pros and cons, is a great way to keep a clear head—and a clear head makes good decisions.

Even though you'll want to do some negotiating with your immediate family over the ways your goals will affect your lives together, the point of that negotiation stops where your mutual concerns end. Have the courage to say, "This is what *I* want in life even though somebody else may not judge it to be worthy." Any goal is a worthy goal: from changing the way you look to changing your career or changing your approach to finding love.

Once you've examined your own goal, figure out what your first step will be. Ask yourself what needs to happen before you can accomplish it. Include both the big moves and the little ones—even if those little ones are as minor as getting your hair cut before you go out for interviews.

No goal is too inconsequential to give clear attention to. No goal is too *large* to set your sights on. And no goal is unacceptable unless it's immoral or illegal.

If your goal, like mine when I left Highland, is still a little vague, don't let that stop you, either. Maybe your inner voice is reminding you that you want to leave public relations, but you don't know exactly where you want to go or even if you want to keep working. Maybe you're thinking about having a child. You could call your goal, Creating My New Life. Maybe point A is simply checking the balance in your savings account. Point B might be a visit to your old friend Betty in Minnesota, who just stepped off the fast track at the age of forty to have a beautiful little boy named Bob. After you come back from visiting Betty, you might realize that while you adore your nephews and nieces and godchildren, you're not sure you're willing or able to devote the sort of complete attention to an infant that Betty clearly devotes to Bob. You might decide that you can find plenty of fulfillment in being an active and loving aunt.

Or you might come home thinking how content Betty and her husband seem. How Betty never looked happier in her life. And most important, how you never got tired of holding that baby yourself.

That gut reaction is where you start. Your heart tells you what you want: now you use your head to get it. You lay out the ABCs of it, and start with A.

You can and should depend on your gut reaction when you're trying different lifestyles on for size, but that's not the same as letting fear or embarrassment stop you from taking any of the little steps you need to accomplish a change. That's where you need to let your head take over. If you feel a "no" coming on, or you cannot visualize your result, use the decision list to pinpoint where the hang-up really is. Deal with that, and then either proceed or readjust.

A smaller goal might be to re-landscape the south side of the house. What you see in your mind's eye is a beautiful trellis of roses along the wall. But you put off doing anything about it because you're not sure you have enough time to devote to it, and you've heard that roses are an expensive pain in the neck to raise. Your first step might be to invest a few dollars in a book about roses, or to visit the local nursery or botanical gardens to talk with people there and take a look at *their* results. Maybe those roses take a lot *more* trouble than you dreamed—but you love them so much you decide it's worth it. Or maybe you find a happy compromise when you discover that old shrub roses and rugosas require much less attention than hybrid teas—and you love them just as much.

Finally, give yourself a break and remember that *you do not have to map out the rest of your life right now.* I never do. In fact, my goals seem to change direction in a major way every five years or so. Just about as frequently as I get a professional makeover—about once a year—I do a new goal list, to check in with myself and see if I'm on track.

It's the process of goal setting, and not the goal itself, that gets you on your way. In most cases, going after something that turns out to be the wrong choice for you isn't going to take you off on some fatal detour.

It's not like getting on the expressway going in the wrong direction. If you stop and alter your course, chances are you'll discover that no matter what you've been doing, you've been making *progress*. You've still moved a little closer to that new place where you really want to be.

You can always trust your inner voice to guide you and give you courage when you need it. Take that first step, and keep putting one foot in front of the other, come hell or high water, until you get there. The world being what it is, you probably *will* have to wade through some high water, and maybe even fight your way through a little hell, to get where you're going. But you may also discover that the smallest, most specific steps you take ignite the most spectacular results!

Chapter 8

Way, Way Over the Rainbow

"Adversity is the first path to truth."

—ANONYMOUS

Nearly all the dreams I'd visualized while I worked my way through adolescence came true in the summer of 1972, but there was an unsettling surprise waiting for me on the other side of the rainbow. Achieving my childhood dreams just wasn't enough for me. I might have been safe. I might have been loved. But I wasn't content.

My kind and generous first husband was in his forties. He'd already scaled his mountain. He'd created the life of his dreams, and he was very happy with who he was and with the life he was living. He built his buildings. He played golf and gin rummy. He deserved what he had, and he enjoyed it. But I was just beginning to find out who I was. And the more I found out about myself, the more I knew that I had just begun to scale my own peaks.

I got impatient. And in the quiet and leisure of the country clubs where my husband spent so many sunlit hours out on the golf course, I kept remembering what my mother had said to me so many times as a child. I could have whatever I wanted.

I didn't want to live someone else's dreams. I wanted to make my own. I didn't want to be dependent. If I didn't have my own position and my own authority, I wasn't really free. I was determined to have my own career and make my own mark.

Though the fascination disappeared a long time ago, at twenty-five I was fascinated by the entertainment and movie business. My degree was in television communications, and since childhood, my fantasy life had been wrapped up in the movies. In Highland, when you weren't working, what else was there to do but dream about the movies?

Although I now know that Robert Muir and I would have eventually parted, it might not have happened quite the way it did or as soon as it did if I hadn't made a move that turned out to be the biggest wrong move in my life.

It actually began before Robert and I were ever married, when I rounded up my two friends from Grey Advertising and together we began to produce television ads for Robert's malls, and a pilot for a TV magazine series.

Robert Muir knew that I loved my work. He respected my business sense and supported me wholeheartedly, and I continued to broaden my contacts in the advertising and entertainment business.

In 1976, when a friend invited me to a party where I'd be able to make some important new contacts, I was more than eager to go.

That's where I met George Barrie. I knew perfectly well who he was: He was the CEO of Fabergé, which owned a feature film company called Brut Productions. Brut was hot in the mid-seventies, and Barrie was a Hollywood kingmaker. If you were a star, he could give you a fat, high-profile sponsorship contract with Fabergé. Cary Grant had one, and so did Farrah Fawcett and Joe Namath. If you weren't quite yet a star, he could make you one—as he did with Margaux Hemingway. If business was your talent, he could take you all the way to the top of one of the most powerful and glamorous companies in the world.

G.B. was brilliant. He was notorious. People lined up to meet him. And I joined them.

A new little voice inside me egged me on. Needless to say, it wasn't my inner voice. It was the seductive, rationalizing voice of ambition and immaturity. It had very little to do with who I really was. But the words it spoke made my heart race.

I had come so far, so fast. If it was this easy to be secure and wealthy, then surely all I had to do was snap my fingers and I could become a Hollywood mogul. Why not have the whole *world* on a string? And it only took that one dinner party to convince me that George Barrie could give me exactly that.

In my own way, I was star-struck. And terribly, terribly immature.

Meanwhile, Robert continued to play golf and gin rummy. He also continued to indulge me and spoil me and never say no. I loved and appreciated him, too. But I was bent on finding what I really wanted. I was determined to follow every opportunity.

In some ways, I was like a child who's been told not to put her finger in the flame because she'll get burned. I was curious, and that flame was intoxicating. I wanted so much out of life, I couldn't help but put my finger in that flame.

George Barrie and I started to see more of each other.

I was on edge. And I got edgier and edgier. There were so many changes going on in my life at the same time. I took a job as a production administrator at Fabergé's Brut Productions. My relationship with G.B. deepened. I knew I was pushing at the edges of my life, for better or for worse. I was being drawn by sheer ambition into a situation that, deep down, I knew I wouldn't be able to control. My inner voice was still there, deep inside, telling me I was going over the line. I'd heard uncomplimentary things about the way G.B. treated people, but I was naive and untested enough to think I'd be the one to change him. He was certainly charming to me in the beginning. When you've had one indulgent marriage and very little experience with men otherwise, you feel very self-assured. In fact I was absolutely cocky, and that other voice, that seductive siren call, began to win out.

Robert Muir and I had a very amicable divorce. We remain friends to this day. He understood how young I was. He understood that he was already "made," while I was not yet fully formed. If anyone was in the wrong, I knew it was me. I did everything I could to make the legal and financial details of the divorce work more easily. I kept my personal possessions—including the shiny, out-of-the-blue convertible that had been such a wonderful gift. But I asked for little more than what I had.

I even disbanded the little production company that had given me such a feeling of accomplishment. My ideas about growth, independence, and personal power had become completely tied up in my relationship with the great entertainment CEO named George Barrie.

Now, after five years of living in a movie town, instead of standing wistfully at its edges, I was finally taking part in the excitement 200 percent.

I remember going to the Cannes film festival with him, when he had Faye Dunaway, Oliver Reed, and Michel Legrand with him. Brut was the dominant presence at the Carleton Hotel. Everywhere, the marquees featured Brut productions. We had the best suite at the Hôtel du Cap. There were all these people revolving around G.B.'s schedule. There were paparazzi trying to get pictures. Stars would cross the room at restaurants to speak to him.

It was like being in a movie of a movie. Just being in the proximity made you feel like a star yourself. Believe me, it was overpowering for a girl from Indiana who had a lot of fantasies about the world of Hollywood.

In my later position at Fabergé, I still traveled with movie stars. Cary Grant was on the board of Fabergé, and I often accompanied him when he made personal appearances for the company. Once we flew to a factory in Canada where he greeted all the women workers, and on the way home he serenaded me with old vaudeville songs.

For this, I got paid!

Sometimes I had to pinch myself. Once, when I was living in a Fabergé corporate apartment, G.B. asked me if Cary could stay as a guest. One morning I stood in front of the mirror putting my makeup on, when Cary walked in the door and started asking me quite argumentatively why it was that women wore that stuff. Cary didn't really approve of makeup on women, despite his corporate affiliation.

Even while I countered him point by point, part of me was thinking, "Not only is Cary Grant standing in my apartment, but I'm putting foundation on my naked face right in front of him, as if it were the most ordinary thing in the world."

With G.B., I thought I was basking in the glow of power. I moved into a suite at the Beverly Hills Hotel, and I felt as though I were linked to the very center of the universe. I felt like Cinderella at the ball with the very same people I used to read about in magazines all around me. I couldn't believe how glamorous it all seemed. The people . . . the parties . . . the private jet. I thought I was on top of the world.

But what I discovered was this: misery is the same at 40,000 feet in a private plane as it is at sea level.

The real irony of my relationship with G.B. was that the most valuable things I learned from him didn't have anything at all to do with Hollywood.

Two years after I joined Brut as a production administrator in 1976, Ted Turner bought it out. I moved with G.B. to New York, and took a job as a marketing executive in Fabergé's New York office. Outside of the hard lessons I would learn about myself and G.B. during those years, the most useful things I learned from George Barrie were about the cosmetics business.

G.B. knew the cosmetics business inside out, and he gave me a complete education. He was famous for his enormous half-moon desk, which was always completely covered with creams, lotions, shampoos, mascaras. Every category and sub-category of cosmetic or grooming product under the sun found its way there, sooner or later. Usually sooner. When it came to developing quality products that flew off the shelves, the man was simply unbeatable.

The one great legacy of my years with him—and it is priceless—was the intense, hands-on business education I received at the hand of the master. G.B. made me the guinea pig for all his new product lines: "What do you think of this fragrance? Are you attracted to this cream when it's plain white, or in this jar, when it's colored blue? Does this lipstick feel good? Do you think the color is the same on your mouth as it is in the tube? Which of these two shampoo submissions do you think has the better consistency? And which do you think the consumer would prefer? Do you like this advertisement? This spokesperson? This jingle? This slogan? Would it make you buy the product? Why?"

From him, I learned what it took to create a new product, how an idea is born, how to respond to a customer's needs. I learned how to tell the difference between good and poor-quality ingredients, and how to work with chemists in research and development. Publicly, George Barrie and I were a glittering couple with a golden agenda, flying in his private jet, partying with stars. In terms of my career, I was learning some of the most important lessons you can learn about consumer products. But in our private lives, the power that had attracted me had turned into a terrible game I could only lose.

It's hard to say whether everyone knew from day one that I was the boss's girlfriend, but I believe they did. G.B. was always surrounded by a little entourage of hangers-on, who were basically terrified of him.

They seemed to stick around twenty-four hours a day. And whenever G.B. wasn't around, they'd tell me to get out while I could.

But in my ignorance, I didn't listen. I thought I could change him. In fact, I made that classic mistake of believing it would be different with me than it had been with other women. "No," I'd say, "you don't know what you're talking about. This time around, things will be different. This is going to be a spectacular life."

But G.B. was the kind of man who'd make a lot more promises than he kept, the type who promises you everything but gives you nothing. He had a pretty cavalier attitude toward the truth. When I first met him, he told me he was separated and that his divorce would be final in a matter of weeks. Those weeks turned into four years. And for all of those four years, while we worked together and I lived with him off and on, he'd tell me, "Any day now, the divorce will be final." And what he said next—"I love you and want to marry you"—also meant something other than what I thought it meant.

Many nights lay ahead when I would miss not only Robert Muir's affection and generosity, but even his golf games and gin rummy nights. There would be nights when I would have sacrificed quite a bit to have the privilege of calling myself a "golf widow" once again. When I became involved with G.B., I couldn't see far enough ahead to perceive how this entanglement would become a threat to everything the Navlan and Paulsin women of Indiana had ever taught me—everything I held dear.

But hindsight's always twenty-twenty. When you put on the blinders, you give up your peripheral vision. And for the most part, what was on center stage now looked pretty darned good.

G.B. and I flew to Las Vegas in August of 1980, after his divorce came through, and got married. By then I already knew, deep down, that this wasn't going to work.

It was when G.B. was drinking that things were really rocky. He's a brilliant man, and when he was sober he had a certain vulnerability about him, and he was protective of me, too. He had almost a paternal sweetness at those times. It was one of the things that made it difficult to leave him. That and the degree to which the taunts and criticisms that came my way the rest of the time wore my self-esteem threadbare.

"Georgette, don't be stupid. Do you think you'd get anywhere in this business if it weren't for me?"

"Georgette, surely you don't believe any of these people are actually interested in *you*. I'm the only reason they hang around." After a while I started believing everything he said.

It was tough trying to dig yourself out of a relationship with G.B., because when it came to manipulation, he was world-class. When he wasn't tearing me down, he was telling me what a great success I'd be, what a great success we'd be together. He was apologizing for the drinking and the quarrels. He was penciling in trips to the South of France, just the two of us together.

Then, overnight, the trip would be canceled, the dream postponed, and the berating and drinking would begin again.

When you keep believing that someone like that will keep his promises, that things will change, you start to berate yourself. You say to yourself, "I couldn't possibly be this stupid. I couldn't be any more stupid than this if I tried."

And, incredibly, even though you understand that you don't *like* this man, you think you're in love. I did. I think it's probably the case with most women who get into no-win, abusive situations. In order to rationalize the abuse, you have to think it's love. When you begin to ask yourself why you let this person take advantage of you, and can't come up with an answer, ultimately you lose all self-respect. When you get that far down, you don't like yourself, you don't like where you are, but you don't know where to go. You really don't know how to get out.

I became convinced that I was incapable of doing anything. Most of the time I was miserable. All I had was my career, and if I left G.B., that would be blown to bits. I'd lose my friends and contacts, lose the status that being half of a succcssful married couple gives you. And status and power seemed terribly important to me. I had painted myself into a corner with gold leaf. It was like being in prison, with myself as the jailer. It was right out of the film *Days of Wine and Roses*, except that I didn't drink.

Sometimes you have to hit bottom before you bounce back, and for me the bottom was lying in that dark bedroom listening to the phone ring, knowing it was G.B. on the other end, ready to say terrible, hurtful things to me.

For a time, I'd pick up the phone and listen for a moment or two, then hold the receiver away from my ear, then hold it close long enough to say, "Fine, whatever you say," before holding it away again. I might not know exactly what he was saying, but I had a pretty good idea. And even with the receiver a few feet away, I could hear the anger and malice in his tone.

It was a little game I was playing with myself, pretending to be there when I wasn't. After a while I simply stopped answering when instinct told me G.B. was on the other end of the line. I told myself that whatever terrible things G.B. had to say to me and about me, it wasn't the real *me* he was talking about. I reached down deep through all the hurt, the feelings of inadequacy and worthlessness, found my inner power, and summoned the strength to leave him.

Consciously, and intentionally, I started dating other men. That broke the spell. Soon it was done: the separation, at least, was official.

I knew that what lay ahead in the divorce proceedings would be painful.

When G.B. hired the infamous Roy Cohn to represent him in our divorce, my worst fears were confirmed. I also knew my days as a vice president at Fabergé were numbered. Cohn threatened me—with losing my job, with cutting off my support, with selling my house and putting me on the street. Sure, he scared me. But with my Feminine Force back on my side I could be scared, but I couldn't be stopped. And when Cohn realized that, he backed down.

G.B. also harassed and threatened me. There was a set of gold and white china we'd bought together that I was very fond of. He started to call me up to say he wasn't going to give alimony payments unless he got the china—a possession which, of course, he'd barely noticed before we separated.

But I kept going. I kept working at Fabergé, and putting money away.

And I made one of the most important decisions of my life: *I decided that I was never again going to be dependent on anyone else for my well-being.*

As I walked the halls of Fabergé, I knew that no matter what anyone said about me, it wouldn't hurt me. I wouldn't let it. Even in that inevitable moment when G.B. fired me, I was going to be fine. My self-esteem would remain unimpaired, because his opinion no longer mattered to me. I knew I would never, ever again choose to be with a man who didn't really love me. Sure, sometimes I cried. Sometimes I was lonely. But far better to be alone. Far better to be dreaming my *own* dreams and creating my *own* realities. I began to enjoy being alone, just sitting in my apartment and planning my next move.

With my marriage over and my job on the line, it might have looked like I had nothing.

But really, I had all I needed.

I had myself back.

Chapter 9

Humble Pie

"You may be disappointed if you fail, but you are doomed if you don't try."

—Beverly Sills

My mother says that after George Barrie and I divorced, she wanted to send him a telegram thanking him for giving me the opportunity to discover my real values. It was half a joke, made after the real pain of our relationship had begun to heal, and not one I would have found very amusing ten years ago. But I know what she means.

The truth is, I was bewitched by power. I was simply too ambitious to see that, and it took a few years of misery with G.B. for me to understand it at gut level. When I left him, I understood all too well that pure power, when not rooted in values, is worse than worthless. It's destructive. It's exhausting. It rains misery on you. It takes your trust and your joy away.

Those years took me down a few pegs. Let's call a spade a spade: I was humbled. On the outside I may have looked very determined, but on the inside I was becoming more thoughtful, more forgiving, and more self-aware. I'd learned the hard way that the trappings and the raw substance of power didn't count for anything. What still counted for something—for almost everything—were the basic values that the Navlan and Paulsin women of Indiana had so wisely taught me. Without dignity and self-esteem, nothing else mattered. Not power. Not influence. Certainly not money.

Nothing.

It was time to get reacquainted with my values.

G.B.'s late night calls continued throughout our separation. For a while I listened to him. Then I held the phone away from my ear while he talked. And finally I just stopped answering altogether.

I didn't like playing possum in my own home but it did the trick. And then I got up in the morning and went about the business of creating my new life.

Part of that consisted of taking stock of what I'd never do again. All too many women will recognize the abusive pattern of my second marriage. You stick it out because you want to believe that tomorrow everything will be okay again: "It's just another bad week at the office. It'll all blow over by the weekend."

For a long time I told myself, "Hey, I can handle this." First it was, "I mean, he did finally divorce his wife, didn't he?"

When you're an overachiever, you have a hard time accepting defeat or saying "I misjudged this. I was wrong." You have a tendency to hang in there longer than most.

So I told myself, "G.B. has so much to offer me. I know all his tricks now. I just have to handle them better."

Then I said, "I cannot admit I made this big a mistake."

And then, "I have no other structure in my life, so I've got to make this work, no matter what!"

But somehow, things never improved. Instead, they got worse.

When you're in a situation like this, the final stage is thinking, "Well, maybe this *is* all my fault. If I change, if I try harder, if I act smarter, if I become more attractive, *then* everything will work out."

It may take months or years before you figure out that nothing will work. And when that moment finally comes, you wake up and say to yourself, "I'm not so bad. In fact, there's nothing wrong with *me*. So who's he kidding?"

Himself.

A man who manages to convince you that everything that's wrong with your marriage is your fault is a man who's tipped his hand: he's an abuser.

Abusive men will also do everything they can to separate you from your friends and family. That's another telltale sign. G.B. used to tell me that I didn't have any friends. All my friends were his friends. They were only interested in me because I was his wife. Part of this was true. Our friends *were* his friends. And once we separated, many of the parties faded away. But I did have real friends—and it took me time to understand who my real friends were.

He'd also tell me my family was no good. Back in our California period, he and my brother George had been good friends. Often, they went out drinking together. But when G.B. came home he'd always manage to get in a few digs about George. Soon those digs were not so subtle. Slowly, G.B. was crippling all my personal support systems.

What's so amazing about this time-honored method is how successful it proves to be. By undermining your self-confidence and cutting you off from people you love and support and who love and support you, the abusive husband keeps reinforcing the belief that *everything you have and everything you are is dependent on being with him.*

How beautifully this system creates its own energy and feeds itself. It's a veritable perpetual motion machine. What it's grinding on though is you. There's no way to stop it.

Walk away. As fast as you can. No. Don't walk; hell, run!

Even then, it may not be over. But however low you may go, you still have the power within to end it. All you have to do is release that power.

I know a woman whose husband, during their divorce, took her wedding and engagement rings from her bureau while he was visiting the children and gave them to his girlfriend. And that wasn't enough for him. Next, he came back and took all her furniture.

I know a woman whose ex-husband threw her through the door of a shower. I know a man who threatened to fight his wife for custody of their two toddlers because she'd charged a thirty-five-dollar restaurant meal on their joint credit card the week before their separation became final.

It doesn't matter. You've still got to pick yourself up. You've still got to tell yourself, "Hey, the next one to go through that door is *not* going to be *me*!" You've got to tell yourself, "It may *look* like he's the one holding all the chips, but he is mistaken and that's *my* trump card.

Because I'll do whatever I have to do to get through and out of this. And that will be more than enough."

It's harder if you have children: Where do you go and what do you do? Again, you get yourself up off the floor and move to point A, and then on to point B. You move from family members to friends to support groups. Come hell or high water, you do whatever you've got to do. Abuse of any type—physical or emotional—is not something you should have to live with under *any* circumstances.

This is a touchy area. So many women with children are in this position, and our system of laws doesn't really protect them. There's still a double standard there, and that has got to be changed. In the meantime, you need to ask the advice of experts if you're in this spot. What *I'm* qualified to tell you is that whatever's required to free yourself of this situation, you absolutely must find the power within you to do it.

Mother used to tell us that if any man ever hit us—even once—we were to pick up the hardest, heaviest thing within arm's reach and stop him in his tracks. If you hurt a man enough, Mother said, you'd never have to hit him again. But she insisted that you had to take a stand on the first blow. If a man knows that hitting you has no consequences, he'll do it again. But if he's as frightened of you as you are of him, he'll stop, and the pattern you establish will be a different one. The point is, if a man ever hits you, fight back in any way you can. Preferably by leaving him.

Take my mother's advice however you want to, but I think it's valuable as a metaphor. The point is not that life doesn't deal blows. The point is how you perceive them. If you perceive them as defeating, knockout punches, that's what they'll be. If you think you can get up, you will. You will and you must. To actually make life better, you have to believe it can be better. Without that belief, one punch can be a knockout.

You have to refuse to become a victim, because the victim is the one who gets hit and hit again.

The ability to get out of a bad marriage in one piece, to get past it and find happiness and thrive, is something that starts in your head, just like anything else. So much of life is a self-fulfilling prophecy.

Yours may be a traditional marriage where the wife runs the house and the husband brings home the paycheck. Or you may have a two-career household with a mortgage, school tuitions, and other expenses that require both your incomes to maintain. It doesn't matter. The dissolution of your marriage won't just mark the end of an emotional partnership. It will threaten your whole way of life. But you can rise above it. You can triumph.

If I could do it, you can, too.

Remembering and talking about my second marriage is still hard for me. I'm not proud of my choices, and I'm not proud of my assumptions. Ten years later, the only reason I am motivated even to mention those years is to let you know I've been there. I'm not giving you advice from the isolation of a gilded tower. I've been there. Boy, have I been there. And I've come out on the other side and thrived.

When I woke up from it all and examined what seemed to be my very limited options, I asked myself, "What's the worst that can happen?" I realized that at worst I'd have to go back to Highland and live with my mother. And I thought, so what if it's "running home to Mother"? What would be so terrible about that?

I'm here to tell you that once you walk out, once you ask yourself the question "What's the worst thing that can happen?" and realize that whatever it is, it's better than what you have now, an amazing thing happens.

You start to get strong. And you start to heal.

Looking back, it seems to me that my second marriage taught me four important things. And I'm sure these are the things Mother was referring to when she said that this unique, once-in-a-lifetime experience prepared me for the man of my dreams.

First, I would never again abandon my sense of values in order to serve my ambition.

Second, the next man in my life was going to have strong values. His values were going to have to match my basic values, the ones I'd just reclaimed; otherwise it just wasn't worth it. At the age of thirty-five I'd learned the hard way that although power is devastatingly sexy, unless it's grounded in values, you're in for a miserable time.

Third, I'd never marry just to be married. A bad marriage can put the happiness of every single one of your remaining days in jeopardy and I'd just flirted far too seriously with this possibility.

And fourth, I'd make sure my future husband and I agreed on the basic responsibilities of marriage by discussing them *before* we exchanged vows.

Marriage comes with some assumed responsibilities. You can change or modify those responsibilities, but to do that, first you have to talk about them. Discussing three key issues—I call it The Marriage List—with your partner *before* you marry ought to give you a good idea of your level of risk.

Please. If even one woman has this conversation with just one man before she takes the leap and saves herself heartache as a result, it will help me to know that some good came of my own folly—*and* of revealing it. But don't do it for me—do it for you. Because waking up one morning to discover that you and your Romeo have nothing in common is the rudest of awakenings. And not only that, to get yourself in that situation is irresponsible.

If the two of you can't come to agreement or a happy compromise—and certainly if you can't even have the conversation—the risk of marriage is not worth taking.

THE MARRIAGE LIST

Basic Responsibility #1:

Unless the two of you explicitly state otherwise, it is assumed that if you marry someone you are going to be faithful to him, and vice versa.

Fidelity may not be important to some people and I can't judge them for it, but it is extremely important to me. If you are to have a successful marriage, the decision to revise this basic assumption about marriage must be made *before*—and not after—you become husband and wife.

Basic Responsibility #2:

Entering into marriage implies a joint responsibility to bear children. It also means that you and your partner respect preexisting family commitments that each of you may have, such as supporting or caring for an aging parent or children from a previous marriage. If such a commitment exists, you both have to understand what that means. You can't just say, "Well, now that we're married, that changes things."

Basic Responsibility #3:

Finally, I think the two of you should be very honest about what your goals are, careerwise, and how those goals may impact your family life. You can't change horses in midstream, so if your career is vital to who you are—or if being a full-time homemaker is vital to who you are— make sure your mate knows that. To assume your goals are his goals without clearly communicating them is irresponsible.

A partner who suddenly tells the other, "I can take care of you, now you don't have to go to school, now you don't have to work," is a partner who is not being responsible to a basic commitment of marriage, which is to honor each other's goals. And the partner who doesn't make his or her goals clear—before that ceremony takes place—is equally irresponsible.

The last thing I learned from the G.B. years was perhaps the most important. It was that I'd never truly be able to guarantee my own happiness 100 percent until the reins of my financial well-being were held firmly in my own hands.

I learned that I could enjoy the lifestyle that being married to a powerful and well-to-do man can offer. But that doesn't mean I'm going to put my security into *anyone's* hands but my own—no matter how exemplary that someone may be.

You can call it insecurity. I call it being realistic. You never know where the next turn in the road is going to take you. You may encounter flak where you least expect it—on the Concorde to Paris or on the most ordinary shuttle flight of your life. So pack your own parachute.

Call it insecurity, but also call it pride. Most of us want to feel that we're married to an equal. That's something that cuts both ways. It's easier for me to feel like an equal in a relationship with a man when I'm in charge of my own financial well-being. It's the way to match independence with independence. It's the same attitude my mother had when she set out to prove she could care for her family no matter what the circumstances. Believe me: It's an attitude that a secure man will *absolutely* appreciate.

Especially believe me when I tell you this:

When push comes to shove, *no one is going to take care of you but you.*

Chapter 10

Don't Mistake His Good Fortune for Yours

"A woman must have money and a room of her own."

—VIRGINIA WOOLF, *A ROOM OF ONE'S OWN*

"I'll wear your ring, I'll cook and I'll wash, and I'll keep the land. But that is all. Until I've got my dowry safe about me, I'm no married woman. I'm the servant I've always been, without anything of my own! Until you have my dowry, you haven't got any bit of me. Me, myself! I'll be dreaming amongst things that aren't my own. As if I'd never met you. There's three hundred years of happy dreaming among those things of mine, and I want them. I want my dream. I'll have it and I'll know it!"

MAUREEN O'HARA TO JOHN WAYNE IN JOHN FORD'S
THE QUIET MAN, REPUBLIC PICTURES, 1952

Unless you were born under a lucky star and into a trust fund, or your Uncle Edward made a killing in the stock market and is leaving his portfolio to you, your financial security is ultimately going to depend upon you and you alone. Having a husband who can make you materially comfortable is essentially another form of luck. Whether or not he is materially comfortable—indeed, whether or not he remains your husband (unless someone's come up with a way to abolish divorce and death)—is something that is ultimately beyond your control.

I don't know about you, but I don't want to depend on luck. I like to know that if I do A, B, and C, I'm going to arrive at D. Whether I get lucky or not. Like my mother taught me: If I get good grades, I get to go to the circus.

So let's talk about love and money. In any marriage, yours or mine, love and romance are one thing and money and security are another. They mix about as well as oil and water, but in the lifetime partnership called matrimony, you need both, You *deserve* both.

You're nodding. Or maybe you're not nodding, you're yawning, because this seems so obvious. But let me ask you a few questions anyway:

1. Do you know where all the financial and insurance papers are kept in your house (or in which bank they are held)?

2. Do you know how much your car insurance costs? Your mortgage? Your health insurance?

3. Do you know what the monthly overhead or "nut" is for your household each month?

4. If your husband is the sole wage earner in your family, does he have a life insurance policy? And, if so, do you know the details if the unthinkable were to happen?

5. Are you familiar with your husband's will? Is it up to date? Are you comfortable with the provisions made for you and your children—if you have or expect to have any? Do you have a will of your own?

6. If you are considering marriage and you have your own financial assets, have you considered making your own prenuptial agreement with your fiancé?

7. Do you have your own independent form of financial security, such as your own savings account, investment fund, or pension plan— whether you work or not?

Believe me, the most experienced, savvy, and yes, even wealthy married women—even and sometimes especially married career women with their own substantial earning power—have been known to fall into a blissful but dangerous state of ignorance as far as their financial security is concerned. I'll never forget the *60 Minutes* piece on the Bel

Air–Beverly Hills bag ladies. After divorce, they were out of their mansions and living in their cars—parked out on the street.

I know, because it could have happened to me, the girl who spent all those hours of her childhood and adolescence raking over her budgets.

As soon as I married Robert Muir, all of that went out the window. Yes, I still shopped at Sears, but our real overhead was something I didn't pay attention to. He was wealthy. He knew how to deal with money. What a relief it was not to have to count every last Kleenex any more, or fret over dry cleaning bills! Maybe our father had died and left us, but finally someone was taking care of me!

Sure, I ran my production company and produced my ads and did the decorating for his real estate developments and malls. But as far as personal financial awareness was concerned, I blissfully let it all go. And so when we were divorced, I knew nothing. I didn't know how much anything cost—from my car insurance to those dry cleaning bills. I had to start again from scratch. I had to go back to those daily budgets I'd made in high school. I had to make phone calls and find things out.

With G.B., it was no different. By now I had my own salary, but he was my boss, so he was *still* in control. I knew when I rocked the boat in our personal life, the financial hourglass was going to start running out.

So did he. And he used it to his advantage. It was one of the ways he manipulated me. It was a big part of why I stayed around as long as I did and was so miserable as long as I was.

Men are brought up to compete. As boys, they participate in competitive sports, and as men they compete in business. They become risk-takers through competition. Girls, on the other hand, all too often are given the message—either overtly or covertly—that we don't have to compete. We just have to be nice, and we'll grow up to marry a man just as nice as we are who will take care of us.

The message is, someone else is going to make you safe—whether it's your husband, your father, your mother, or your government. And ironically, accepting the myth that someone else will make your life risk-free is actually the biggest risk you could take. It puts your well-being right smack dab into the hands of another. It walks you right up to the edge of a cliff. Some women—and often it's the ones with the longest list of achievements, the most public attention, and the most advanced degrees—can't even bring themselves to look over the edge to see how far down it goes. They just jump right off.

No matter what your status in life and no matter what the quality of your marriage or any other personal financial partnership may be, please do *not* abdicate the responsibility for your own material well-being to anyone.

Ever. Period.

It's not always fun. Sometimes you'd really rather be visiting your mother or walking your dog than paying your bills. *Ignore your personal balance sheets at your own peril.* Do it and you put your own freedom on the line. Do it and you strip yourself of security and put your dignity and self-esteem at risk.

Once you put your survival into the hands of any other human being, you are at his mercy.

If you're lucky enough to be a full-time mother or homemaker, you can still have independent financial security. And it will be just as important for you as it is for a single woman. Because if you don't make those arrangements, you've built your house on a sand bar.

If you are married, you start by sitting down with your husband and asking him what the financial provisions are for the family. If he tells you, "Don't worry about it, I've taken care of it," you say, "Darling, I am an adult and I have a responsibility to myself and to our family in addition to my responsibility to you. So although I appreciate it, 'Don't worry about it' just won't do."

You then go on to explain that you want the specifics and the details, so that if, God forbid, the worst happens, you are not left at the mercy of other people.

There's no easy way to do it. You just have to sit down and speak clearly but lovingly. And if your husband still resists, that should tell you something.

If he actually refuses, then you've got to make a decision for yourself. Maybe you call the insurance people on your own to find out about the car; ditto the bank to find out about the mortgage. Or you go down to the bank on your lunch hour and pull the papers out of the safe deposit box. Start building your own files of information. Or pick a third party to come in and sit down with the two of you to help him understand your need to have this information and this control over your own life. Decide what works for you. Despite the emotional challenge of all this, it's worth it. You must understand everything that is going on in your husband's financial life insofar as it concerns you and your family.

Now I'm going to tell you something that may shock you.

Remember the three responsibilities of marriage I listed in the last chapter? I'm going to add a fourth one, for your eyes only. It's a lesson I took from Baba and her money under the mattress.

Basic Responsibility #4:

Once you are married, make sure you have money of your own that HE DOESN'T KNOW ABOUT. It doesn't matter where it comes from. It *does* matter that it stays your secret. Ferret away a few dollars of the weekly household expenses and put it into a small savings account that no one knows about. Take a part-time job. Start a business in your kitchen. Take advantage of the savings plan at work and don't tell anyone, *especially* not your husband. Think of it as your children's future. Think of it as your rainy-day fund. Call it your under-the-mattress money. It will do more than anything else to assure you your freedom.

If you marry a wealthy man or a man who has been married before, there is also the matter of the prenuptial agreement.

I've signed one in each of my three marriages. I had an emotional conversation with each husband first, but it's a no-win situation. When you sign it, you give away any rights you might have to your husband's property. But if you refuse to sign it, he can say you don't have his best interests at heart. There's nothing to be done but grin and bear it.

After that, you do need to make sure that assets you create after you're married go under your name. The deed for the New York apartment is listed in my name, so there's no mistake. The only things I *know* I have are the things I control in my own name. I run my financial life entirely on that premise, because that way I can't be disappointed or surprised. I don't want my security and my family's security to hinge on someone else's largess, no matter how good or well-meaning that person is. Now, that may be my own problem, given my history, and of course there has to be a degree of trust in life. I'm more than willing to trust my emotions to my husband. I'm willing to trust my contentment to my husband. But I am not willing to trust my money to my husband—and Robert Mosbacher is the finest, most decent man I have ever known.

If the tables were turned now, I would demand a premarital agreement with my husband. I wouldn't marry anyone without one. I've counseled my sister not to marry anyone without one. If you have any assets at all I counsel you not to marry without one; it doesn't matter how kind, generous, or wonderful your fiancé may be. To suggest that creating a prenuptial agreement will hurt a marriage is ridiculous. A marriage is either going to work or it isn't, whether you have a premarital agreement or not.

Having one doesn't mean you don't share. It just means that both of you are *free* to share—out of love and generosity, not out of necessity.

Which leads me to the ultimate path to freedom. For me, it's the most compelling one of all: creating your own income.

After G.B. and I broke up, there were friends of mine who thought that a bad marriage and a rough divorce were reason enough to kick back and coast for a while.

Utter hogwash.

Totally counterproductive.

I knew well before I lost my job what I wanted to do. What it was time to do was find a company to buy, and the means to buy it.

There were plenty of people who thought I was crazy. I hardly had the financial wherewithal to buy a company on my own. And I hadn't been a very high-level executive at Fabergé. I was just vice president in charge of licensing, and one of many corporate V.P.s. Sure, I did deals and I managed, but I did not acquire and I did not do strategic planning, or any kind of planning beyond my own focused managerial responsibilities. I certainly was not involved in the big picture and the big numbers that resulted in the bottom line of Fabergé's annual report.

However, I had discovered that I was good with numbers. I had an affinity for numbers.

And if you understand one budget (which is not that hard), you can understand them all.

There were those who were telling me that no one would ever see someone with my qualifications as CEO material. No one would take

an ex–vice president of Fabergé seriously as an entrepreneur. Especially a woman ex–vice president. And *especially* an ex–vice president
who had been married to the boss.

I didn't listen. I knew I could trust my judgment on the soundness
and profit potential of a company. I knew I understood consumer
products, that I had a flair for aesthetics and beauty, and that I could
market the heck out of any product that was worthwhile, at whatever
the price.

I knew the company had to be consumer-oriented, because consumer products were what I knew, and I knew that I understood budgets. So I started educating myself by doing what I called "due
diligence" on companies that intrigued me. This meant that I spent all
day poring over annual reports, analyzing numbers and assumptions,
and finding out whatever I could about them.

Meanwhile, I was also dating and falling in love—and eventually, I
married. But I had learned the hard way that financial independence
was imperative, and I had learned, too, that I could not sacrifice that
goal to a relationship. Make no mistake: my marriage is a source of real
growth and joy. Both my personal responsibilities to Robert Mosbacher and the social responsibilities we share are sources of genuine
pleasure. Although I take delight in sharing Robert's life and his good
fortune, I don't mistake his good fortune for mine. That belongs to him
and to his children.

Robert is secure enough to respect all my attitudes in this regard. He
understood from our first date that I believed in building my own
career and my own security. And I knew I needed—and thrived on—
the challenges building a career would bring.

If I knew anything about myself when I was fired by Fabergé, it was
that I was a born marketer. As I began to research acquisitions that
might make sense for me, I focused on areas where I knew I could
work my own kind of magic: consumer-oriented companies with great,
arresting trademarks, excellent products that I knew something about,
and unexploited marketing potential. I looked for companies whose
market share I could expand. I knew I could take a business that was
promising and turn it into a double-digit success. If I heard through
friends or associates that one of these companies was in need of a new
partner, so much the better. Big or small didn't matter. Being able to
tick off items on my requirement list did.

When a company met all the criteria, I'd go forward and price out my ideas to find out whether they were feasible. And if they were, I'd go courting.

One of the things G.B. had said was turning out to be true: Most of the friends I had during my marriage with him disappeared when the marriage fell apart. So had the parties and the fun, although by the end of that ill-conceived marriage anything fun was just a distant memory. It was just me and the silence, and my family at the other end of the telephone line. I didn't even have a dog.

I was learning one of life's toughest grown-up lessons. Where there is a divorce, more often than not the friends go with the power partner, and the power partner isn't usually the woman. Most of the invitations went to G.B., and not to me. My job was gone. My lifestyle had become a lot more modest. There was no more car and driver, no more hotel suites. I wasn't surprised that material aspects of my life had changed, and changed pretty dramatically, but I didn't resign myself to that idea. I felt lonely. But if I had to choose between being alone and spending an evening with anyone who was going to waste my time with negative messages—and that inevitably included a few well-meaning friends—I knew I would do a better job of keeping myself company.

I had a tough few years in there, before I met Robert and even after we started dating, when what I wanted from him—marriage—didn't seem to be in the picture. I sat alone in my quiet apartment, studying and watching the companies I was interested in, hiring consultants out of my savings account, and crunching numbers.

The silence got deafening at times. But there were other times when I'd get so involved in what I was doing, hours would pass without my noticing it. There were times I'd sit down thinking "Well, I put in a long day. I'm going to go to bed." But I'd follow a train of thought I'd been working on, and it would lead me in a new direction. I'd see a problem in a different light. I'd see a way to *improve* my business plan, and I'd go for it.

I had some of my longest conversations with my inner voice those days and nights. If my inner voice had been my best friend in the past, now it was my guardian angel. Time after time, it kept me on the track. Time after time, it reminded me that even though Cinderella's fairy godmother wasn't going to materialize in the kitchen and make all my wishes come true, I had a better ally in creating the reality I wanted. My own Feminine Force was my strongest friend, and boy, did I need that friendship.

For the first time since I'd been a child facing the prospect of growing up without a father, I was keenly aware that the life I lived wasn't going to be built by a man. What my life became was going to be entirely up to me. *It was my own to create.* Although I wouldn't avoid the invitations that still trickled my way from the remnants of my old social life, I wasn't going to invest any time worrying about them. I resolved that I would understand which friendships in my life were predicated on power or were a couples-only deal. I would take part in that social life only when it was convenient for me.

What was becoming clearer to me was my own identity. I knew that there was absolutely no reason why, from this moment forward, the power in my life should have to come from a man. I was capable of creating my own identity and my own power. I was capable of being liked for myself alone, and being a social asset for myself alone. Taking full responsibility for that, as well as for my own financial security, was the challenge I was facing.

It's the challenge you face when, as an adult with a chunk of your life already behind you, you finally discover and rediscover your strengths.

And do you know what? Discovering and using those strengths won't just be one of your biggest challenges. It can also be one of the most thrilling things you'll ever do.

Chapter 11

Strength Building

"Herein there is nothing to be afraid of, but everything to hope for."

—TERESA OF AVILA, *LIFE*

"Without you, I'm nothing" is a line that works just fine in old torch songs, but in real life it's a crazy idea. It's the feeling that if you don't have that particular man in your life or you don't have that particular job, you haven't got anything. Some women who know in their heads that this isn't true can't seem to get their hearts to accept it. I know women who can't enjoy travel or movies or dinner parties or much of anything now that they aren't part of a couple. A particularly painful experience or loss has stopped them dead in their tracks.

Of course, the time you spend with your loved ones is time you cherish, but the time you have to yourself is precious, too, and should be savored.

One of the most powerful ways you can help yourself build a new life is to focus on the things that make you *you*. Without him or them or it, you are still a whole person with real interests and real talents. Having some time to yourself is a golden opportunity to discover and *re*discover what those talents and interests are.

SOLO SATISFACTION

If you've been in a less-than-terrific relationship, you may have discovered that your partner and the relationship itself has played far too big a role in determining how you spend your leisure time. I know women who feel that their husbands are so uninterested and patronizing about the things they like to do that they can't even enjoy those things when their husbands aren't around. If you miss any of the small pleasures you used to have in your life, now is the time to rediscover them. Now is the time to be utterly and totally yourself.

Julie, a friend of mine, is a good example. Her ex was a photographer, and one big wall of their apartment was covered with his work. After she and he broke up, that wall of photos seemed to lay claim on her surroundings. But she couldn't bear to get rid of them. They were part of *her* life—pictures taken on trips to favorite places, photos of the kids. She considered taking those pictures down and storing them for a while, but then another, better idea hit her. She painted the walls a bright shade of peach, covered a big overstuffed sofa in chintz, and totally changed the look of the room. It helped her to change her attitude as well—to an attitude of taking control of her life. Making small changes, taking those baby steps were important to her sense of strength.

Getting some of the little pleasures back into your life and learning how to take over your own space are small but important pieces of building your strength. A bigger challenge is building strength in the other territories of your life—your career and your goals.

Strength building is like decision making. Knowing who you are, and what you want, is the bedrock of self-confidence. One of the worst things about truly destructive experiences and relationships is how they can confuse your sense of who you are. They can cloud your dreams and obstruct your vision.

In fact, turning *any* major corner in your life can feel like a rough passage, and you may find yourself thinking, "I don't really know *what* I want. How can I go after what I want if I don't know what it is?" Or "I've spent my adult life taking care of a family. I did my time learning how to run a household and be a good mother, but now that the children are grown and out of the house, I really don't *know* who I am any more."

There's an effective way to discover the answer to these questions. And it's an equally effective way to get yourself going if those dreams about your future are already starting to take shape.

It goes back to what you love. You started finding out what you love a long time ago—maybe all the way back to the time you still thought the stork brought babies, and the only thing you knew about raising children came from your experience with a drink-and-wet doll. Looking back to see what you've loved in your life is another way of finding a role model in yourself—a way to rediscover things you may have forgotten that the child in you still knows.

I flourish in the cosmetics industry. My first job outside the house was doing my neighbor's hair in styles I copied from magazines. That was one of many early experiences that taught me that *what I enjoyed could sustain me*. Acting on that observation has never proved me wrong. Whenever I build a goal from something I love to do, it doesn't matter how many challenges and "failures" come my way, that goal is golden. There's opportunity, if you examine it carefully, in so much of what you do. There's gold "in them thar hills." It just has to be mined.

Think about your own experiences when you were a child. What did you love to do or excel at when you were seven? When you were ten? Thirteen? Sixteen?

When I was seven, I was organizing my brother and sisters into a team, and figuring out how to convince them to clean their rooms by turning it into a game. At ten, I was teaching those same kids to budget by sending each of them through the aisles of the grocery store or variety store with a dollar bill. At thirteen, I was sitting in that top balcony at the opera watching the beautiful singers on the stage and the glamorous men and women sitting in the front row. And at fifteen, I was setting hair.

It's not too hard to see how those apparently disparate things would translate into a career as a cosmetics entrepreneur, is it?

Other talents you discover through trial and error. I discovered later in life that I was very good at deal making—numbers, negotiations, and sales. That was a significant step past budgeting, and it was a skill I discovered largely through trial and error. I used deal-making skills to achieve my goals in everything from television production to redecorating houses. When necessity presented itself, I found I had a knack.

Advocacy was also something I always had an interest in, but it wasn't something I really understood or acted on until I was married to Robert Mosbacher. Trial and error have also taught me what areas are *not* mine to conquer. When I was living in L.A., I desperately wanted to get into the movie business. I even had a walk-on part in a movie. That was one possible door into the industry, but the experience made it clear to me that acting was *not* the door for me. I'm not exactly a triple threat—can't dance, can't sing, can't act—and even a bit part was enough to tell me I should stick to producing.

Trial and error is one way to discover your skills, but there are other ways. Sit down and ask yourself this: What makes me feel productive? What gives me that feeling of accomplishment, that feeling of fulfillment? What makes me feel exhilarated? What makes me feel challenged, totally engaged, and practically electric with energy, as though I'm using all my circuits—all my intelligence and all my wits?

What you're asking yourself, in other words, is "What makes me feel *alive*?"

Make a list. Yes, another list. And this one is one of the most important ones you'll make.

Did you have a knack for managing other kids like I did, or were you more like my sister Melody, who, according to my mother, used to keep rocks and frogs in her dresser drawer and today lives a fulfilling life as a mother of three and grandmother of two in the hills of Tennessee?

Did you like to teach as a child, or did you like to dream? Did you get a kick out of high school biology? Were you your phys. ed. teacher's favorite student, or the art director of every poster committee? Were you the class clown? Were you the only girl in your neighborhood with a go-kart? Did you build a doll house that all the other little girls on the block envied, or did you tell the best scary stories, or were you the one who always got your scout troop out of the woods?

Make a list of what you were good at then and what you're good at now. A list of skills. A list of things you've really loved. And don't forget those skills that seem to you to be the normal, everyday requirements of adult life.

You have all kinds of identification in your purse—driver's license, credit cards, bank cards, and so on. They give all the numbers, but they don't say very much about who you really are. Think of this as a list of your *true* I.D.

Your Feminine Force I.D.

Ask yourself *What did I really like to do when I was six or seven? What was I really good at?*

What did I love to do when I was nine or ten? When I reached adolescence? When I was twenty?

What do I like to do and what am I good at now?

After you've made that list, add up what you see there. Find the patterns. See what still excites you.

There's nothing silly or self-indulgent about this exercise. No one doubts that children rehearse adult roles—that's the reason educational toys are so successful. No one questions the value of the chemistry set the prize-winning scientist played with when he was nine, or doubts that being elected vice president of the senior class had something to do with a state governor's career. It's simply chauvinistic not to take the roles that girls rehearse as seriously as the roles we typically think of as boys' roles. And it's only sensible to take a look back over your shoulder when you come to a new fork in the road. Just remember that this isn't an exercise designed to keep you headed down the same path you've always followed. It's a way to discover which *new* directions are likely to be the most promising.

Spend some time asking your own family about the memories they share of your childhood. Call up the sister you were close to, or that friend who was with you at summer camp the year you remember as the best year of all. You don't have to tell them what you're up to. Chances are they'll remember some special moments in your childhood that will tell you something about yourself that you've forgotten, and trigger other memories as well. Chances are you'll be able to return the favor.

What about those adult skills you don't think of as skills? Put them down on the list. If you moved to New York from a little southern town and learned how to get where you wanted to go on the New York subway system without risking your life, that's a skill. If you put together very good dinner parties, think about how many things you do to make them succeed. Like putting together a clever combination of people for your guest list. Juggling the budget for food, wine, flowers. Scheduling everything in the kitchen so that the vegetables are ready before the roast gets cold. Don't forget that you also negotiate with all kinds of people to make your parties a success, from the mom-and-pop butchers down the street, to employees at the supermarket who have to deliver your order in the next half-hour, to the snooty manager of your local wine store whom you convince to give you discounts. Think about it: How many men do you know who could pull off a four-course dinner for eight?

The skills you've developed as a homemaker and hostess are not very different from those a man develops in the business world. They are *management* skills, pure and simple.

My friend Rebecca, who lives in Florida, has small children. Before she decided to make her family a priority, she was a pastry chef. Rebecca still loves to bake pastries. Robert and I always look forward to seeing her, because she's great company and a wonderful friend. But I have to admit there's another treat we look forward to at Rebecca's dinner parties: dessert.

We weren't the only ones who appreciated Rebecca's skill in the kitchen. One day someone said to Rebecca, "Look. For goodness sake, why don't you just bake some of your specialties to sell at Christmas time? You have a lot of friends who'd jump at the chance to buy cakes and pastries from you."

Rebecca considered the idea. It was a way to do something she loved—and make some money—without leaving the house or taking too much time away from her children.

She tried it. She sent out cards to people she knew, announcing that she would take orders for Christmas goods and including a delivery schedule and price list. By Christmas, all of her friends had bought a cake from her. I ordered a decorated Christmas cake, a cheese cake, and other assorted pastries that I served throughout the holidays.

Her Christmas "bake sale" was a success, and Rebecca learned a few things about organizing her kitchen to accommodate the extra baking, and how to schedule this new job around her domestic life. She realized she could expand a bit, so her next step was to take some samples of her wares and visit some of the small local restaurants that didn't have their own pastry chefs.

Soon she had added two restaurants to her list of happy clients.

Last time I heard, all the small restaurants in her vicinity were featuring Rebecca's cheese cake or Rebecca's chocolate mud pie, and Rebecca had hired four assistants—two of them full-time. Her business prospered, and she still lived on her terms. She was bringing a second income into the house doing something she loved, and she was still "at home" and able to devote time to her children.

Rebecca discovered how what she enjoyed could sustain her. Notice how she moved one step at a time. She developed her business at her own speed, taking on only as much as she was confident she could handle. Her thriving small bakery all started with a few cards sent out to her friends and acquaintances.

My venture into the entrepreneurial world was more of a leap, but I'll let you in on a little secret. When I first set out to acquire my own business, I didn't quite realize what I was getting into. I didn't know how much I still had to learn. Looking back, I admit I had a lot of nerve. If I'd realized at the time how little I actually knew about the realities of cash flow, cash management, profit margins, contingency plans, manufacturing screw-ups, inventory control . . .

Ugh! Help!! I might never have dared to do it. But thank goodness I did dare. Otherwise, I'd never have found La Prairie.

Chapter 12

And He Said He'd Never Get Married Again

"We can only learn to love by loving."

—Iris Murdoch

Meanwhile, I had to build some strength back into my personal life.

It was a muggy August day in 1982, and I was about to take a one-day business trip to Houston for Fabergé. My divorce from G.B. had become final just the week before and I was dating again.

It wasn't always pleasant. After failing at two marriages I wasn't at all sure I would ever meet the man of my dreams. I was even less convinced that I deserved to. There was no way around the fact that when it came to men I'd been a darned fool. My judgment had been horrible, my motivation worse, and I'd been completely naive. I now knew there were a lot of things in life worse than being a golf widow, and I'd given myself the dubious privilege of finding out what they were firsthand. Youth and inexperience had been no excuse. I only wished I could regain some of that youthful determination of mine.

Sure, I was out of hell and I was healing, but when you glue a shattered vase together you can still see the cracks. And even when the glue is the best you can find, you wonder what it's made of, and whether it'll really hold.

Whenever I caught sight of myself in the mirror I saw a spider web of flaws invisible to the casual observer. The knowledge that they were largely self-inflicted made it even worse. I asked myself a million questions: Would I ever trust anyone again? Could I ever again believe that men would find me desirable and worthy? And worst of all: Had I already squandered my relationship allotment? After everything I'd put myself through, could there possibly be another man in the world willing to commit his life to me?

I'd grit my teeth and put those questions aside as my inner voice told me that no matter how I felt about love, I had to keep trying. Somewhere out there, there was a corner to turn, and if I didn't find it, it wasn't going to be anyone's fault but my own. I was just going to have to talk myself through it. If I stopped to think about all the reasons "why not," I was never going to go forward.

So what that G.B. had come to take my china? I bought my own, and I signed my own mortgage papers. I had learned, as every woman should, that I was the source of creating beauty and joy in my life. From now on, I'd create my own home to my own taste and then invite guests over to enjoy it with me. Not only that, but I was going to cultivate friends who would invite me out because they valued me for myself, and not because I was attached to a powerful husband.

And as far as new men were concerned, no way was I going to just sit and wait for them to come to me. I was going to use the same strategy for dating that I did for reaching my business goals.

Why should women wait for the right man to come calling? If your goal is to have the right man, don't wait for him to call. Go out and use the same skills that you apply to reaching a goal. In short, go out and get him. What are you waiting for? What do you have to lose? And you can have fun in the process, don't forget that. Remember, you can't get anything you don't ask for.

I went through my address book, made an A, B and C list of prospects who might know single men, figured my approach, and talked right through those "no's."

"I'm single now," I'd say. "I went through two marriages, and the second one was horrible, but that doesn't mean that I don't trust men or I don't want to go out with any. The guy doesn't have to be my next husband and he doesn't have to be Casanova. He just has to be a nice man."

I quickly found that my obstacle lay in convincing my friends that my date *didn't* have to be Mr. Perfect. They just didn't think I'd want to go out with nice Mr. X or Y. They thought that no one they knew would be good enough for me, and it took all my powers of persuasion to convince them otherwise. I quickly discovered that being attractive and accomplished didn't necessarily draw men to you like a magnet. If anything, it was a deterrent.

"Oh, Georgette," my friends would say, "you couldn't possibly need me to set you up. Who could I possibly know who would appeal to you?"

I was not above begging. Coupled with persistence, that was what usually worked.

Was I embarrassed?

No.

Never let embarrassment get in the way of achieving your personal goals, either. It's nothing but a shackle on your happiness. What's the worst thing that can happen? That your friends think you're forward? Is that going to ruin your life, or, for that matter, your friendship? And if a friend does introduce you to the man of your dreams, won't it all have been worth it?

If I were ever single again, and I don't plan to be, I'd add a few more strategies to this one. Since I have an apartment in New York, I'd go to the F.A.O. Schwarz toy store on Fifth Avenue on Saturday afternoon when it's loaded with divorced men and their children—these are caring fathers. Second, I'd keep my eyes open at the auction houses and museum shows, because a man who shares my taste might also be a good prospect for sharing my life. Last but by no means least, I'd make a habit of taking Adam, my lovable and much-loved King Charles Spaniel, for long walks through neighborhoods where the eligible men of my choice lived. There's no conversation opener like man's best friend.

Once I figured out how to persuade and cajole my friends, the supply of blind dates they arranged for me was pretty steady. Yes, the percentage of jerks on my dance card was large. And although I'd said he didn't have to be Richard the Lion-Hearted, sometimes I did end up face to face over a linen tablecloth with an apparent descendant of Ivan the Terrible.

But I didn't let that stop me. A cold call is a cold call whether you're looking for the love of your life or a steady paycheck. In either case, it's going to be that eighteenth call or the appointment that you are too-darned-tired-to-make-and-keep-and-it-just-started-sleeting-and-hailing-out that ends up being the one that will change your life.

Or at least that's what I told myself, even when one disappointment after another made me just that more sure that love was never going to happen to me. Although on the outside my attitude was so smooth you could bounce a dime off it, inside I still beat myself up constantly.

"How'd you end up here, Georgette?" I'd ask myself. "I mean, here you are in the humiliating and quite uncertain situation of having to start your life over from scratch at the ripe old age of thirty-five. And it's not like you didn't ever have anything, either. You did, and you were reckless. You threw it all away."

In those moments, nothing I had or was fighting for in my career seemed to count for much. One minute I'd be sure I was worthy of love, and the next I would get that sinking feeling in my stomach that reminded me that I wasn't worth anything but the bill of goods I was selling myself.

But still I forced myself to pick up that phone. "Nancy? Molly? Henry? Hi, how are you, it's Georgette. Don't you know any nice single men?"

Inevitably, they would. And I was set up with a lot of different men. From fabulously wealthy, successful men all the way down the line. In the process of marriage, divorce, and dating I learned one extremely important thing: the most important quality a man can have is to be generous—not rich, but generous. A man who isn't generous with his money isn't generous with his love and affection. And if there's one thing we all need, it's LOVE AND AFFECTION!! If he's stingy with his money, time, spirit, or any other resource he holds dear, he's going to be stingy with his love, too.

And so it was that I came to land in a Houston hotel near the Galleria mall, where I reviewed my schedule for the next twenty-four hours: back-to-back meetings, and, oh yes, a blind date that a girl-friend who knew I'd be visiting Houston had set up.

I groaned out loud. The date was set up for dinner in one hour. Although I liked this woman a lot, her taste in men could be pretty crazy.

"Georgette, this is nuts. He's bound to be a wacko," I said to myself. "This one can't possibly be for you."

"Snap out of it, Georgette," I finally said out loud. Then I took a shower and went through the ritual of putting on my makeup, plenty of hair spray (it's hot and humid in Houston in August), and a blue silk sheath dress.

Grimly determined, I got into the elevator.

When the doors opened again, there was only one man in the lobby and he was sitting on a bench right in front of me. He smiled at me.

"No," I said to myself. "Couldn't be. No way. Too good to be true."

He was movie-star handsome. He had piercing blue eyes, and that smile just lit up the whole lobby. And this was quite a big room.

I was so taken aback that even when he stood up and walked toward me I couldn't stop talking to myself.

"No blind date could be this good-looking, Georgette. Just doesn't happen, can't be."

"Hi," he said, smiling again and reaching out to shake my hand. The smile was just as good the second time around. "I'm Robert Mosbacher. I thought we'd go have dinner around the corner. There's an excellent restaurant in the Galleria."

"Okay," I said.

"Oh, by the way, I have a convertible. Do you mind if I put the top down?"

Well, of course I minded after I'd just spent God knew how long getting my hair just so.

I smiled.

"Oh, no, not at all."

Quality is something I know when I see it. And I knew it the moment I met my husband.

I can't remember what the restaurant looked like, and I have no memory of what I ate. I was transfixed by Robert. It was the usual first-date conversation of introductions and small talk, but I instantly felt safe and protected. Almost immediately the two of us were laughing. And we kept laughing. Not only was the man gorgeous and courteous, but he was very easy to be with and I could tell that he thought the same of me.

He was charming, honorable, and intelligent. He didn't say much about his business dealings, but the little he did say told me he was also ambitious and result-oriented. His words and his actions were respectful of both my femininity and my power. I quickly discovered that, like me, he was conservative and his family meant everything to him.

I'm still an old-fashioned girl in a lot of ways. I love doors opened for me, chairs pulled out for me, and men standing when I walk into a room. I need and expect to be treated like a lady—and you should too—and I also like to be treated equally in terms of what I offer intellectually and professionally. And, by the way, I don't share checks.

Robert was a gentleman. A real gentleman. And, most important, he absolutely radiated integrity.

And with that realization, the fear that had kept such a grip around my heart began to loosen.

"Trust yourself, Georgette," my inner voice said. "Just because you made one disastrous mistake doesn't mean you're predisposed toward making the same mistake forever."

I don't know how, but in one fell swoop I just decided to will those scars right out of me. And I did. My faith in life was restored. I'm here to tell you that it can be that simple.

When Robert dropped me off at my hotel I was afraid he'd hear my heart pounding. I could. Before we parted he told me he had an office in New York and got there a couple of times a month. He didn't make a specific date, but he did say he'd call.

Then I marched right upstairs, picked up my phone book, and called my friend Susan Glesby, who comes from one of those fine old Texas families.

I was in luck. She picked up the phone.

"Hi, darling, I just had this blind date with a guy named Robert, and I need some information."

"Oh God, Georgette. You caught me drying my hair. I'm running late. Can't this wait?"

"Sure. I was just wondering if you knew this Robert Mosbacher. I'll talk to you later."

The hair dryer stopped dead, and when she spoke again Susan was practically yelling.

"*You had a date with Robert Mosbacher?* Well, I suppose I'm going to be late. I and practically every other woman I know would *kill* for a date with Robert Mosbacher. I mean, he's only the second most eligible bachelor in the world."

"The *second* most eligible bachelor in the world? If he's only the second, then who's the first?"

"Prince Rainier of Monaco. Since Princess Grace died, that is."

"Prince Rainier? Oh no, I don't think so. Monaco is a very small principality, Susan. Texas is much bigger than Monaco. Now, tell me everything you know about him."

Apparently Robert was quite well known in Texas, where he headed his own company and was very active in civic and community activities. He had been widowed about fifteen years after twenty years of marriage, when his wife and college sweetheart, Jane, was discovered to have leukemia. Tragically, Jane had passed away within a year of diagnosis, leaving Robert with four growing children, the oldest of whom was just a teenager. Completely devastated, Robert married a short time later, forming a prominent alliance with socialite Sandra Gerry that quickly ended in divorce. So he had been twice hurt and devastated.

If there was ever an argument for the existence of love at first sight, then I am living proof that there is such a thing. Because I fell in love with him the minute I set eyes on him.

Next, I did what any powerful and determined possessor of the Feminine Force in my position would do: I waited for the phone to ring.

But, just in case it didn't, I channeled my nervous energy into forming Plan B, which was quite simple and can be summed up in a single sentence. It went like this: "If he doesn't call me within two weeks, I'm calling him."

Every day I checked my messages. My mother called. My sister called. My brother and my friends called. But no Robert. So I whiled away the time working and developing Plan B, which consisted of what I'd say if I had to be the one to pick up the phone. My script went something like this:

"I thought I'd just give you a call and find out when you're going to be in New York. We could go to the theater."

Amazingly, I didn't have to implement Plan B because two weeks to the day after our blind date, Robert called. He was going to be in New York for a board meeting and he asked me out for a date.

We had a fabulous time together. As we shared our pasts, I realized that this was a man who had had his own struggle over the relationship between worldly power and privilege and real values.

As Robert is fond of saying: "Influence is something you have until you need to use it." The experience of his first wife's death had been a humbling one. It had brought home like no other experience could that the things that really make the world go round—love, family, security—are much more important than any amount of power or influence, that they can't be bought with all the money in the world, and that without them all the power and influence in the world doesn't mean a heck of a lot.

Now don't get me wrong. I'd rather be rich and miserable than poor and miserable, and anyone who tells you otherwise is a liar or a fool. But wealth cannot protect you from real loss. Wealth cannot protect you from heartbreak, and wealth cannot protect you from feeling terrible about who you are inside.

So we found out right away that although both of us valued the ability to make an impact on the world, we were realistic about the place of power in life and about what was really important. We were both thoughtful because we had both lived through losses.

I also began to notice the interesting differences between us. Robert was understated, soft-spoken, and tough in a very quiet way, while I was flamboyant and tough in a more direct way. Still, it was clear that we each used our individual style to pursue similar goals—to create results in business, and to build security for our families. The contrast in our styles only made things more interesting.

I was now sure that this was the soul mate I had been visualizing.

"You know," I joked over dessert, "I do believe I'm going to marry you."

Robert laughed, and I could tell he was flattered. But although he took it as a joke, he also firmly disabused me of the notion.

"I hope you'll understand, Georgette, that I'm never getting married again. I'm not a young man, and I have four great kids. Twice is enough. I want to put that on the table with you up front. I wouldn't want to mislead you."

I ignored him. There's *no* part of "no" that I understand.

"I have tickets to the opening of *Cats*. Want to fly up and go with me?"

"Sounds like fun," he replied, perhaps thinking the case was closed. "I'd be delighted."

As I walked the halls of Fabergé during the day, I smiled. My ex-husband G.B. wasn't totally without conscience, and as our interaction had dwindled, his interest in me had dwindled along with it, until little was left but a kind of brooding passivity.

Until I went on a cruise with Robert, that is. Somehow, G.B. found out, and I came back to a locked office door and the news that there was no reason to go inside because he'd thrown all my things out.

And so, as I stood in front of a locked door, my years at the company ended. The symbol of the closed door was ever so fitting. But even though he and I were already divorced by then, and even though I had spent a year getting reacquainted with my inner voice, the pain I felt at that sight was not only startling—it was unsettling. All my old terrors and insecurities came right back up and hit me in the face as if they'd never left. Without my job, how was I going to take care of my grandmother? How was I going to protect myself? Could I really make something of myself by myself, or was it all just a fantasy?

How quickly it can all come back to you. Confronted with that final salvo, even my new relationship with Robert and the recovery of my inner freedom were cold comfort. Nothing helped but a new series of down and dirty conversations with my inner voice. I had to go home, look in the mirror and go through my Feminine Force affirmations. Again and again.

"It doesn't matter, Georgette," I had to remind myself. "Even if you end up on the street you'll find a way, Georgette. You'll put one foot in front of the other until you get there."

Meanwhile, my budding new relationship continued to grow. Once I got over the shock, I had to thank G.B. for being the one to show me the time had come to bring down the final curtain on that act in my life. It made it that much easier to turn all my attention and determination toward the future.

A long-distance romance is wonderful and difficult at the same time. It's wonderful because it's so romantic. But it's difficult because one minute you're on cloud nine, and the next you get that inevitable sinking feeling that always comes when it's time for the man you love to leave.

That's the way it was for me and Robert. Sure, I already loved and implicitly trusted the guy. Despite his protestations to the contrary, after that second date I never doubted that he was "the one." Still, one minute it was bliss, and the next minute I'd be alone again at my dining room table with my annual reports and my cold calls and my silence. Of course, I didn't accept Robert's protests. The way I saw it, anybody who marries twice will marry a third time. But *he* thought he meant what he said. And he certainly hadn't made me any promises.

My work was cut out for me. I was going to have to change Robert's mind, and it was going to be a formidable task. The man clearly loved me, but would not admit he loved me.

That was the reality of the situation, and I had to go from there. So I decided to make sure he understood that life *with* me was much better than life *without* me. I wanted him to realize that life without me would leave a major void. This had to be done by bringing a quality of love, caring, and affection into Robert's life that he presently lacked. I wanted him to see that the love I offered him was so powerful that the chance of losing it would become even more unappealing to him than the idea of getting married again.

This was a pleasure for me to do, because I already loved this man down to the deepest core of my soul and it is true I am adventuresome by nature, while my husband by nature is an over-achieving, all-around great citizen and workaholic. So I was willing to share his activities with him and make compromises with him just as readily as he was to share my activities and make compromises with me.

Boy, did we have fun. We traveled, boated, danced. He taught me about the oil business, and I taught him about cosmetics. At first he didn't take me completely seriously, but he learned to, and he was charmed. I added adventure to his life everywhere I could. And it worked. One day I happened to mention to a Houston friend of Robert's who went back thirty years, that Robert and I had just come back from Monte Carlo.

The man looked at me in amazement.

"They must have struck oil in the Mediterranean if Mosbacher went to Monte Carlo," he said.

I wanted to keep up with my movie contacts from California, so with a little cajoling I got my buttoned-down preppie to mingle with that glittering crowd. It was, for him, an earth-shattering lifestyle change. What can I say? The guy has driven the same old car for ten years.

At first, he was suspicious, but then he relaxed and had a great time. Since I've always loved the theater, instead of sitting around and waiting for Robert to figure out by osmosis that I wanted him to ask me, I followed up my *Cats* suggestion with the Bronx Zoo. Robert wasn't wild about the idea, but I sold it to him by telling him that this was one of the greatest zoos in the world, and that going to a zoo with another adult is completely different from going as a parent—you appreciate the animals for yourself, instead of for your children. And not only did he come, but soon he even began to develop a taste for my taste.

Robert quickly came to love and appreciate the dimension I added to his life, and to recognize that these events were experiences he would not have had otherwise. Consequently, when I wasn't there, there was a hole in his life. In this respect, getting my own needs fulfilled actually moved the relationship forward. The life I introduced Robert to, the things that surrounded me, and my interests, gradually became just as attractive to him as I was—part of my appeal.

However, although Robert and I would eventually talk to each other quite a bit when we weren't together, at first there was nothing in those interims but dead silence. The vulnerability in those moments was compounded by the fact that my old fear had come back again, in a new form. I might have been a cool customer, but every time Robert left me, I became terrified I'd never see him again, just the way I'd felt as a child when Mother went off to work. I knew it was just a mark of my deep feelings for this man, but that knowledge didn't make things any easier.

There were times when I thought the obstacle was bigger than I was. There were times when I wondered if I had misjudged things and Robert meant what he was saying about never getting married after all. Time and time again I had to tell myself that he loved me but just wasn't capable of admitting it.

Meanwhile, our relationship was continuing to evolve. Not only were Robert and I having more and more fun together, but I began to spend much more time in Houston. At the same time, my business goals were beginning to reach critical mass. I was never going to give up my business life or financial independence for Robert—and he never, ever doubted that. Because I was already "made" that way when we met, to his credit this was not a problem for him. But in all ways we began to operate not only as romantic partners, but as more and more of a life team.

In particular, his respect for my horse sense grew. One morning after I'd dissected the annual report of a major American consumer-oriented company, I sat down to breakfast with him and said, "Robert, there's something here. There's something really here. And it has an energy unit to spin off. Why don't you come in on this one with me?"

I told him that I would put the deal together and spin off the energy unit to him at a good price. I structured the whole deal for him as we finished our coffee.

He wasn't quite ready to take me *that* seriously. In those days, I pored over my deals, and he pored over his, and never the twain would meet. Back then he was a little chauvinistic in that respect.

Not anymore.

Because seven months later that energy unit was sold off at a $300 million profit by someone else.

After missing out on that one, Robert sat up and took notice.

Our growing closeness didn't help me in any way to breathe easy. If anything, it made me more anxious. I wanted legitimacy so much, and it was as though everything I'd ever wanted in a man was being dangled in front of my nose and then pulled away again. I was desperate to find someone who would say something that would soothe me, so desperate that I did things I'd never done before and will never do again. I even started going to astrologers.

I had to be honest with the guy and bring up the idea of marriage in all seriousness. I'd already asked two men to marry me, with some success. Why stop now? He refused. For a while, the fact that I was interested in getting married and he wasn't was a running joke between us.

One weekend on his boat I even caught Robert singing lyrics to a very interesting song in the shower. It went something like this: "When an irresistible force such as you, meets an old immovable object like me . . ."

But soon the humor was exhausted, and the subject became a source of irritation and fights.

Two years in, I had to ask myself a hard question: Could I go on in this relationship as it was without being married? I knew that I could not. We were spending every weekend together, which, of course, is more or less what we do now that we're married, but the relationship was missing the commitment that was so important to me.

Emotionally, I am just very conservative. I need to be legitimate to be happy. Maybe it's because of an early loss, but I really don't know why, and ultimately it's inconsequential. That's just the way I am. And I'm honest about it.

For me, part of being a pragmatist means that I want to deal in the realities of my life in order to go beyond them to create new realities. Part of the reality of romance is that couples who love one another commit to one another. Right now in our society, that commitment is expressed by marriage. It may sound a little esoteric, but there is something about legitimizing that commitment through marriage that's like affixing your signature to a check. The check can't be cashed until you sign it; that doesn't mean you don't have the money in the bank. Similarly, only marriage turns your commitment into a bond. Once you're married, your commitment becomes sacred. Before that, it's just talk.

Some traditions, even if they're not necessary anymore (and in some ways I do think we're evolving beyond the point where we need that "piece of paper"), are nonetheless very satisfying to observe. Marriage is a pledge of fidelity and emotional support. Public acknowledgment of your commitment makes you happy and other people socially comfortable. And if you're going to have children (and I always kept that possibility in the back of my mind), you want to make life as stable and carefree for them as you can. No matter how enlightened most of us have become, there is still a stigma attached to children who are born out of wedlock. Your kids will have to fight their own battles and make their own choices in life. But why complicate it for them? Let's face it, having two loving parents gives the children the extra security they need.

Twice I threatened to leave Robert if he didn't marry me, and twice he said he would, but backed out at the last moment. My inner voice might have demanded a marriage license, but I just didn't have the heart to follow through on my threats. My heart was saying, "Count me out on this one." Even as I was threatening to walk out, every single time *he* left *me* I had that uncontrollable fear I'd never see him again.

But finally, in February of 1985, the moment came to face down my dragon. It wasn't anything in particular. My feelings and will just suddenly synchronized into an iron conviction that I deserved marriage, that I would have marriage, and that if I couldn't create that relationship with Robert, well then by God I'd have to go on and create it with someone else. I hadn't been able to go through with my ultimatum before, but now I knew that not only could I, but I must.

I'd rather be with Robert, boy would I rather, but if I couldn't, I loved and valued myself enough to move on. So what if I'd tried twice to leave him and failed? That didn't mean I wouldn't be successful this time.

Call it Feminine Force.

So I told Robert that I wasn't going to see him again.

"Try to get through a week," I told him.

This time I could tell by the look in his eyes that he really believed I wasn't coming back. And well he should have.

Nevertheless, as I flew back to New York, my heart left its usual place in my chest to loll in my mouth.

The days went by, and Robert didn't call.

I was absolutely miserable. But I resolved that I still had to move on to whatever the resolution of the situation was going to be. I knew I couldn't live this way very long and also keep my sanity. I also knew I couldn't make the decision for Robert, that he had to make it for himself. All I could do was make him see that it was time to make the choice.

So I called a friend and said, "I'm going to try the oldest trick in the book, my last stab. I've tried everything else. I've got to find the richest, highest-profile, most handsome younger bachelor in New York and date him. Who would that be?"

My friend gave me a name.

I had another friend in California who knew this gentleman, so I called him and told him he had to set up this date for me.

"Yeah, sure, Georgette. I'll get back to you."

"No," I said. "I can't take any chances on this one. You might get back to me and you might not. So put me on hold and get him on the other line right now."

And God bless him, that was how I got him to set up the date for the very next day.

I made sure that absolutely everyone knew I was going out with this guy. The two of us hadn't had but three dates when I answered the phone and heard Robert's voice on the other end of the line.

He was very calm. It was a Monday. He said he was in New York and asked if we could have lunch. I said fine. I might have sounded cool, but I was trembling. I could tell by the tone of his voice that he knew I hadn't been bluffing. He sensed the new intensity of my Feminine Force. He knew in his gut that this time I had the will power and the character to stick by my guns. If I was going to create the life I felt I deserved, it meant either I was going to be married to the man I loved or I wasn't going to be with him at all.

First we went to Sotheby's to look at paintings, and then we went around the corner to a little restaurant on First Avenue called Adam's Rib. I remember because Adam is Robert's middle name and because later I named my dog Adam. We had a very civilized lunch together, but I still didn't have a clue as to what would happen next.

"What do you think, Georgette," Robert said finally. "Should we get married on Friday?"

I began to tremble.

"We've been through this before, Robert. I don't believe you. Twice you talked about a date for this and then canceled it."

"Yes," he said, "but this time is different. I realize you're dating someone else. And I've been dating too. But I've asked myself whether I want to live my life with you or without you, and I know what the answer is. I want to live it with you. So if marriage is what it takes, that's what it takes."

"I don't believe you," I said.

"Okay," he said. "How about Friday?"

Thursday I flew down to Houston. The plan was that I would pick Robert up from a meeting he was having on Friday and drive to College Station, Texas, where Robert knew a minister. We wanted to keep the wedding quiet, and College Station was located in the only nearby county in Texas where Robert's company didn't have oil production.

I remember picking out a wine-colored silk dress with a matching jacket, checking the time, calling my mother, who was elated, getting into the car, and wondering what would happen next. I was a wreck, incredulous, hoping against hope he wouldn't change his mind again. Not only did I fear he'd never go through with it, but I also knew I'd played my last hand. If he didn't marry me this time, it was over. There was nothing more I could do.

And what happened was that Robert got into the car and we drove to College Station. We walked in the door, got the license, went to the church, and were married by the minister.

By the time it was time to say our vows, I was crying so hard I could hardly say, "I do." I could barely believe this was actually happening.

Meanwhile, beside me, the man who had resisted this day for years was repeating his vows with total calm, dignity, and love. He had made his mind up, was finally sure he was doing the right thing, and that, as far as he was concerned, was that.

It was March 1, 1985, less than four years after I'd fled G.B. to a phone booth only to find that I had no one to call.

We drove quietly back to Houston and spent the evening no differently than we spent any other. And then Robert came with me to New York.

Aside from all his other attributes, Robert is wonderfully caring and protective. Often I feel he's like a guardian angel, watching over me as I venture toward my goals.

"Make sure they know about your softness and warmth in this book," he says. "You're nowhere near as tough as you say you are."

Well, not as far as he's concerned I'm not. Nor as far as anyone I love is concerned.

I treasure that about Robert, that he has who I am at heart and tries to protect it. I love that he knows who I am, and is my advocate, and watches over my activities—not to control them or correct them or somehow compete with them, but to help make me even more of who I am.

People often ask if marriage changes a relationship. They ask if marriage changed our relationship. After all, when we married we were both grown and fully developed adults with our own careers. And we already spent all our weekends together, entertained together, confided in each other . . .

Actually, the only change in our relationship was a new sense of permanence in the way things already were, and a sense of security and ease about what they would continue to be. And that was all I had needed. I had wanted to know that we could plan our future at leisure, that each of us could always count on seeing the other's family at Thanksgiving and Christmas, that if either of us decided to buy a house or launch into a new career or make any major move, the other one would be expected to not only give an opinion, but to accept the decision. That was what my inner voice had told me I deserved: nothing less and nothing more.

Although it is certainly my frank preference to bank my own money and live on my husband's, I gained little in permanent financial terms. Robert and I had, of course, signed a prenuptial agreement, which essentially waived any community property rights on either side. I'd married a rich man, but I wasn't rich. I had learned the distinction through hard-earned experience, and I wasn't going to forget it.

To the shock of some of our friends, I did not give up my business plans or my work weeks in New York. And neither did Robert expect me to. That was another lesson I'd learned far too well to forget ever again. I was finally married to a man who loved and cherished me, a man I knew would never hurt me and who understood and respected my goals. But meanwhile I was more determined than ever to continue to pursue my own destiny and scale my own mountain—to have complete financial independence and stability of my own.

Chapter 13

You Want That Man? Here's How to Get Him

"The average man is more interested in a woman who is interested in him than he is in a woman with beautiful legs."

—Marlene Dietrich

Let's start with the basics. You've met him. You walked your dog in the right neighborhood. Your accountant set you up with one of her other clients, according to your exact specification. Or you walked into the museum on Saturday morning and saw the most attractive and thoughtful-looking man sitting on the bench right in front of your favorite Matisse.

He's a gentleman. He pulls out the chair and opens the door.

You're a lady. You glow inside and out, you're warm and attentive—and you don't share checks.

You've also asked yourself two questions and answered them both to your own satisfaction.

First question: What is the most important quality the man of my dreams should have?

Second question: Does this man have it?

Here's my answer to the first question. Two words: *generosity* with *integrity*.

I've touched on this point briefly, but it bears repeating. In my experience, a man who isn't generous with his resources, no matter how many or how few he has, won't be generous with his love or caring either. So if generosity in love, caring, and affection is important to you, every time you meet a man, take a look at this bottom line indicator.

What exactly do I mean by generous?

It depends on the man.

A generous man is one who wants to make your life more comfortable and exciting, using whatever resources are available to him.

Remember, a wealthy man is not necessarily a generous man. It all depends on the man. There are very busy men who show that they're solid gold by being giving with their time. They help you with your errands. Or they may read to your child from a former marriage. Maybe they cook for you. Perhaps they make time to visit your mother in the hospital even though there's a drop-dead big project at the office. Now *that's* generous. And heartfelt and caring.

There are men whose greatest gift of generosity is one of spirit. They may have little to offer you financially, and you may not care (after all, you're responsible for yourself). But they will fully and wholeheartedly support you in your choices and dreams.

Generosity is a relative term, and it comes in all shapes and forms. What they all come down to is the willingness to just "be there" for you in whatever way you need. And, of course, you're just as generous with him.

If you think the most important quality a man could have is something else entirely, then more power to you for knowing what you want and need. Just make sure you know what that quality is, and then do not neglect to determine whether or not the man you are interested in has it.

Whatever that most important quality is, seek it out. Demand it. Expect it. And don't be cheap with yourself. A "little" generosity isn't generosity at all. Expect a lot. *Always* expect the best for yourself—the best in love, the best in warmth, the best in caring. And, in my opinion, if you find a generous man, you're already halfway home.

If a man does not possess this most important quality, don't go any further with him. Sure, read this chapter, but practice on someone else. It's just not worth it. You'll be cheating yourself out of something that you need, want, and deserve. A happy life alone—and your happiness starts with you—is far, far preferable to an unhappy life together.

A German *Vogue* photo for a profile on the "professional woman." That's my actual briefcase, my ubiquitous cellular phone, and my frequent office companion, Adam Mosbacher.

22

23

To Georgette + Bob MacEnroe
With warm regards —
from Richard Nixon
1-23-89

29

28

24

25

Clockwise left to right:
with Parisian Mayor
Jacques Chirac, Lech
Walesa, Barbara Bush,
General Norman
Schwartzkopf, former
President George Bush,
former President Ronald
Reagan and Empress
Farah Diva, former
Israeli Prime Minister
Shamir and Mrs.
Shamir, and Henry
Kissinger and former
President Richard
Nixon.

26

27

30

What can I say? I love
getting dressed up . . .
and I love being a girl.

31

32

Isn't Adam the cutest?

My happiest role, as entrepreneur, at the helm of my own company. And believe me, it's worth the blood, sweat and tears to have your independence.

34
PREVIOUS PAGE:
Finally, my childhood
dreams become a reality,
and yours can, too.

And if he does have it?

How do you turn a moment into a lifetime?

Here are my ten proven techniques.

Quite frankly, most of what I've ever consciously learned about making a man feel good around me I learned from my mother. So here are Georgette and Dee's suggestions for what to do with the man of your dreams once you've found him. Oh yes, my husband threw in his two cents, too.

Hard-core feminists may not like them.

So what? It's your move. And it's my pleasure.

MY TEN PROVEN TECHNIQUES FOR TURNING A MOMENT INTO A LIFETIME

1. Cultivate "The Look"

If you do any research on great *femmes fatales* throughout history—and I mean from the French court favorites through modern heroines like Jacqueline Kennedy Onassis and behind-the-scenes political powerhouse Pamela Harriman, you'll find they all have one characteristic in common. And that is the ability to silently and wholly lock on to a man with their attention.

The women who practice this art have the technique down to the point where they are so completely and genuinely engrossed in what a man is saying that they don't even see anyone else enter or leave the room. They're that focused. Harriman is so celebrated for this talent that they call it "The Look."

My husband knows Pamela Harriman, so I asked him. "Well, Robert: What is it about her?"

"She's sexy," he said.

"What exactly makes her sexy?"

My husband confirmed that it was her ability to look a man right in the eye and, just with her interest and concentration, make him feel as though everything he says is brilliant. She does it without ever having to have those words pass her lips. In fact, if I could give you just one piece of advice on how to develop a relationship with a man after you've met him, it would be these two words: *Be attentive.*

And I mean attentive. If you come by this talent naturally, exploit it.

If you don't and not all of us (including myself) do, do whatever you can to develop it. Never let your eyes roam. I don't care if a flying saucer careens into the room and two little green men get out. Your job is to stay absolutely focused.

Be attentive with your ears, too. Really listen to what your date is saying so that you can respond genuinely and spontaneously. Get him to talk about himself. Center the conversation around him—what he's doing, what he wants in life, and who he is.

I never consider attentiveness a sacrifice of Feminine Force or a form of confinement. On the contrary. I expect that everyone I meet can teach me something, that I can draw it out of him, and that we'll both benefit from the process.

No, every conversation won't turn out to be as scintillating as a tête-à-tête with Henry Kissinger. However, remember that enjoyment of life does require some participation. So don't just sit around and wait for someone else to entertain you. Get the ball rolling.

2. The Art of Conversation

Ultimately, what a man likes most to talk about is himself.

How do you get him to do it?

You ask questions. Be a reporter, if you will. Question him about his business and his hobbies. Ask him if he has children, where he went for vacation last year, what kind of car he drives, what his favorite food is, how he spends his weekends. ASK, ASK, ASK!

No, he won't think you're nosy. And, of course, you exercise obvious judgment about how far you can go. I mean, don't ask him how much money he makes. But aside from that, there's no trick to conversing but doing it.

When you practice the Art of Conversation, a man's answers will always provide you with the clue to your next question.

The most artful conversation often starts with something very simple. And I mean really simple, like clothing or personal appearance: "Oh, that's an interesting tie." Or, "Does that red hanky signify anything?" Or, "Have you always worn a moustache?"

Is he left-handed? You can develop a whole conversation right there!

Start by picking any one of these openers: "Did they try to get you to switch to your right hand when you were a child?" "Can you write with both hands?" "President Bush was left-handed. They say left-handed people have special talents. Do you believe that's true? What are yours? Does left-handedness run in your family?"

Once you get a yes, run with it: "Oh, so you have a brother who's left-handed. What does your brother do? Is he older or younger than you are? Oh, you're the oldest in the family. Oldest children are sup-posed to be very responsible. Are you?"

Or, "Do you have your own company? Was it scary to start it? What kind of professional background do you need for something like that?"

Now you're off and running.

Some men you will always have to draw out, while with others, all you have to do is ask one question and it's as if you turned on the faucet. But it's *okay* to draw a man out as long as you always look him straight in the eye and listen to what he has to say. It is *more* than okay. He'll love it!

As far as general subjects of interest go, most men like to talk about politics and sex. And you can always assume that whatever's on the front page of the news section or the business section of the newspaper will be of interest to a man (and, of course, to you, too).

On the other hand, don't *ever* be intimidated if what he knows isn't what you know. Everything *you* know is more than enough.

If you're interested in a very distinguished history professor, get the ball rolling by telling him you were *lousy* in history, if you were. Don't be shy. That's a *great* conversation opener. Or, ask him, "What do you think are the most significant moments in history?" Then just listen to the answer, and it will give you your next question.

Point A to B to C to D. That's all you need to give yourself the gift of gab.

3. Flattery Will Get You Almost Everywhere

Men haven't come as far as women have when it comes to self-esteem or inner power. Let's face it, they may look tough but they all need to be coddled.

I, for one, can't really blame them. I *love* to be told that I have a good smile, or that I'm smart, or that my new hair style looks great. So why shouldn't they?

It will be no challenge to compliment a man you find attractive. So just remember to do it often, with great charm and style, and immediately.

Be especially sure to compliment a man who needs to be reassured about something. But *always tell the truth*. False compliments always fall flat. People know what's true about them and what isn't. Don't you?

Robert had to get some glasses recently, and he wasn't too happy about it. So when he put them on I said, "Robert, how is it that you can put on a pair of spectacles and still be incredibly handsome?" And not only did I mean it, but he loved every minute of it!

A compliment is not a capitulation. It's a demonstration of power. Your power. If he can't take it, it's his problem. But I bet you anything, he'll take it. And take it. And take it.

4. "I'm Game"

This one may surprise you. But *never* play hard to get unless there's a very good reason for it. Be available and be supportive.

I remember being cross with Lyn after a man she'd just met in Texas asked her to go shooting with him. Even though she liked this gentleman quite a bit, Lyn proudly reported to me she'd turned him down because she doesn't believe in shooting birds.

"Lyn," I said, "that is not the point. Next time say, 'Oh, I've never been shooting. I'd love to give it a try.'"

Now, I get exasperated for Lyn because I love her so much. In a way, I feel as if I raised her. I'm very protective and maternal. And what I was telling her was just what Mother told me.

But the fact is, Lyn didn't have to shoot anything. All she had to do was learn *how* to shoot, and if she didn't want to shoot a bird she could just say so honestly.

To say "no" to a man before you even understand what it is he's asking is ridiculous. So you've never shot a bird and you never plan to shoot one. Fine. That doesn't mean you can't go out there and shoot clay pigeons.

By the way, I go shooting. A woman just can't be married to a Texan and not know how to shoot.

A man who asks you to join him in his favorite hobby does so because he wants to share something he cares about with you. Not because he expects you to excel at it. So get out of the way of yourself. You can always learn. I just plain don't subscribe to the play-hard-to-get theory. Remember, *men love a woman who's game.* Your attitude will show him that you are an individual with principles and tastes of your own, and that, what's more, you hold yourself to a healthy level of esteem. You need not prove this by saying "no" or "maybe later."

What really interests men are these two little words: "yes, now."

I used this approach to court Robert Muir. If he wanted to play golf, sure I'd play golf, even though I'd never done it before. I was game to try anything. So you want to go to Hawaii? No, I don't need two days to get ready; I'll be waiting on the doorstep in half an hour.

There are women who consider this level of agreeableness pandering, but I don't. It's a way of sharing a man's life. That way, when you're not around, he'll miss you.

5. Make Your Needs Attractive

I love the theater, and I love to go dancing. But when I met Robert Mosbacher, although he liked these activities he often liked others— sailing for instance—more. So we sailed. *And* we went to the theater and danced. I made my needs attractive to him by taking the initiative in getting them filled. For instance, you know how I feel about opera; I've been going since I was twelve. Robert really wasn't at all fond of the opera. But I didn't let that stop me. Instead, I researched the schedule and took him to the most whimsical, entertaining operettas in the Houston and New York repertories.

These days, Robert enjoys the opera. That's because when we go, I first make sure that the performance is going to be a flat-out extravaganza: the greatest sets, voices, and costumes possible. And I don't force him to sit through the whole show. We often leave after one act.

For me, the compromise is worth it. I don't get to see the whole show, but it becomes something we can enjoy together. And my husband appreciates me all the more for it. The trick here is to avoid making your proposition into a matter of quid pro quo. If you do that, you're turning the fun and enchantment into a form of debt repayment. That's unappealing to anyone. So hold on to the fun and enchantment, and keep your partner's needs in mind at the same time.

6. Express Yourself

When I was working on this chapter I asked Robert what he liked in a woman. (I always think it's a good idea to be direct and go straight to the source.)

"That one reminds me of a story I heard about a man with three daughters," he offered without hesitating. "The man was asked which one he liked being with the best, and he said, 'The middle one, because she likes me the best.' "

So here you have one pretty reliable answer to the age-old question, "Is a woman more desirable when she desires a man—and he knows it?" The answer is yes.

Never be afraid to show your warmth and affection. Never be afraid to put your arms around someone. I touch my husband a lot. I stroke his hand. I stroke his face. Everyone in my family is warm and demonstrative. We always have been. And over the years, I've observed that men respond positively to this kind of contact.

This instinct for warmth and nurturing isn't necessarily sexual. We all need to make contact and be contacted through terms of endearment and touch. I know the difference between warmth and sexual aggression, and so does a man of quality. (If he doesn't, forget him.) Men like human touch. Don't you? It shows caring; it shows connection, it shows a man that he is not alone in the world. A man responds to a warm, self-confident woman. She's someone who clearly has something to give and is comfortable both with herself and with him.

A final note: I proposed to all three of my husbands. None of them said yes the first time. You just keep talking over that "no" until you get a yes. Are you fabulous? Are you warm? Can you tell he loves to be with you?

You have power in this relationship. You are worth it. Do not hesitate to be the one who asks him to dance. It'll also be good practice for success in every other arena in life—including business. It's essentially the same technique: To get what you want, you have to *ask*.

7. Don't Be Afraid to Show Him Who You Are and What You Want

Robert also recalls that on our first date I conveyed a certain combination of glamour and directness. He liked the fact that I was both a very feminine woman and very blunt at the same time, even when I said things that might be found provocative. (For instance, on our second date I informed him that I was going to marry him.) Robert also says he liked the fact that I wasn't afraid to speak my own mind and that I didn't play games.

Why?

First, men find a plain-speaking woman very sexy. A woman who clearly knows what she wants and is no shrinking violet conveys that to a man. She also controls her own pleasure—in all senses of the word. Men like a woman who is familiar with life's pleasures. Men find it a real turn-on to meet a woman who is as strong as they are. The prospect of "conquering" an equal is more of an accomplishment. And there are a lot of men who just plain don't like to play games. My husband's one of them. "I like the man/woman relationship," he says. "I've known women who play games and women who don't. And I choose the latter."

Finally, show a man that you're loyal. Men look for loyalty in their partner as much as women do. We all want to know we have someone to count on.

Don't be afraid to show a man all of who you are, and don't be afraid to express candidly what you want from the relationship. Don't expect a man to read your mind. Flex your Feminine Force. You deserve to be fulfilled.

8. At Your Leisure and at Your Pleasure

Being game and saying "Yes, now" is the way to go with a man—*with the exception of sex*. Never have sex unless you want to—and *when* you want to. If you say "no" and he then makes saying "yes" a condition for the pleasure of his continued presence in your life, then you just let him leave. It's very, very simple. You control the agenda. And if he doesn't like that, then too bad.

Listen carefully to these important words: You will *never* hold a man any longer or get him any faster because you said "yes" or "no" to sex earlier or later in the relationship. As far as that old adage goes, "Why buy a cow when you can get the milk for free?" I think the point is irrelevant—although your grandmother may not. Because ultimately, sex isn't what "does it" for a man. What makes a man want to commit to you is his interest in *you*, *all* of you, and sex flows out of an interest in being with another person.

Yes, there are some men who may want you just for sex. And if sex is all you want from a man, that's fine—as long as, of course, you take the necessary precautions. A woman who practices Feminine Force is just as responsible for preventing pregnancy and protecting herself against all forms of communicable disease as she is for securing every other aspect of her well-being. I'll say it again and again and again: If you don't take care of yourself, who will?

It all comes down to your inner sense of moral judgment. You have to listen to your conscience and always make a ritual of checking in with your self-respect before you make any decision about sex. If your decision—whatever it is—makes you feel good about yourself and about the relationship, then you can't ever go wrong.

My personal philosophy, however, is to make him earn it. The harder he works to have intimacy with you, the more he'll value it.

9. The Art of Compromise

He likes steak houses; you're a vegetarian. He simply must ski; you crave the beach. He has a chance to move up the ladder by moving to California, but you want to stay close to your family in Michigan. Every relationship has its "little" battles and "big" battles. Experience tells me to advise you not to get caught up in the little battles and to save your fire for the bigger ones. If going to the restaurants Robert likes instead of the ones I like makes him happy, then this is a battle I'm glad to surrender. So all other things being not equal, make sure you're the one to tip the balance. You may have to give more in your relationship. You may be more liberated than he is. You may have to make more compromises. If this describes your relationship, then don't make big issues out of little things.

So what are the "big" things and what are the "little" things? That's different for all of us. The ability to make the distinction is what distinguishes the women from the girls. Once again, it's just a matter of practice.

You don't compromise your power when you give in to your man in ways that show him support and affection. To be able to compromise and still feel good about yourself is power itself.

10. If I Were a Single Woman . . .

I'd call my friends and ask them to set up dates and to take me along when they went out. I'd force myself to go to certain events I'd rather not attend.

It doesn't matter how boring something sounds. The fact of the matter is that you're at least one hundred percent more likely to meet a special someone among other people than you are at home alone.

Also, don't be afraid to go out alone. You do not need a man to go anywhere. In fact, the very event you felt you could not attend alone because you were not part of a couple may be the one where you *meet* your true other half. Never be afraid to ask your married friends or your family to invite you places. Sometimes you just have to be a pest and ask if you can come along. That's life.

The easiest way in the world to meet men, and not too many women know about it, is to get involved in politics. Politics is a field defined and dominated by men. And, although those of us who practice Feminine Force are quickly revising the world of politics, at the moment it's still run by men. So turn that negative into a positive. Get involved. You won't only help to change that definition, but you'll also be entering one of the few remaining life arenas where you are sure to encounter a man-to-woman ratio that runs wildly in your favor.

You can get involved at any level—from the local board of the smallest community on upward. The two of you will already have something to talk about: a candidate, an issue, a goal. And not only will you be meeting men and changing the power structure; while you're at it, you'll also be participating in the process that makes our country great.

Chapter 14

Success Is the Process of Not Accepting Failure

"Failure is impossible."

—SUSAN B. ANTHONY

At the same time Robert and I were courting, I was pursuing courtships in the business world. Now that I wasn't working at Fabergé, I was looking for my own mountain to scale. More than once I had to pick myself up and start over after I'd fallen off. Remember, getting where you want to is a series of small steps. A to B to C . . .

My first serious courtship was with a small cosmetics company that was up for sale. When I decided to go into business for myself, I targeted consumer products and specifically cosmetics because these were what I knew. But I still couldn't quite believe I could play in the arena that men played in. I didn't have the confidence and courage I needed to go after a bigger company. I picked a small firm partly because it *was* small.

Though this particular product sold in retail, I thought it had excellent potential in mail-order, and the price was right. So I ran background checks to see if what the sellers were claiming about their company was true. I hired a consultant and did a national check to verify the company's store image. I confirmed their sales volume. I verified that the company itself owned their formulations.

When my consultant brought me the results of the research, all my instincts about this venture were confirmed. When we ran the projected numbers, I found I'd been right about the opportunities mail-order distribution presented. The company seemed perfect in nearly every way.

I'd been budget-conscious all my life, and now I was determined to maintain my independence. From my savings, I calculated I could live on the money I had for about three years.

I was using my own dining room as my office, so my business overhead was about as modest as it could be. But I still needed a secretary, and cash to cover the cost of my independent research—consultants, heavy long-distance telephone bills, occasional travel, supplies, and support services. I was in the process of a total remodeling of my life, and that three-year cushion was my security blanket. I'd have to raise the cash for the deal from outside.

If I knew anything about myself, I knew I was a born marketer. With all other systems on go, I knew I could sell an investor on the virtues of this acquisition, and I made the first move before I'd lined up my backing. The product was good. The company was a manageable size. It wasn't going to cost a fortune to close the deal. So I built a business plan that showed potential investors where the return on their investment would come from and laid out the assumptions behind my numbers. Then I made an offer.

Now, understand that I had no track record in raising venture capital or buying a business. What I did have was an innovative plan. I was proud of that plan. I was confident that even though I was sailing into new waters raising venture capital, I'd be able to pull it off.

I was still in the early stages of talking to investors when the seller backed out.

I tried to sweeten the deal. I renegotiated the timing. I went back and forth with the corporate management until it became clear: this was simply a deal that would not be made.

I never got the chance to find out whether I could line up the backing or not. It was an enormous disappointment, and the night the deal fell through I opted out of a fancy cocktail party, called a friend, and went to a tiny Italian place around the corner for a quiet, consoling dinner.

The next morning I pulled out my old notes, lined up a stack of stockholder reports I hadn't looked at yet, and started over. I was back on the horse again.

I looked at a little cosmetics company owned by Revlon, and liked what I saw. I got up my nerve, made a couple of cold calls, and met with management. A very exclusive Italian leather goods boutique with a particularly fabulous advertising campaign caught my attention for a while, and when it did I started thinking about the potential for expanding the line to include belts and scarves.

I was just an unemployed corporate manager, sitting at home in her dining room eyeing name-brand franchises. I scrutinized company after company. I was reaching as far as I could imagine reaching.

As entrepreneur J. Peterman said, "Success is the process of not accepting failure."

Remember when I suggested you pay attention to what you love because what you love is probably what you are good at?

Well, the answer to my prayers turned out to be literally right under my nose.

During the course of my research I'd begun to notice that many cosmetic companies were owned by large pharmaceuticals, and that there was a trend among these to divest themselves of their cosmetics divisions. The skin-care products I was using were from La Prairie, a subsidiary of American Cyanamid, and I loved them. As far as I was concerned, this was a company that had a unique, very high quality niche in the cosmetics market.

La Prairie had caught my eye three years earlier, with a quiet advertising campaign that featured real women like Ann Getty and Judith Peabody. The La Prairie skin treatment line had been developed by Dr. Armand Mattli, at his clinic La Prairie in Montreaux, Switzerland. Hundreds of well-known people had visited the clinic for treatments against aging; it had a client list that included Winston Churchill, Pablo Picasso, and Marilyn Monroe. When the company branched out into skin care, it drew on fifty years of success and a reputation for advanced research and the highest quality ingredients. It seemed to me to represent the best of what European skin-care scientists were producing.

There were other things that made La Prairie particularly attractive. When the clinic sold its cosmetics branch to American Cyanamid in the early eighties, La Prairie was such a small part of the American Cyanamid world that no one messed around with it. No one tried to save a few cents by cheapening the packaging, or by revising the formula. No one lowered the quality or tried to reach a huge mass market to make a bottom line. So La Prairie was positioned right at the apex of a very competitive market, with distribution limited to the most exclusive department stores in the country—Neiman Marcus, Bergdorf Goodman, Saks Fifth Avenue. Anyone who owned La Prairie would own that exclusive niche.

I thought about what I could bring to the line and I came up with ideas that excited me. La Prairie was already the best of the best in skin care, as far as I was concerned. They had a full line of purifying gels, exfoliators, and cellular balancing complexes based on their anti-aging research, but they had only twenty-one products on the market, while most skin-care companies offered more like fifty.

When I discovered that La Prairie might be available, I already felt that cosmetics should be treatment-oriented. I demanded it, and I was certain other women wanted it, too. La Prairie offered the perfect opportunity to expand a great trademark with a cosmetics line that matched the treatment line in terms of quality and positioning.

I began to do preliminary due diligence, and I liked what I saw. The moment for expansion was perfect.

I decided to approach the parent company with a cold call.

They told me they didn't want to sell, but then I heard through other channels that American Cyanamid was planning on divesting their whole cosmetics division, which also included Geoffrey Beene and Niki St. Phalle, to Sanofi, a French pharmaceutical company.

The rub was, American Cyanamid had decided it was more advantageous to them to divest the division whole. They didn't want to sell it brand by brand.

Then I learned that the division couldn't be sold to Sanofi without the approval of Nina Ricci, the fragrance company that was already part of the Sanofi holdings, because of a clause Robert Ricci had negotiated into his contract with the parent company. This was significant information. It told me Robert Ricci held the trump card in this deal. Another important fact became clear: Like the other two companies in the American Cyanamid portfolio, Nina Ricci was a fragrance company. La Prairie was not. If I was right, Sanofi's primary interest in this acquisition wasn't going to be La Prairie.

All of this information allowed me to form a plan of attack.

Here is one of the most powerful observations about business I can give you. Putting together a deal isn't much different from playing a game of treasure hunt. You take your first clue and let that clue lead you to the next. One person or one detail always leads you to the next question and the next answer. It's a process that's really based on nothing but simple logic and tenacity. There is no trick to it.

As Pat Harrison, head of the National Women's Economic Alliance, says, "In the past, work was a mystery to women. But when we get into it we find that there's no mystery and no magic to it. Women have to spend less time thinking, 'Am I doing it the right way?' and start thinking, 'Am I *doing* it?' "

My next step was to call Robert Ricci in Paris and ask if I might come in and see him. We met, and I asked him if he knew whether Sanofi wanted to spin off La Prairie. He said he thought they might. I told him a little of my plans, and he placed some phone calls of his own. The next thing I knew, I was meeting with Sanofi's lawyers. I asked them what they wanted for the line. They came back with a figure.

This was the deal I had my heart set on, and I knew I'd have to put all my security on the line. The prospect was a little easier to deal with by then, because by then I was married and I didn't have to worry about food, clothing, and shelter. If I failed, I'd have to start all over again, but I wouldn't be out on the street.

But I did *not* intend to fail. I was going to make it work. Putting all my security on the line was the move that would make this deal fly, and that's what I was prepared to do.

The figure that Sanofi came back with was, I felt, high. But there are those moments in life when you just have to go for it. I said fine, subject to my formal due diligence, and then I gave them my letter of intent.

I knew I had to move fast. Once word got out that Sanofi was going to spin off La Prairie, one of the big companies would go after it and I wouldn't stand a chance. And I wasn't wrong in my prediction: Once they heard the news, Avon, Estée Lauder, and Revlon all made overtures.

I did my due diligence—the background check on Sanofi's presentation—and we began to negotiate price. As we negotiated, the deal of my dreams fell apart three different times.

I'd looked at a lot of other companies by then, but I wanted this deal passionately, and each time the deal fell out I thought it was dead. Over. Gone.

But I bit the bullet, talked myself up, and kept negotiating. For a year I kept negotiating. This was a deal that should have been made in two months. But since life isn't fair, I just had to deal with the reality of the situation. I kept phoning. I kept flying back and forth to France.

I was frightened to death. I lost sleep. I cried. I stayed up all night reworking the same numbers over and over again, checking my personal assets, adding in what I could count on from backers, and asking myself again and again if I could make this work, if I could stick it out. I was putting my security blanket on the line, but that was only a small piece of the money I needed, and I was going to have to answer to my investors as well as to myself.

I was talking to potential investors the entire time I was negotiating with Sanofi, and in those conversations I often felt insecure. Yet I knew that each time I approached one, I had to come off as supremely confident. As one after another turned me down, I had to be strong and not get discouraged. I had to sell my vision to my investors, and convince them that I could make that vision a reality. I had to continually shore up my *own* belief that I could make this deal happen—and that I could make it succeed.

It *was* going to happen. For an entire year, I spent every waking moment struggling to stay focused and to believe in myself against all odds. I endured the pitying stares of people who thought I was just plain crazy. I plugged my ears when I called friends on the phone for support—and heard instead, "So, is this what your marriage is going to be like?" It was almost as if they were hoping my marriage would fail, because in their opinion I was neglecting it by pursuing this deal. On top of the anxieties of the deal itself, I had to stay stalwart in the belief that I could simultaneously be a loving, attentive wife *and* a tough businesswoman.

Robert Mosbacher had no problem with that. Behind the scenes, he was encouraging me every inch of the way.

How did I pull it off?

Well, it wasn't magic and it wasn't handed to me. I was successful for the same reasons that other people are successful: I trusted myself and I did my homework. Look at your own life. Most of the things that you have accomplished have happened because you believed in yourself, because you put the time and effort into making a solid plan, and because you were unrelenting in the pursuit of your goal.

I used the very techniques that I talk about in this book. I put one foot in front of the other; I relied on my inner voice; I accessed my Feminine Force; I made a plan based on the A to B to C principles; and I persisted. Working my way through the unknowns, the hidden obstacles, the naysayers, and my own deepest fears, I realized that I had what it would take to accomplish this goal. If I had let myself be overwhelmed and paralyzed by the size of the job in front of me, I never would have made it.

Instead, I broke it down into little pieces, pieces that I could manage. It wasn't magic and it wasn't handed to me. And contrary to those who would like to believe that my husband secretly financed my acquisition, the truth is Robert Mosbacher did not invest one dollar in La Prairie. I was able to buy La Prairie becaue I did my homework. I found and cultivated each investor on my own. With the exception of the smallest investor, no other investor even knew my husband. But they knew me, they knew my business plan, and they knew the company. That's how I raised the money, and that's how I succeeded.

At the moment of closing, I was at my lawyer's office. We had been there for hours signing final documents. The high point of the day came when an assistant walked in to announce that the funds to close the deal were moving through the Federal Reserve System to the seller's account.

That was the moment I became the owner of the company. I excused myself, went into someone else's office, shut the door, and cried. I couldn't call Robert. He was out of town and not available by phone. So I dried my tears, walked back into the office, and finished signing papers. Then I went home to bed, got up in the morning, and went to work.

In a way, the battle had only just begun. Because even though I had won a long war and was feeling the exhaustion of a battle-weary victor, nothing approaching a conqueror's welcome awaited me. On the contrary: now I had to prove I could do what I said I would do!

HOMEWORK AND RISK

I'm not a high roller. I can't be. I won't risk anything I have on a hunch. I have responsibilities to too many people—right now I'm my mother and grandmother's primary source of support. Most women have responsibilities that are more like mine than those of players who like to roll the dice, and values more similar to mine than to theirs.

But I do take calculated risks. There is no other way to stay in the game. And I'm going to let you in on a little secret. The difference between a calculated risk and rolling the dice can be expressed in one word: homework.

Taking a calculated risk means that I went through your business plan with a fine-toothed comb. I analyzed the assumptions behind your numbers; I researched your field; I made phone calls and thoroughly checked out the mechanics and claims of your business. After all that, I went with my gut.

I had already learned to ride my instincts in smaller risk situations and analyzed the results before going in on a big one. I had already practiced learning how to listen to my inner voice. In a way, researching and marketing a product, whether it's for your own business venture or within a large corporation, the process is the same. What you are doing is using your own intuition, training, and life experience to find a way to fulfill other people's needs.

As you develop your product and explore your market, imagine what messages your customers' inner voices are giving them. How do they want to grow? Who do they really want to be? Then develop a product or service that will help them get there.

You do your homework as you create the blueprint for your product. You identify your customer, plan your marketing, and set up a good financial model. You make sure that you won't need any unexpected infusions of capital down the line, and with every step you ask yourself the following questions: What's at stake here? How much of this stake can I afford to lose, and still survive? I only need to hold on by a thread, but I want enough to let me hold on.

Your inner voice is what tells you when you've done enough homework and it's time to make a move. Eventually, after doing all the research and thinking and question asking, you go with your gut. There's no other way.

All the due diligence and reading I did before I went into business for myself sharpened my instinct for knowing what a good deal was. In a sense, the research itself was a matter of going with my gut. I hadn't consciously thought, "Okay, now I'm practicing tracking and researching businesses so that when the time comes, I'll have honed my skills enough to be able to take a successful leap." I was just pursuing what I loved—what required all my wits and totally captivated me.

But all those practice hours I spent at my dining room table with my figures, my telephone, and my annual reports paid off. Still, no matter how much you think you have every little base covered, unexpected things will always happen. What separates the winners from the losers is that winners are able to handle problems and crises that they never *imagined* would occur. You hit the floor, but what counts is how fast you can get up and regroup.

Failure is simply part of the equation.

When I tried to interest Robert in the energy unit of one company, he was still learning how serious I was, and he didn't bite. When the energy unit of that company was sold off in just the way I had outlined to him, I got confirmation of my abilities. When the deal for the small cosmetics company fell apart, I learned more about how to tie a deal down with the seller. And each time I called an investor, pitched my plan, and got put off, I'd fine-tune my pitch a little according to what I'd learned from my failure. I was filling in the gaps of my knowledge, and succeeding by failing. All of this led me to La Prairie, and even though closing that deal was a challenge, when the time came, I was up to it.

When my investors looked at my results, they saw that not only did I meet the numbers I'd laid out in my business plan, I'd actually doubled my projected operating profits. In the three and a half years that I owned the company, we achieved double-digit growth without running a single ad. And three and a half years after I bought it, I was able to sell the company at a healthy profit.

I had achieved my goal. I was financially independent. I'd be able to support myself and my family for the rest of my life, and I'd never again be dependent on someone else's power to achieve my own personal goals. I was a power center in my own right.

LOOKING FORWARD TO
SUCCEEDING BY FAILING

When boys play football and baseball and basketball, they learn something that serves them well all their lives. Even championship teams lose some games along the way. What the players understand is that losing comes with the territory. Failures, they know, are part of the process of *winning*.

Sometimes, not getting what you want can lead to a whole new opportunity—something far better than what you first set your sights on.

The career of former Secretary of Labor Lynn Martin is a good example. You probably know a lot of women like her. You may even be one yourself. A few years back, Lynn was a school teacher and mother of two who left her job to be a mother full time. When the kids got old enough, Lynn went back to her teaching job. She grew frustrated with many of the problems she saw as a teacher—problems in education that she thought started with the local school board. If she could change things at that level, she could make a difference.

She ran for a seat on that school board, and won.

One thing led to another, and soon Lynn was involved in local politics on a larger scale. She excelled in her new career. Sometimes she was surprised at how good she was at it.

With each success, Lynn Martin grew stronger and more confident. Eventually her confidence in herself grew so strong that she decided to undertake a formidable challenge: to run against Paul Simon, Illinois's popular Democratic Senator. The odds against her winning against Simon were enormous, and Lynn lost her Senate bid soundly. In fact, she was trounced.

But in the meantime, the highest levels of her party were sitting up and taking notice. They weren't focusing on a failed campaign. They were saying, "Who *is* this woman?" They were impressed by her tenacity. They became equally impressed by her command of the issues, her speaking style, and her campaign skills. They wouldn't have known to look at those things if she hadn't had the guts to go up against Paul Simon. She proved she was part of the team. Her party was so impressed that then vice presidential candidate George Bush asked Lynn to be the surrogate for Geraldine Ferraro in his rehearsals for the 1984 debates. And when Bush was elected President in 1988, Lynn was named Secretary of Labor. She became part of his "kitchen cabinet." In her defeat, Lynn Martin had become a real winner, and today, her name is on more than one list of potential presidential and vice presidential candidates.

The lesson?

Failure may be just a step toward your eventual goal.

When confronted with a "failure" situation, always look under the surface. You do that by focusing on the *heart* of your goal—not just what it looks like on the outside. Remind yourself of what it is you're really after. Then think about the ways the failed attempts brought you closer to the real goal.

THE "POSITIVE" FAILURE: A REQUIRED COURSE ON THE PATH TO SUCCESS

Every "failure" is going to represent an opportunity to change a negative into a positive. Some failures may be telling you that you need to do a little more homework. Or that you need to make a few changes in yourself to reach the goal you're after.

And some failures are experiences that will point you in different, better directions.

Take the case of my color consultant, Jennifer Balbier. Jennifer is the very talented independent consultant I hired to help me develop my color palettes.

Jennifer spent years on the corporate side of cosmetics. When she started out in 1970, most of the women in the business were beauty consultants. She decided she wanted to be in marketing, but to be in marketing you had to spend time in sales. So she spent about eight months going in and out of drug stores from 42nd Street all the way up to Harlem in New York City. This eventually won her a trainee position in new products, and over time Jennifer worked her way up until she became vice president of marketing at a major company in Los Angeles. Her next step up came when she landed a position as corporate vice president of a major New York company.

As luck would have it, less than a year after Jennifer landed her new post in New York, the company she joined became the target of what everyone thought would be a friendly takeover. The takeover turned out to be anything but friendly. A lot of heads rolled, and although Jennifer wasn't fired, her treatment by the new management developed ominous overtones. Jennifer stayed long enough to size up the situation. Then she took the bull by the horns.

She went in to see her new supervisor and said, "Look, it's pretty clear to me that I'm going to be history here before long. If we could work out some kind of settlement, I'll leave quietly."

Still, when Jennifer walked out of her office for the last time, she had some emotional struggles ahead of her. Just eight months after she'd left a good job in Los Angeles, she found herself out of a job and collecting unemployment in New York. It was hardly the situation she'd imagined when she left L.A. It's a real shock when you wake up to discover that even though you're doing a bang-up job, you're going to lose that job anyway. At this point Jennifer started doing some long, hard thinking about her next step.

In the meantime, however, people had started calling her. "Look," they'd say, "until you get another job, why don't you consult on this new product for me?" Jennifer picked up a consulting job here, and another one there. Soon she was developing everything from fragrances and lipsticks to bath and body formulas—with different kinds of companies, from mass market to niche. It quickly became apparent that not only didn't she need a "regular" job, she was pretty darned successful and happy doing business on her own. She began to wonder why she hadn't bailed out sooner!

Jennifer makes her success sound easy, but in fact it took guts to reassess herself and plunge ahead when the clock ran out on her so unexpectedly. Jennifer was able to recognize that grim surprise as the wake-up call it really was. If she hadn't lost her job, she might never have stopped long enough to hear her inner voice tell her that her real goals lay somewhere else.

Jennifer Balbier's success also illustrates the power of the point A–to–point B principle. Jennifer didn't plan on going into business for herself, but she was making all the preparations she needed to do it. She was well trained in her field. She made a lot of important contacts. Early in her career, a mentor had even suggested that she specialize in new products because no one else was doing it—so she did. It wasn't until years later that she reaped the results of that work. Goals A, B, and C primed her for goal D.

To reach success, you have to push past the failures you're bound to encounter along the way. But every once in a while it's a good idea to take another look at the prize.

I know more than one executive who's found herself out of a job and then goes through what seems like a long period of doubt and struggle trying to map out a new course. Two years down the line I've had those same women say to me, "Oh, Georgette, things are really falling into place now. I can't *tell* you what a difference it's made not to be in that old job any more. Oh, I am so *happy* not to be there!"

If circumstances turn the tables on you, you may be more ready to rise to the occasion than you think. You may discover that you've been waiting for an opportunity to grow and surpass your present circumstances for a long time. You just hadn't realized it.

Deciding when to cut your losses is a matter of judgment. In my husband's words, sometimes you drill a dry hole—and it can take courage to face up to it when you do. But as frightening as it sometimes is, you may discover that a decision to cut your losses is one of the most liberating decisions you've ever made.

Jennifer Balbier has been in business for herself since 1986, and she does well enough to support a full-time assistant. She gets called in on almost every new product in the business. She has her own thriving company now, called The Pink Jungle.

Jennifer got where she is through pure Feminine Force. When she first went out on her own, she consulted with Procter & Gamble, and discovered that of all the consultants they brought in on that particular project, she was the *only* woman—and the only one without an M.B.A.

"In fact, that's why they brought me in here. While everyone else was talking numbers," Jennifer says, "I was talking product—you know, color and shine. So whenever they saw me coming they'd all say, 'Here she is, Miss Pink Jungle.' I decided that if I ever incorporated, that's what I'd call my company."

Moral of the story?

Necessity really can be the mother of invention. And dire necessity may turn out to be a fertile place for your imagination and creativity to take root. Jennifer Balbier might have tried to go out and find another corporate position when she lost hers. Instead, she discovered that the best place for her to exercise all her creativity and her smarts was out there on her own. The "jungle out there" turned into her own jungle—and she turned an unfriendly takeover into the best job of her life.

Chapter 15

Guts of Steel: What's the Worst That Can Happen?

"Seek, and ye shall find."

—MATTHEW 7:7

MAKING THE LEAP

Striking out on your own isn't easy. Yes, it takes commitment. Yes, it's risky. But starting your own business may be the one risk you can't afford *not* to take. And whether or not you want to consider it seriously right now, I think it's a good idea for you to stick your toes in the water, risk-free, by reading these pages.

Pat Harrison, the head of the National Women's Economic Alliance, became an entrepreneur twenty years ago when she started a firm that specializes in environmental issues. "When I started out," she says, "people would ask me, 'Who do you think you are? *This* is the way things get done.' But if you believe that you have to do things someone else's way, you'll never go very far.

"Women for the most part don't look at life like a candy store. And they *should*. The first thing you need to do is to understand that everything is available to you, if you know what you want."

LIFESTYLE ENTREPRENEURS

A growing category of entrepreneurs today is what M.I.T. professor Edward Roberts calls the "lifestyle entrepreneur." She is generally not someone whose main goal is to make a new mark in the community of the wealthy and powerful. She is a person who goes into business for herself in order to comfortably support her chosen lifestyle, and provide her with the freedom she needs to pursue all her goals. She tends to be more interested in creating value than in manipulating the money market. Sure, there are men who are "lifestyle entrepreneurs," but this is a particularly promising avenue for women—women who may be seeking more opportunity, freedom, and challenge than what's available in the corporate culture.

Today, women are creating their own businesses at twice the rate of men, and that trend will continue. By the end of 1992, the number of employees at women-owned businesses surpassed the number of those employed by the Fortune 500. Women have not only started their own businesses; we've also been quite successful at it. During the decade of the '80s, U.S. entrepreneurial revenues grew 99 percent overall, while revenues of entrepreneurial enterprises led by women grew by 140 percent.

Clearly, many women are out utilizing their Feminine Force in business.

Why is it so hard to think of success stories about women and to find business role models in women? Frankly, the press would never write about me as a businesswoman if it wasn't a kind of sideline to the tabloid stuff. One of the first women ever to grace the cover of *Fortune* was Madonna, and she appeared there for her "marketing savvy." I admire Madonna's marketing savvy myself, but *Fortune* didn't put her on the cover for her business value.

When women chosen to be on the covers of magazines are either Madonna or the "trophy wife," a distorted and inaccurate image of the American businesswoman is perpetuated. Male CEOs aren't chosen to appear on *Fortune's* cover by dint of their glamour or what's presumed to be their brazen materialism. Successful women shouldn't be, either.

The media may adore twenty-two-year-old whiz kids from Silicon Valley, but the country is full of women who work quietly and steadily without all the fanfare. Lillian Katz, founder of the Lillian Vernon Company, started selling Christmas ornaments and wrapping paper off her kitchen table fifty years ago, and she now has a $700-million-plus company with an exceptional pre-tax profit.

Outside of getting the cover of *Fortune*, the rewards of going into business for yourself are great.

Think about it: You own the company. You call the shots. Your financial security and your destiny are in your own hands. Instead of other people creating jobs for you, you can create jobs for others. When a woman runs the store, she can make her own rules. She can implement Feminine Force on a grand scale. Though we work just as hard, women are often more flexible, less concerned about politics, and more consensual in business than our male counterparts. When we choose to make it a priority, we can also structure our businesses in ways and on scales that harmonize better with the responsibilities we have in other arenas of life.

If the idea is even remotely appealing to you, start doing a little homework on it. Even if you do not know exactly when or how you will go into business. Even if you're not sure what your product or service might be. This is another point A–to–point B situation.

I hardly blossomed as an entrepreneur overnight. From doing my neighbors' hair in high school to selling shampoo in college, I built on my experience. From the time I helped Robert Muir in his business to my years working at Fabergé, I always did a little more than was required of me.

Always do more than is required of you. Go the extra mile. If it doesn't pay off now, I promise you, it will later. Developing my understanding of the way the numbers worked helped me move into my own licensing division at Fabergé before I left the company, and I eventually gained enough confidence to go into business myself. I was prepared to take that leap.

That doesn't mean I leaped without looking. It was two years after I left Fabergé before I closed my first deal. I was taking a big step, and I wanted to be sure of my footing. Taking your own time is part of the difference between a calculated risk and rolling the dice.

But there are also going to be instances when you can use time pressure to your advantage—to prod you into making a move you really are ready to make. When the La Prairie deal started shaping up, I hadn't figured out exactly how I was going to capitalize the venture, but I knew that if I was going to have a chance at it, I had to make a move fast.

You can move from point A to point B in as simple a way as consulting your inner voice every time you read a business or trade magazine or anything else that inspires thoughts of striking out on your own. Ask your inner voice, "Is this a product that people will buy? Who will buy it?" Or, "Is this a service people really need or will pay for in this financial climate?" And always, "Would an investment in this enterprise make sound financial sense for me?" If you're already daydreaming about breeding and raising pedigreed dogs or getting into mail-order knitwear, test those dreams with the same sort of questions. Do your own "due diligence."

Go through advertising in local magazines or on bulletin boards and ask your inner voice which ads seem likely to attract more clients and business, and why. Walk past shops to see which windows attract the attention of different types of people. Ask your inner voice what it is they're seeking. Pay attention to conversations in which your friends and acquaintances voice their wishes and complaints about the products and services they use. All of these are ways to do research on the potential viability of a product. Practice and test your instincts in everyday, risk-free situations, and you may be surprised at what you discover.

The next step, which you can take in your own time and on your own terms, is to think seriously about how you are going to reach your customers. You need to know both who that customer is going to be and how to reach her. The only way you can sell a customer is to know what she wants. And the only way you can know what she wants it to know who she is. That's one of the most important tips I can give you. You need to know *everything* you can about your customer. What does she look like? Does she have kids? Especially in the beginning, you need to focus on exactly who your customer is. That's what will guide you in developing the specific details of your product. That's what will show you how to reach him or her.

My friend Rebecca, who started the baking business you read about in Chapter 11, is a perfect example of a "lifetime entrepreneur." Her first small step in marketing research was simply to send out cards to her friends and acquaintances, to let them know they could order cakes and pastries from her for Christmas. The response she received at that stage was her first indication that what she did well could also be a source of income for her family. Her second step was to discover which local restaurants didn't have their own pastry chefs. She went on from there.

I know other examples of women who have started their own profitable cottage industries. A Texan friend of mine is a grandmother. Ceramics is Nanette Finger's hobby. She derives great satisfaction from working with her hands, and her avocation became such an integral part of her life that she had a ceramics kiln built in her home. One day she made a ceramic bowl for her dog with his name on it. Everyone who came to her house was totally taken with it, and the next thing she knew, all her visitors asked if they could order dog bowls from her. Soon Nanette was fielding orders for Christmas presents, and hostess presents, and for all sorts of other occasions. Today there are eight women making bowls and related ceramic products, and she's extended her market by getting listed in a good mail-order catalog.

Baking and cosmetics are areas that are traditionally feminine, but women certainly aren't restricted to that territory. I recently met a congresswoman in New Orleans who had been a housewife all her life. Her kids were grown and she'd never worked outside the home. But one day she got angry over the way some of the local issues were being handled in New Orleans. She got involved, and discovered there were plenty of people who felt as she did. She ran for city council, and won. In 1992, she ran for Congress, going door to door to raise the money for her campaign, and she made it to the U.S. House of Representatives.

My particular passion led me into a position as chief executive officer of my own corporation. The passion of the woman from New Orleans landed her a seat in Congress.

As you consider what you love, you may conclude that it's time to start a business of your own, or that it's simply time to get a new job. Maybe your best assets are in sales, or administration, or problem solving. These skills are needed in all sorts of enterprises. Never assume that something is too far-fetched to come through. And never be embarrassed to inquire about a job or to seek backing for a venture of your own. You'll never get what you don't ask for. Call everyone you can think of who might be able to help you achieve your goal.

Go for it. Bite the bullet. Put your blinders on. Get single-minded. Call anyone you might think can give you a lead—even that person you just met once for five minutes. Rehearse what you're going to say, then put away any second thoughts, pick up the phone, and call.

No matter how difficult it is to do some of these things, they will ultimately pay off. Nine times out of ten, it's that extra phone call or that extra resume you sent to a place you never thought would come through that gets you the job. I was on the phone to Sanofi once or twice a week for two years. It was the one hundred fiftieth call that landed La Prairie.

Never worry about being perceived as overly aggressive or pushy. If someone thinks you're pushy, what is the worst that can happen? That you don't get the job? Well, you definitely won't get the job if you don't go after it. Life has sure taught me that. And "going after" something doesn't mean you just get up to the door: you've got to push it open.

If you're perceived as aggressive, so what? It's not a blight. You're not marked for life. Better to be perceived as aggressive than to sit there waiting for life to happen—and letting it pass you by.

As Pat Harrison says, "Entrepreneurs are people who enjoy asking questions and aren't afraid of looking stupid. Especially women entrepreneurs, because we haven't been in the game as long as men have. On the other hand, women have always been entrepreneurs. Women who organize church suppers and charity drives—volunteers like those have skills that put CEOs to shame! But when you ask those women about it, they'll say, 'It's nothing.' Then you find out what that 'nothing' really is. We never really give ourselves credit. We need to be able to say to ourselves, 'We can do it!' "

You absolutely *can* do it. And one final point: You're never too young or too old to make your own kind of mark in your own kind of time.

You're never the wrong age to release the power within you to create the life you deserve.

WHAT'S SO MYSTERIOUS ABOUT NUMBERS?

When I set out to buy La Prairie, I started with a good business plan. A business plan describes what your business is and how it will work—both verbally and with statistics, spread sheets, charts, and other forms of what are called "the numbers." It demonstrates what profit the business will turn over time, who the principals will be, how the business will work operationally, and what kind of return on their money the investors can expect to make.

If you can make a household budget, you already understand the fundamentals of a business plan. Although business gets a lot more complicated than a household budget, the fundamental principles are still one and the same: you have expenditures each month (utilities, rent or mortgage, groceries, credit card payments, etc.) and you have income (salary, interest, investment income). In a business you want to make a profit, and in a household budget you want to have enough left over to put in the savings account or investment fund. In both cases, you find resourceful ways to make those savings or profits possible. That's what managing a business is. And a business plan is essentially a map of how you're going to manage your business. If you can manipulate a household budget, you have the foundation you need to learn how to construct a business plan.

Here's how it works in business. Let's say you have developed a plan to start a business that sells silver spoons. Your budget states that you will manufacture 5,000 units (that is, 5,000 silver spoons) at a cost of $1.00 per unit. That means your manufacturing budget is $5,000. The assumption behind this number is that you're going to sell 5,000 of these silver spoons in your first year of business and that those spoons will cost you $1.00 apiece to manufacture. Well, if I'm thinking of investing in your company I'm going to analyze this business plan. I'm going to want some research or figures that tell me why you think you can sell 5,000 of these spoons this year.

For instance, if you sold 4,500 last year, where is the eleven percent increase coming from? What is the current state of the silver spoon industry? Are we having an eleven percent growth in the sale of silver spoons? Is that the level of growth the industry saw in the last fiscal year? If the growth in silver spoon sales last year was only two percent, I need some good reasons why you believe you'll get an eleven percent growth this year. What is it about this spoon that will give you that kind of growth in an industry that's growing at a much slower pace? The answer you give me to this question is the assumption behind this number.

The next assumption I'll look at is your cost of goods. What if my own research tells me that the manufacturing cost of silver spoons is

$1.70. How are you going to manufacture your product for $1.00 per unit? Do you have a source that will give you the same spoon for $1.00 that the competition gets for $1.70? Or are you going to be selling a spoon that weighs less or in some way differs from the competition? And if your spoon is not as heavy, do you have another good reason for charging the same price as your competitor who has a heavier spoon? Or will a lower sticker price gain you market share? What will make your customer choose your lighter spoon over heavier ones?

Without knowing the assumptions behind the numbers, investors do not know how real your numbers are. Sure, if I'm writing a business plan I'm going to tell you I can sell 6,000 of these spoons even though I only sold 5,000 last year. Anyone who writes a business plan wants to show numbers projecting a twenty percent growth next year: that's a figure that will make it easier to get backing. But I need to be able to demonstrate what it is I'm going to do to achieve a twenty percent increase in sales.

The assumptions that lie behind the figures in a business plan need to be solidly reasoned. When a potential investor exerts due diligence, in essence she is questioning the assumptions behind your numbers.

If you're investing your own money and your own time, you too need to be sure the assumptions behind your numbers are good. To do otherwise is to ensure failure. But if you run a household or are involved in any kind of business, you've had a lot of experience in examining assumptions behind numbers.

Say your daughter has a wonderful voice and wants to take expensive singing lessons, but your family budget is nearly pushed to the limit. She says she'll cover the cost by picking up extra hours at her part-time job. When you point out that those extra hours on the job are going to disrupt her schoolwork, you're examining the assumptions behind her numbers. You and she won't have a workable plan until those assumptions are reasonable and workable.

If you've spent any time examining assumptions like these, you already have the basics to pick up the skill as it applies to business, if you choose to. You don't really have to know how to crunch the numbers: You just have to know how to read them.

An M.B.A. can be a foot in the door in the corporate world, but most entrepreneurs will tell you they learn the most by doing. I discovered my talent for questioning the assumptions behind the numbers on the job. I didn't pick up this skill by taking classes.

I just began to read the annual reports and other financial statements of the companies I worked for, even when research like that had nothing to do with my job description. Then I began to read business magazines and carefully digested the words of the executives and entrepreneurs interviewed there. I started to make practice budgets, cash flows, and balance sheets. I questioned people I worked with when I needed help.

The ability to show profit is the name of the game in business. You have to be able to look at each deal and say, what are the essential dynamics here? If success is measured by bottom line profit, how do I get there? There's an old joke that goes, sure the company had 100 million dollars in sales, but it *lost* 140 million.

How do you sell 100 million and lose 140 million? It's easy if it turns out that overhead and manufacturing costs add up to more than your sticker price. Or if you had to sell a million spoons to make a profit but you only sold 800,000.

You don't need to be a mathematical genius to understand how to turn a profit in a business. You *do* have to know how to work the business to turn that profit.

You know the old saying, "If it ain't broke don't fix it"? Don't believe it! Every single day you have to assume it's broke, take a look at it, and see if it needs to be fixed. That's how you stay on top of things and avoid surprises. That's how you develop the ability to react quickly to those unexpected problems that will always turn up. In business, nothing is as inevitable as the unexpected.

GUTS OF STEEL

To create the life you deserve, you have to go after it. The universe that you inhabit flows from you—you don't flow from it. Whatever steps you need to take to create the universe of your choice, you will have to push past predictable feelings of shyness and fear to take them. When fear and embarrassment tell you "no," your Feminine Force will undoubtedly be telling you "yes." And "yes" is the word that creates worlds.

Your goals take shape when you identify what it is you love, what captures your interest and draws on your skills. They take further shape when you sit down and realistically examine your weak spots. If you know that you're weak in certain areas that will be important in achieving your goal—if, for example, you have trouble reading a stockholders' report and it's something you'll need to be able to do—identify that gap and set out to fill it. Read up on it. Talk to friends who are conversant with the subject.

Identifying your strengths and weaknesses in this way is an activity best approached with a sense of adventure. It isn't a time to be judgmental, or to imagine you have some intrinsic flaw because you don't at the moment understand something that others seem to know a lot about. You may discover that you have hidden talents you didn't know you had. You may discover that what you thought were weaknesses are actually strengths.

Strengthening your weaknesses is in part a matter of conquering your fears. You put one foot in front of the other as you work toward your goal, conquering your fears as you go. The same is true of taking the initiative when you want to propose something to a potential partner, investor, or client. It may require that you swallow your pride. If you ask for a favor or even for advice, you run the risk of being rejected. Communicating your goals, especially when there are new goals you've just created as you grow to a new place in life, can be an experience that makes you feel vulnerable. But it's a step that *has* to be taken in order to get to the next step. You can't get to C from A without passing through B.

Swallowing your pride isn't lethal. It might upset your stomach for a few minutes, but the ultimate result may be the life of your dreams. And that's a result that's worth every rejection you encounter.

Nine times out of ten you take the first step in creating your own universe by picking up the phone. That's how you make an appointment for a job interview. It's how you join a networking group or a local gym, how you hunt for investments or raise money or volunteer for a cause. It's even a way to look for your soul mate. But sometimes picking up that phone may seem to take more nerve than you feel you have.

Simply talk yourself through the process. That's how it's done.

This is one of the most important Feminine Force tips I could ever give you: *Don't* let embarrassment prevent you from going after what you want. It's absolutely self-defeating. The worst that can happen is that you get rejected by one person—so what? You have other frontiers, other territory to conquer. Keep the big picture in mind. *You* know you're worthy and that your ideas are worthy, and that's all that really counts.

This is the real secret of guts of steel. Real guts are nothing more than developing your inner voice to the point where it is louder and stronger than the voice of your fear. When you face any challenge, you simply talk yourself through it. And it's a process that will never be complete if you continue to grow. Each new goal you set kicks up its own new fear. Am I good enough? Am I prepared? Will I say the right thing? Will I be rejected? Will I fail? What will the reaction be?

There isn't a day that goes by that I don't ask myself these questions. Every day I talk myself through rough spots and moments of doubt. But I do talk myself through them. Every successful woman I know has to talk herself through them. We all have them. We all deal with them. And as we go, we continue to grow and succeed.

COLD CALLS AND LONG LISTS

Now you have the secret of guts of steel. Here's the system that implements it. I call it cold calls and long lists. Whenever I need to achieve a new goal that involves the participation or awareness of other people, I start by making a list of everyone I know who could be part of achieving that goal. If I'm working on behalf of a non-profit organization, I might be looking for volunteers for an event. If I'm doing a political fund raiser, the list will consist of people whose political philosophy is in sympathy with my cause. If I need to fill a position at the office, the names will be of people I respect in the appropriate field. And if I'm raising money for business, the list will consist of potential investors.

Whatever my goal is, I keep three separate lists: the A list, people I know well and who are good prospects for the goal; the B list, people I know slightly and who might be good prospects; and the C list, who are long shots in both senses.

The next thing I do is schedule time to make my calls and implement the goal. I block out the time in my appointment book, just as if it were a business meeting or a doctor's appointment. Think of it as making an appointment with yourself, and don't break it. Making that appointment is the only way to make sure the goal gets accomplished on schedule.

At the scheduled time, I take my list, go home where I won't be interrupted, and shut the door. First, I review how I'm going to make my appeal. If it's a new and different kind of appeal for me, I might even write down some notes on what I'm going to say. I make sure I've got all the possibilities covered. I anticipate objections. For instance, if I'm trying to raise money for charity, I plan what I'll say if people say "no." Maybe they'll say no because they're uncomfortable about the amount of money I'm asking for. In this case, I'll try to make them more comfortable about it by stressing the importance of the cause, or I'll propose a smaller amount. Maybe they'll say "no" because they don't believe my cause is a priority. In this case, I'll have an answer prepared that explains why this need is more important and time-sensitive than another need.

Once I'm armed with information and arguments, I pick up the phone and start to go down my list name by name. I squelch embarrassment or fear and I listen to my inner voice. I anticipate objections and have answers prepared for them, but I don't hear "no."

This is the first rule of cold calls: you cannot hear "no." You talk right through "no" until you've covered all your approaches or arguments. If I'm still hearing, "Well, I really don't think I can," or "I'm not completely comfortable participating in this," then I do let the call go. However, before I get to that point I make sure my contacts—each and every one—know how important they are to my cause. I make sure they know its virtues. I try to show them how it fits into their own big picture--their own interests and values. I keep selling.

If I still get a "no" I put down the phone and go straight to the next name on my list. I never take rejections personally. That's something men learn in sports and business. And women must learn it, too.

The reality of the situation is that you're not going to be successful with every name on your list—even your "A" list. But you cannot allow yourself to be demoralized by the "no's." When you hang up the phone, check in with your Feminine Force if you have to, and visualize a positive result. If you get a "no" on the first twenty phone calls, I promise you that if you can just get to that twenty-first call you'll get a "yes." As often as not, it's that last call, the one you don't think you can make because you're on the verge of deciding your cause is lost, that gets you the result you want. For some reason, that's the call that comes through. I don't know why. It's just the way things work.

If you find yourself getting embarrassed, keep in mind the worst-thing-that-can-happen scenario. Program your inner voice to remind you, "What's the worst thing that can happen to me? They hang up? They tell somebody about the nut case who called them four times to try and raise money?"

Is that going to ruin your life? Is it going to destroy your universe? Is it going to change who you are?

Definitely not! Not only that, but they will probably have forgotten all about it by the next day, especially when they hear how many other people lined up and supported you.

The list helps you discipline yourself to keep going after you get a rejection. If, after you hang up the phone, you can discipline yourself to say, "I'm not taking this personally. This is normal, it comes with the territory, it's part of the way this works. I am going to be okay. I'm going to do fine," then you're halfway home. Once you have this process down, it's only a matter of time before the tide turns. And it *will* turn.

But you have to be there to see it. It's not going to turn for you if you don't stick around long enough for it to happen. Emotionally speaking, the process doesn't get a whole lot easier with time. Every time I get a positive result from a call, the next call is a little easier. But each time I'm not successful, the next call is that much harder. No matter how many peaks you climb, this doesn't change. I still hate picking up that phone, but I know I have to do it to achieve my goal, and I do it.

That's the bad news. The good news is that tenacity and resilience pay off here as they do elsewhere in life. The woman who'll go just that much farther, who's willing to take just that much more rejection, who will risk falling into another hole and find the courage to climb out of it again, is the woman who is going to succeed. It doesn't matter to me how many "no's" she's heard: that woman is the one I'll put my money on every time.

CHOOSING YOUR RAINBOWS

Remember the story about the leprechaun's pot of gold at the end of the rainbow? The story contains a gem of truth about living your dreams by taking initiative. There *are* rainbows with pots of gold at the end out there, but I want to suggest that you be clever and thoughtful about what rainbows you chase, especially when you need to raise money for business. Where do you go to make those lists of potential advisers and investors?

Part of writing a strong business plan is knowing who the competition is, and who stands to *gain* if you make a success of your venture. These industry contacts should go on your lists.

If you want to offer a 900 service that provides information about different housing markets around the country, for example, you might consider trying real estate companies. On the other hand, you might try existing legitimate 900 services that want to branch out into new areas but don't have expertise in your area. Studying your market will give you clues about which types of investors to target.

Even if they do not invest, such contacts will know who would be interested and they'll tell you so.

In analyzing the market, you'll also have discovered which investors have something to lose if they *don't* get involved. When I went out to raise money for La Prairie, I took a close look at cosmetic distributors, particularly those that currently carried La Prairie. They would have the most to lose if the company fell into corporate hands that had their own distribution channels.

You also want to include contacts who have something less tangible to gain by participating. For example, if you want to start a day care center, you might target activists for children's rights in your community. Even if they aren't prepared to make a financial investment in your plan, they are very likely to know people who will be.

Finally, if you are starting a small business, make it your business to educate yourself about all the investment methods open to you. Below is a brief list of possibilities, based in part on an excellent summary of small business investment options published in the October 1992 issue of *Working Woman*. Use it as a reminder to make sure you're covering all possible bases when you're trying to raise funds, and add your own ideas.

TIPS ON INVESTMENT SOURCES

· People you know. Make sure to include friends, relatives, and business associates. You can expect a quick and often a positive response, but don't expect or even try to raise large amounts through this source.

· Bank loans—a possibility depending on the economic climate of the moment, the strengths of your business plan, and your ability to provide collateral. It also helps if the loan is guaranteed by the Small Business Administration.

· Venture capital funds, particularly those set up by and for women, such as the National Association for Female Executives in New York. There's a good chance more of these will become available to us in the near future.

· Customers who love your product.

· State loan programs.

· Advertising in capital-wanted sections of publications like *The New York Times* and *The Wall Street Journal*.

· Venture capital associations that feature opportunities for investors and entrepreneurs to meet each other.

· Other networking opportunities such as alumni organizations and trade associations.

In the end, raising money is basically a matter of going out there and asking. There are no shortcuts. You can't be afraid of making a fool of yourself. You just have to pick up the phone, make appointments, and ask. The only way to grab that brass ring is to reach for it—every time you go around.

Chapter 16

Attention Is Power

"When I have a brand-new hairdo
With my eyelashes all in curl,
I float as the clouds on air do,
I enjoy being a girl!"

RODGERS & HAMMERSTEIN, *FLOWER DRUM SONG*

These days, I'm more of a beauty role model than a beauty rebel. In the media I've thankfully shed my role as the human equivalent of the parlor game where you guess how many pennies are in the bottle. Instead of guessing at my bra size and clothing budget, reporters ask me how I got what they call "my polished look." And while women may still wonder to themselves if my husband Robert foots my business ventures, what they actually stop to ask me is what shade they should color their hair.

Now it's my turn to answer the question of my choice. And the most instructive revelation I could make on this subject is to remind you of exactly what I started out with in the so-called beauty and glamour department. Because yet again, it's not a matter of what you luck into at birth but what you make out of it.

The most important thing I could possibly say about how to look great is that it's not what you have that counts; it's what you do with it. I was not born especially beautiful or sexy. I started out with just about the same set of natural resources as the next girl. What I did accomplish was putting myself together to get attention.

If you don't believe me, let me remind you that I was not exactly an attractive teenager. And if you don't believe that, just look at the pictures in this book. They say a picture is worth a thousand words, and these are no exception, but let me help you out just in case. Plump? Frumpy? Plain? Awkward? Don't be shy.

And, WHAT ABOUT THAT HAIR?

Beauty? It's ten percent inspiration and ninety percent perspiration, just like everything else.

Creating my look and making myself attractive was and still is hard work, because adult acne, a metabolism that tends to add on pounds no matter what, and off-center teeth are among my ongoing problems.

Making myself look great had nothing to do with resources or contacts or influences. And I only wish it had been nothing more than a simple matter of sunning myself on the proverbial towel after a lucky dip in the gene pool. Remember, when I met my first husband, I was living at my brother's and unemployed. So don't let anyone tell you that spending time to look your best is time spent frivolously. Attention is power, and a woman who looks her own unique definition of what is *her* best is at *her* most powerful. Period.

I am certain that it was becoming more attractive that helped me manifest that Feminine Force, and *not* the other way around. Bringing out my inner glow *was* manifesting my Feminine Force.

As a young woman who attended an Exclusives by Georgette Mosbacher makeover session observed, "You can never make a first impression twice."

Make heads turn when you walk into a strange room and you have achieved a devastating power advantage. You have commanded attention, and your audience is going to listen to what you have to say. Your agenda will get a response. The positive response you get will make you feel better about yourself, which will allow you to make your case even more convincingly. Your growing confidence will continue to be enhanced by the attention you receive, and that circle of radiance will just go on perpetuating itself automatically.

I know this cycle because I live it. I am grateful to say that as far as that circle of radiance is concerned, I know how to summon it up. And I've observed a lot of other women who tap into it and leave those other, so much more vicious cycles of cause and effect behind in the dust. I make people believe I'm beautiful (and a large part of that is confidence and attitude), and in so doing I make them listen to what I have to say. And it doesn't take a genius to create this effect. There is no reason why you cannot add the glow effect to your own life in the way that works for you. And believe me, if you don't, you're missing out on one of life's sweetest rewards for being a woman.

The glow effect kicks in a little differently for every individual woman because "looking your best" is a phrase that means something a little different to everyone. And well it should. For some, it means bright red lipstick and a subtly slinky suit. For others it's jeans, comfortable shoes, and a favorite barrette. Personally I wouldn't be caught dead with white hair, but on some women it looks absolutely resplendent.

To take advantage of the glow effect does not require you to be as thin as the women Tom Wolfe calls "social x-rays." I'm certainly not. Having it all may include having a few extra pounds. It's not a prerequisite to wear a single-digit dress size or a C- or D-cup bra (I don't in real life, just in the Washington press) or to have your nose remodeled. To transform yourself physically so that you radiate that inner glow, you need not achieve a single one of these things.

On the other hand, you may feel that to look your personal, unique best it is an *absolute* prerequisite to lighten your hair or lose ten pounds or have a plastic surgeon give your jaw a new line.

More power to you for knowing exactly what it is *you* want, and not letting anyone else—not your husband, not your mother, not your best friend, and especially not the "experts"—talk you out of it, either.

YOUR OUTER GLOW TRANSMITS
YOUR INNER VOICE

What really burns me is when so-called media experts make the charge that we women wear make-up or dress nicely because outside influences—magazines, advertising, men—said we should. I frankly think that idea insults our intelligence.

To exercise your power is to make any choice for yourself that you want to make, including the choice to define beauty your way.

To be beautiful means to radiate your inner power and self-esteem however you choose to, from *all* of the options and advice made available to you or that you seek out. And these can include advertising, magazines, plastic surgery, your mother, your best friend, or even "experts"—if, and only if, you decide what they have to offer is what you want.

Watch out for the theoreticians of anger who will try to dissuade you from this. Watch out for the women who argue that beauty is a myth perpetuated to keep us down and that the pursuit of beauty is evidence of a backlash against women unleashed by male capitalists out of greed and fear. Watch out for the people who tell you that you don't know how to listen to your inner voice and that your choices are dictated by other people who are making you miserable.

Let's face it, we're not that easily manipulated. We're not that stupid.

In *The Beauty Myth* theoretician Naomi Wolf describes a "ritual of self-abasement" carried out by women. Looking at a picture from a fashion magazine, these women chant "the well-known formula: 'I hate her. She's so thin.'"

Now, I have no doubt that some women perform this particular ritual. But I'm here to make a different contribution based on my own experience and the experience of women I know—women who are not anorectic and whose happiness and self-esteem, to borrow one of Wolf's metaphors, does not rise and fall like the stock market based on their perception of how closely they resemble pictures in fashion magazines.

If I want to lose five pounds, it's not because I saw a six-foot-tall sixteen-year-old model with seven percent body fat leaping through the pages of *Vogue*. I may appreciate the photograph as a beautiful image but my motivation doesn't start outside me. It starts inside me. The fact that my own clothes don't fall or fit the way they usually do, or the fact that I feel uncomfortable when I sit down or have to walk up a few flights of stairs—those are the things that motivate *me* to lose weight.

If I want to make a change, that change begins with me. I fit the information presented in magazines into my understanding and image of who I am, not vice versa. If a fashion magazine ever did make me feel bad, it would be because I had already done a number on myself.

When I was growing up, Mother didn't beat herself up. She didn't groan with anger when she got on the scale, or restrict her diet, or deprive herself. Neither did Grandma and neither did Baba. As a result, I never learned to associate beauty and power with deprivation. I never learned that to be female was never to be beautiful enough. On the contrary. I learned that being a woman was something to be proud of, and that make-up was fun, not torture. I learned that there was no conspiracy behind using hair color to express who you are. If anything, the conspiracy was ours. The point is simply to look better, and that's precisely why we buy beauty products, not for some ephemeral hope in a jar, but for a little realistic sprucing up.

Show me one woman who doesn't feel more powerful in her own unique way when she looks *her* personal version of great. That glow consists of both inner and outer radiance, an inner and an outer beauty. Both start with your role models. Both start with your image of yourself—not someone else's image of idealized beauty. And, most important, both start in your head.

SMALL CHANGES AND SPECTACULAR RESULTS

When I went on the road for La Prairie I never once met a woman who felt good about herself who wasn't also proud of the way she looked. During these department store events, which were held all over the country, it wasn't difficult to pick out the women who didn't have a good self-image. We could all see them coming across the floor. It was a look—a certain lack of crispness and glow. Sometimes there were hunched shoulders, or gray skin, or a hair style or a lipstick color that clearly hadn't been updated in years. But although the individual specifics might vary, what they all had in common was that it clearly had been a while since they had looked at themselves with much in the way of hope or affection. And the time had come.

Usually, these customers already knew that we knew. So many of these savvy ladies had consciously come to the store for help. So many times as we sat down together the conversation would start, "Well, I've been through a lot. I got laid off and I have two kids." Or, "I lost my parents," or "I've been so ill and now it's time to live again." Or, "I'm getting divorced. I've lost fifty pounds and a lot of things are starting to change in my life. I really want to pull myself together now. That's why I came."

After the makeover was finished, these women would immediately look in the mirror. And instantly, they'd smile. That smile was a smile of knowledge. A corner had just been turned. We knew it, and they knew it. The alchemy of a major transformation had just begun.

It's hard to feel good about yourself on the inside if you don't like what you see on the outside.

In my experience, it's usually small changes and refinements that add up to a big effect and make you glow the brightest. To make the transition from my own "before" picture to my "after" picture, I only did a few things: I lost a few pounds, I had my eyebrows tattooed in because they were practically nonexistent, and I used make-up to emphasize my best features and play down the ones I like less. And of course, I became a redhead. And I didn't see a big-name hair colorist—a local beauty parlor in Chicago was just fine, thank you. To recreate myself I did nothing but follow my inner voice, make a few changes, and go through a little trial and error.

I still experiment. These days, I continue to reassess and refine my look about once a year. I factor in the probability that sometimes I will make a mistake. I made one a year or so ago when I decided that short hair would be more youthful on me. After I had it cut, I realized that on me it looked harsh. Now I'm growing it out again. No harm done—few beauty changes, barring cosmetic surgery, are irreversible. And trial and error is the name of the game.

The truth is, there are many virtually foolproof products available to us. Today, there are so many tools and so much expert advice out there that we don't really *have* to make a lot of mistakes. You can change your hair color by washing it in the shower—and you can wash that color *out* in the shower. If you can't afford braces, you can have your teeth bonded in about four hours for a fraction of the cost. You can press on nails, you can change the color of your eyes with contact lenses. Isn't it wonderful? There are so many things available to women—affordable, simple to use, foolproof, and *accessible* ways to make changes and improvements in your looks. You don't have to be able to afford to go to a salon. And you can no longer say you want to look better but don't know how to do it, because there are products that practically do the job for you.

I don't really need to tell you anything about before-and-after transformations. Pick up any magazine, and you'll find them. The proof is in the doing—that's why those pictures are there and why they have so much appeal. Have you ever looked at one of those and decided you wanted to be the "before"? If you want to be an "after," go be an "after."

You don't have any excuses. As the ad says, *just do it*.

When the time came for me to evaluate who I was inside and how I could express that through what I had to work with physically, *definition* became the theme behind all my key changes. At the time I reinvented myself I didn't always know this. I just followed my intuition and applied what I'd learned through trial and error. Looking back I see that each of these changes fell under that category. I defined my hair color, my eyes, my face, my body. And as I did, I defined who I was.

My sister Lyn is a different story. Physically, Lyn and I don't look that much alike. Lyn is smaller and more angular than I am, although I can give her clothes and they alter very well. Since the time she came to work for me five years ago, first at La Prairie and now at Exclusives, Lyn has also reinvented her look and found her own glow effect in the process.

Lyn was always pretty. But now she's beautiful. No, I take that back—she's not beautiful, she's *spectacular*. Ask Lyn if her look has changed, and she'll groan.

"Oh, if you could only have seen me," she'll tell you. "I was so timid, so shy. I had no self-confidence. I didn't walk as tall or smile as wide."

Only when prodded will Lyn provide the outer details, because to her they seem secondary:

"Well, I used to be a little heavier. I've lost about ten pounds. And for a long time I was always changing my hair—at La Prairie, everyone knew me as the 'hairdo of the week.' One week it was long, the next it was short. One week I'd part it on the left and the next on the right. It was pretty drastic."

Believe what she says. It got so bad that one day when Lyn cut out a magazine picture of a hair style she liked and said, "Georgette, this is what I want," without even looking at it I ripped it up into a dozen pieces and said, "Lyn, I am tired of this *hair* obsession!"

But even as Lyn kept changing her hair style, something interesting was happening. She was gradually lightening the color and it was looking better and better.

What Lyn was doing was matching the way she looked with the way she felt inside. She was carving out a new life, shaping a career, and growing and changing in the process. Sometimes the interior and exterior changes had to catch up with each other.

Shortly after the magazine picture incident, everything finally came together. Lyn's new short hair style looked both pretty and professional, and the soft blonde color complemented her fair skin and light blue eyes.

Lyn hasn't changed her hair lately—but don't push her. She's feeling much more confident about herself than she did when she first started working with me, but she *continues* to grow. Did I like all of Lyn's different hair styles? No, not all of them, and neither did she. But some of them were great, and through trial and error she's found the one that suits her perfectly. The theme of Lyn's reinvention wasn't *definition* but *confidence*.

Clothes, cosmetics, hair styling and color, body size, cosmetic surgery—all of these are variables at your disposal to play with and explore using your own smarts to figure out what reflects the inner you, and what doesn't. Trust your own ability to re-create yourself. When you are through and have perspective on the process, you'll probably see that your transformation had a theme, too.

I have my "before" and "after" shots just like everyone else. "Before-and-after" is not like falling off a cliff into a new country. It's more like a continuous cycle. Don't deny yourself. Remember, attention is power—and a unique opportunity to celebrate being a woman.

COSMETICS AND HAIR STYLES

If you want to reinvent your face or your hair, start by looking at yourself objectively in the mirror and thinking about what you want to change. Listen to your inner voice and see if there is any way you can use your personal history to help you achieve your goal, the way I did when I decided to become a redhead.

Perhaps the most subtle and powerful change you can make is in simple maintenance. Make sure your grooming is perfect. Is your hair clean and cut well? Are you taking good care of your skin and your nails?

Beyond that, your options are limited only by your desire and, possibly, your fear. I know some women who are so used to neutrals, even a bright lipstick frightens them. But come on. Are you really going to let a tube of wax or a bottle of dye push you around? Eliminate the fear factor, because unless it's your nose, whatever you change you can always change back. You can also start gradually. Nothing you do with your hair, your cosmetics, or your style of dress is ever permanent. That's part of the fun.

As far as color is concerned, your aim *always* should be to glow. That's the real appeal behind cosmetics. When you apply them well, they radiate the real you. Used correctly, they make you appear to be standing under a very flattering spotlight. Cosmetics are less successful when you use them to hide you or disguise who you are.

The basics of application are simple and reflect this principle. First, always use a nice foundation to give yourself a finished look. A little bit of lipstick and a little bit of blush on the top of your cheekbones will light up your face and make you glow. I put the slightest touch of blush on the outside of my eyes because it opens up the face and gives that wide-eyed look. Your eyes are one of your most expressive features, and they should glow, too.

To get that glow effect in your eyes, all you really need to do is apply a little mascara, and then, for those who are a little more adventurous, a little eye shadow. If you aren't sure about eye shadow, stick to the smoky, muted shades. Colors like this will never scream. And by the same token, always avoid frosts. Frosts are like neon and will accentuate every tiny flaw and crease in your skin. Use either one or two colors, and if you use two use the lighter shade on the whole lid and a darker one in the hollow below the brow bone, blending to the outer corner of the eye. You don't need four eye shadows, even though there are a lot of cosmetic companies who will try to sell you those four pads.

If you have a nicely shaped mouth, play it up with a bright lipstick. If you have a small mouth, use a more natural shade of lipstick or extend your lip line with a pencil. A lot of women make the mistake of sloping the lip line down as they come to the corners, because they want to hide what they perceive as a flaw. The irony is that this actually ends up making the mouth look smaller. Trace the line along the outer edge of the lips and take that pencil all the way to the corner. Remember that one of the biggest assets anyone has, man or woman, is a good smile.

Personally, I don't believe any woman has to categorize herself into a "summer, winter, spring, or fall" to look her best. The "seasons" system or any other limited color palette strikes me as an example of pigeonholing. Why limit your options?

I say you can wear *any* color—it's just a question of making adjustments according to your particular skin tone. I'm a redhead, for example, and I'm not supposed to be able to wear red. Well, look at the cover of this book. Red is my favorite color—I love it and wear it happily.

There is no reason in the world to let your age define you, either. Mature women have just as much reason and right to look as good as nineteen-year-olds. Why should you stop caring how you look just because you've passed fifty or sixty or seventy? I'll never forget the wonderful ninety-year-old woman who presented herself for a makeover when I was doing a department store appearance for La Prairie in Pasadena, California.

We all saw her coming, and everyone behind the counter froze in alarm.

"We can't do a makeover on *her*," my colleagues gasped.

"Why not?" I said. "I'll do it." I love to put color on people's faces and love personal contact, so it was a pleasure. I really got into it. I finished with mascara and red lipstick, and it looked darn good, too. When the makeover was complete, this ninety-year-old lady wanted to buy quite a few of the cosmetics I'd used. I was startled. I was dealing from my own preconceptions, and I actually tried to talk her out of buying some of those products, because I felt guilty about selling her things that I didn't think she'd continue to use.

My new customer pulled herself up very straight and said to me, "I beg your pardon. I love the way I look and I have a boyfriend. Just because I'm ninety doesn't mean I can't look terrific and wear makeup. I'll take the mascara, thank you. AND the red lipstick."

The next thing we knew the boyfriend showed up, and he was at least ten years younger than she was.

There are those who are going to see all this as something frivolous. To those who say beauty should not be an issue I say, wake up, get real, understand that there are realities in this world, and take advantage of them to work in your favor. As women, we're fortunate to have many creative ways to redefine ourselves. We can use make-up and color to enhance our appearance, and it's a privilege. It's a pleasure. It's a celebration of who we are.

If you want to be the one who sets your cap on bringing down "the beauty myth," I salute you. But the majority of us have different goals. We want to use every tool available to us to reach them. And if we gain an edge and get a kick out of looking terrific, that's not a bad goal in itself.

No, I don't deny my femininity. Yes, I like it when the opposite sex says I look good, and yes, I like getting attention, and yes, I love it when my husband is admiring. Don't you?

Sometimes a cigar is just a cigar, and sometimes a lipstick is just a lipstick. Sometimes looking great is just looking great.

Sure, we all have busy lives and important things to do. When we put ourselves together we figure out how to do it quickly. We discover how to organize ourselves and simplify our beauty routines.

But think about it: Why should we feel guilty about spending time on ourselves? Women tend to be the caretakers in most situations, and that's fine, but who is going to take care of us? Even if your kids and your husband usually come first, you need some time to take care of yourself.

Grooming and maintaining yourself is not pampering yourself. Why should it be exceptional? It should be like brushing your teeth. Regular maintenance is something we should be able to commit some time to, without feeling we have to apologize for it. You shouldn't have to wait for your birthday to get your hair done.

It's great to be able to go to the drugstore and buy hair color and manicure supplies and do it all yourself. But there's a downside to that self-sufficiency. Not so many years ago, women used to go to the beauty parlor once a week. It was a place to relax, to gossip. It was soothing. It was invigorating. It was fun. It was a modest reward for working Monday through Friday, and a way to revitalize yourself for the Monday to come. It was what gyms and club locker rooms are to men. They get their massages and their haircuts there; they hang out and watch sports and have their bull sessions there. They feel entitled to those small pleasures, and they make time for them. Why do women need to feel guilty about spending a Saturday afternoon at a salon?

I think we need to start a new movement:
I say, BACK TO THE BEAUTY PARLOR!

YOUR WARDROBE

Thrift shops—including consignment shops and non-profit shops that benefit specific charities like hospitals and schools—are still a great way to dress on a budget. You'd be surprised at the names and quality you find there. I was. When my first husband fell for me, I was wearing a hand-me-down. A good-quality previously owned suit or dress can get you through an interview, a dinner date, or a formal affair. Good thrift shops offer a range of styles, from classic to more avant-garde. If you asked me how to make a tiny budget go as far as it could toward re-creating your look, I'd tell you to forget about buying clothes—no matter where they come from. I'd spend my money making sure my existing wardrobe was clean and pressed and in good repair. The rest is incidental. When I was earning money pressing other people's clothes, I was struck by how a skillful pressing could make the most unpromising garments look presentable. I still notice and admire a well-maintained wardrobe, and I am not alone. When your grandmother told you to replace those buttons and press those pockets and collars, she was right.

When you do have some money to spend, purchase classics. Classics never go out of style, and they go everywhere. The little black dress? Still nothing like it. It's amazing how far one of these will take you—morning, noon, and night. All you have to do is add a scarf, pin, belt, or a jacket to give yourself a new or a different look. A classic black dress can be anything from a strapless sheath to a long sleeved, turtle-necked, black sweater dress. And one will do it. I have no problem seeing the same outfit over and over again as long as it's clean and well-maintained. Looking great is looking great. Period.

Today I can afford to buy what I want, but I prefer to keep my wardrobe simple. It's just plain easier to get dressed when you wear one-piece outfits that don't require much coordination or accessorizing.

I've designed the little jersey dress as the cornerstone of my wardrobe. I have it in at least a half dozen colors and with small variations in style—in red with buttons, in powder blue, in purple with a dropped waist and a little flare, and in coral, with puckers around the neck. I also have a collection of jersey jumpsuits in black, navy, red, and rose. This jumpsuit has a regular neck, long sleeves, a soft shoulder, and zips up the back. It's very flattering to wear day or night—and moves effortlessly from a day at the office to a dinner date.

A wardrobe can be simple and work hard for you and still express who you are. You don't have to look as if you stepped off an assembly line in order to be practical. Conformism and practicality are words women join at the hip much too often. Self-expression and practicality are words we have the right to associate more.

For you, simplicity and classics might mean something entirely different. You may base your wardrobe on the pant suit, tunics and leggings, floral dresses, or on Chanel-style suits. To find your own sense of style, exploit fashion magazines. Ask yourself what you consider stylish, and then ask yourself what you see in the magazines that reflects your personal sense of style. And if you see something you particularly like or admire on someone else, never be embarrassed to go up and ask her where she got it or how she did it. I do it all the time. You'll be amazed at how most people are more than happy to give you information—even strangers. And what fun you can have following up on the answers. This doesn't just apply to reinventing your appearance, either. If I see a beautiful work of art, I'll ask who the artist is just as easily as I'll ask someone where they got their hairpin. Career, office, catalogue shopping, you name it. Never be afraid.

And while you can always solicit the opinions of those whose taste you trust, whether it be your old friend or the salesperson, never let anyone dissuade you from your personal style. If you are comfortable with yourself inside and that feeling radiates outward, no matter what your style is, others will be comfortable with you, too.

DRESSING FOR THE OFFICE

Women are always asking me what to wear to the office. Unfortunately, as our options expand, so has our confusion. Business majors at Indiana University, my alma mater, ask me if they really have to spend money on that dull blue interview suit. Women already in the work force are curious about my philosophy on bright colors, feminine cuts, and big jewelry. The big underlying question seems to be, can women be themselves and still be "appropriate"? Again, it's that age-old question: Can we be feminine and be powerful at the same time?

My answer to the business majors is simple. The reality is that the dark, conservative suit is often still the standard uniform in the game called getting a management job.

So if entering business is your goal, why on earth risk blowing your chances just because you didn't follow a dumb rule? You know who you really are under the navy gabardine, so do what it takes to get the job.

And once you get it, just throw that suit away.

You keep a job on the merits of who you are, not how you look, and once you prove your value the trappings become incidental. Follow your own intuition and sense of what works as you balance your sense of style with your sense of what's "powerful." Bright colors, feminine lines, and graphic jewelry are all appropriate. The question you want to ask yourself is not what *is* appropriate, but what *isn't* appropriate. Appropriate options are much more numerous than inappropriate ones. Just listen to your inner voice. As Grace Mirabella has said, "Businesswomen have for the most part wanted clothes that express something more than business savvy . . . Men like to show what team they're on—in sports, at war, in business. But a woman flies her own personal flag."

Generally, there are only a few looks that I would avoid for business. The looks to avoid are pretty obvious, and your inner voice would probably prevent you from choosing them in any event, but here they are anyway:

—going without a bra
—wearing a skirt so short that it is overly revealing
—décolletage
—see-through fabric
—sequins in the daytime
—the lingerie look, even if it's a camisole under a suit
—four-inch-long fingernails (they interfere with your work)

Aside from those, if you feel appropriately dressed you probably are. Pants are perfectly appropriate for business. I wear them all the time. When you follow your gut in business dressing or dressing for any social occasion, you may find you want to make minor changes from situation to situation within your own comfort zone. I do. For instance, if my husband wanted me to wear a skirt instead of pants to a political function, I would wear a skirt, in my style. However, if he asked me to go buy a pin-striped shirtdress from Brooks Brothers, I'd flat out refuse. The Brooks Brothers look is just not my look. It's a great look for someone else, but I just plain will not compromise the basics of who I am. I'm game to make adjustments (as long as I still feel like the vibrant, powerful woman I know I am). But I won't wear anything that makes me feel as though I'm diminishing my Feminine Force.

And if you like long nails with red polish, I find that to be fine for the office as long as the length doesn't interfere with your work and is not distracting. However, although I wear red nail polish to business meetings, I wouldn't wear it into a board meeting. I'd go with a more neutral color. Yet I don't feel that I'm compromising who I am or my femininity in doing that. I'm not giving up nail polish, I'm just changing the shade.

Within the context of who we are, it's okay and even preferable to be reasonable and practical. And while we may resent being dictated to that way, we really shouldn't. What we are really doing is controlling other people's impressions of us—not the other way around. So what's the big deal? After all, men have always played by these rules. They've always had to wear suits and ties to the office. Changing your nail polish to go into a board meeting doesn't mean you are not effective in that board meeting or that you are not equal or that you are not independent. It just shows that you are reasonable and practical and interested in controlling people's impressions of you.

Dressing for business travel is another story. Most of us don't have much time left over for dressing, and keeping things simple is one surefire way to save time. I especially avoid separates and suits when I'm traveling, because when I'm busy having to remember to pack a jacket and a belt is just one "to do" too many. Again, my solution is to choose jersey dresses or jumpsuits. In addition to its other virtues, jersey is comfortable, expandable, cleans and presses well, and doesn't wrinkle easily. Because I buy the same dress or jumpsuit in different colors and with slight variations in style, all I have to do is pack one pair of shoes and one piece of jewelry and I'm there. Period. With dresses like these, and a triple strand of fake pearls you're all set, day or night. You don't get bored because you keep changing colors. And for fun you can always add a big pin to the pearls. I have no problem seeing the same thing over and over again, on myself or anyone else. If it looks great, it looks great. Period.

Men only have a limited number of suits which they accessorize differently with shirts and ties. Ease and comfort are the pluses of wearing uniforms, and there is no reason why women cannot appropriate those advantages into our own working wardrobes even as we fly our own flag.

You can simplify your evening wardrobe, too. Personally, I've stopped carrying a purse in the evening. Let's face it, you can't get anything into an evening bag. After all, what do you need? If your make-up performs (and it should—if it doesn't, you need a new brand), one application should get you through the evening. Including the lipstick. My brand lasts all day and through meals—I've tested it myself. And I put my money and my key in my shoe. Even to attend state dinners at the White House.

COSMETIC SURGERY

Cosmetic surgery sure has gotten a lot of attention lately. In *Backlash*, Susan Faludi charged that in the 1980s "gynecologists and obstetricians frustrated with the sluggish birthrate and skyrocketing malpractice premiums traded their forceps for liposuction scrapers. Hospitals facing revenue short-falls opened cosmetic surgery divisions and sponsored extreme and costly liquid-diet programs." Apparently, if doctors go calling we come running. Novelist Mary Tannen, writing in *Allure,* compares cosmetic surgery to African tribal scarification and initiation rites. And *Allure* editor-in-chief Linda Wells, after describing a computer imaging program that shows a woman how she'll age, confides that after seeing how the machine predicted her eyes would look at fifty, she was planning to sign up, knife and all. Magazine after magazine runs true-life stories of face-lifts, often with pictures.

So it seems that one way or another, everyone's fascinated.

Here's my beef with Susan Faludi: never once does she even consider the possibility that a lot of women who have had plastic surgery don't mind the process and actually like the results. They feel that the surgery did something to enhance their self-image. They did it for themselves. There weren't suckered into it. The perception that only a certain kind of woman believes plastic surgery can help her put her best foot forward is sheer nonsense.

Women of all political and social orientations choose cosmetic surgery. Nanette Gartrell, a close member of our family, recently had her eyes done. Nanette is a Harvard-educated psychiatrist who practices in San Francisco. She is gay, specializes in gay issues professionally, and is politically active. Nanette was delighted with the result. She is a perfect example of a very modern, well-educated woman with a very strong sense of herself who has no inhibitions when it comes to understanding the importance of one's appearance. Nanette is only forty, and I didn't think she needed the surgery in the first place. But what I thought didn't matter. What was important was what Nanette thought, and she looks great.

Now, there are, in my opinion, women who have cosmetic surgery for the wrong reasons. Having cosmetic surgery because your husband is fooling around with a younger woman and you think the procedure is going to make you look younger and more appealing to him is having surgery for the wrong reasons. The only reason to make a surgical change is because *you* want to and you know it will make *you* appeal more to *yourself*. And if this is the case, if you feel a face-lift or an eye-lift will make you look better and younger, then why not? This includes women you see who have had so many face-lifts that they seem to be standing in the wind.

So what? The bottom line is that they don't think they look wind-blown; they think they look great. If a woman looks in the mirror and feels her six face-lifts make her look younger and feel younger, then good for her. You may see a plastic face, but she doesn't.

Yes, there is beauty at every age level. There is the twenty-year-old beauty of a face that is often not quite even fully formed, and there is the ninety-year-old beauty of a face that is lined with character and wisdom. But the fact is that we humans are obsessed with our mortality, and a large percentage of us prefer to express our character and wisdom through our words and deeds instead of on our faces.

Once again, so what? Heck, if we're going to be obsessed with anything, mortality is a great thing to be obsessed with. Nobody wants to die. Nobody wants to get old. Anyone who tells you that she wants to grow old is a liar or a darn fool. So where is it written that we have to look old just because we're growing old? What is wrong with wanting to look as young as we can?

TAKING CARE

Finally, never forget that taking care of yourself means just that—taking care. Self-care is a powerful symbol and affirmation of self-love. Health-care professionals now anecdotally confirm that my mother's instinct that looking good would help her to better face the world was dead-on accurate. Statistics show that when women in mental institutions improve in condition, the first thing they ask for is their lipstick. And there is a "Look Good–Feel Better" program currently being run by the American Cancer Society that is very successful with women recovering from cancer and chemotherapy. Even the medical community seems to accept the idea that how a woman looks has a positive impact on her overall healing.

Taking care can be more than a reflection of how you feel inside. It can actually change how you feel inside. A free-lance employee of mine who heard about this book wanted to offer her experiences, and here they are. This woman, a transcriptionist who works out of her home and is the mother of two toddlers, had become obese after her almost-back-to-back pregnancies. Although she was thrilled with the children, she forgot about herself. A period of unhappiness and neglect followed. Next time she looked up, this 5′ 2″ thirty-four-year-old weighed almost 200 pounds. She feels many issues contributed to the weight gain aside from the pregnancies, including the adjustments in her life and her relationship with her husband. But what finally contributed to her transition into weight loss was taking care.

Taking care was a real issue for my transcriptionist. At first, when she realized how heavy she was, she took very little care of herself. She didn't buy flattering clothes and she stopped using most make-up except for eyeliner ("If I don't put it on, my eyes don't wake up," she said, "and with two kids under three you don't get a lot of sleep as it is"). If she started to make this version of herself look good, she reasoned, it would mean that she was *accepting* her weight instead of trying to fight it, and she didn't want to accept it at all. Meanwhile, she just felt worse and worse about herself. Rather than pressuring her into making big changes, the fact that she wasn't taking care of her grooming was just making things worse. Instead of losing weight, she was actually gaining more.

Finally, she got tired of looking and feeling out of step with the rest of the world. She had her hair trimmed and got one of those makeover videos. She bought a few of the products, including softer eye shadow and pencils that were more flattering to her coloring (that early morning eyeliner was a harsh black line she'd been wearing in the same place for about ten years)—and approximated the remainder of the products in a less expensive cosmetic line.

She noticed that she looked soft, and she looked pretty. Even at her weight. She began to feel better about herself and to feel more compassionate toward herself for not being perfect.

And that was when the weight started to come off. And it kept coming off. Once she decided to take care of herself on the outside, she had opened a door to taking care of herself on every level.

So, yes, a little eye shadow *can* change your life. Some theoreticians may sneer, and who knows, maybe it never changed theirs. But my experience and the experiences of others say that yes, it can and yes, it does. Your image counts more than ever today.

You need no approval but your own to re-create yourself physically. And that's true liberation—the freedom not to have to conform to any other person or movement's idea or ideal of what and who you should be.

Chapter 17

Washington, D.C.: The Only City in the World Where You Can Go from a B Cup to a C Cup Without Surgery

"Things do not change; we change."

—Henry David Thoreau, *WALDEN*

C an you keep your femininity and hold your own in an all-boys' club at the same time? When you're a career professional and a loving mother who cherishes many of the time-honored, traditional responsibilities of being a wife, where exactly do you fit in your public life?

These are the questions that faced me in 1989, when Robert and I moved to Washington, D.C., one of the last old boys' clubs in the world.

After his 1988 election, President-elect George Bush chose my husband to serve as Secretary of Commerce during his administration. It was a great moment for Robert, and I was absolutely thrilled for him.

Like all cabinet members, Robert would go through confirmation by the Senate, and like all confirmation hearings, Robert's was going to be broadcast on C-SPAN. Normally, at those hearings, the appointee's spouse—and unfortunately that still usually means "wife"—sits in the front row of the spectators' gallery.

Our story played out a little differently. Before the hearing, a senator on the confirmation committee pulled Robert aside. He quickly got to the point. "Maybe it would be better if your wife didn't come," he said. "Her presence might cause a . . . distraction from the proceedings."

Or, in other words, we senators really don't want your wife here, taking any of the media limelight away from us.

You can imagine how I felt when Robert came home and reported this conversation to me. I was astonished, and at first very angry—not to mention disappointed—at the thought that I might not share this moment with him.

Of course, whether or not I'd attend was my decision to make, and Robert would never tell me what to do. But I did not want in any way to diminish this very auspicious and important moment in his life. I certainly didn't want *anything* to distract from the event—especially not me. So I made my own decision. That's how I came to watch my husband's confirmation from a front-row seat at home, in front of the television.

If the senator thought the media might turn my appearance at those hearings into a circus, he had good reason to think so. As far as I was concerned, the Washington press had had a field day with me—before I even got to town. They'd labeled me "Hurricane Georgette," and gleefully predicted I'd *never* fit in.

It was clear to me that in the next four years I was going to face some real tests.

But I also knew that going to Washington was a great privilege and a great adventure—one I was fortunate to experience because I was married to Robert Mosbacher. That opportunity for learning and growth presented itself not because of anything *I* had accomplished, but I never felt that what I got out of it was in any way diminished by the fact that it came my way because I was the wife of a cabinet member. It was one of the joys and privileges of being "the wife of."

But at that moment, I was first going to have to face the fact that in Washington, perception is reality, and the kind of press that preceded me created perceptions that were going to make life more complicated than I had anticipated. I was discovering that if you get equal satisfaction out of your domestic life *and* your work, you are still something of a trailblazer—and not everyone is going to admire you for it. To make your path somewhat broader than the narrow paths that have been conceived for women, you're going to have to fell a few trees—and clear out a *lot* of underbrush.

Up until the day George Bush put Robert's name forward for a cabinet position, my husband had had no political experience beyond political party activities at a grass roots level and no need for it. Business satisfied him. He was honored and proud to have the opportunity to serve his country in this way, but when he accepted his President's invitation to come to Washington, he stepped into a continuing press story—one that had actually begun with the previous administration.

The way I see it, when the Reagans first came to Washington, they were a relatively unknown quantity to the local crowd. They'd come from California, and they'd brought their California friends with them. The Washington press had a field day with that administration because there was so much to write about: the California lifestyle, lots of brand-new faces, and a President who had been a movie star, no less.

The Bush administration was a totally different story. George Bush had already given forty years of his life to public service. And not only did he already live in Washington, he had also spent eight years as Vice President under Reagan. My personal opinion is that everything there was to write about the Bushes had already been written—except for the fact that they were moving across the street. There was precious little to say about the President's staff, either, as they'd already had a lot of exposure, too.

Enter Robert Mosbacher, a wealthy entrepreneur and an outsider to the political process, a man who'd never been in government or lived in Washington. And, even better, that wife of his was "glamorous" and made no bones about it. I hadn't even shown up yet; I was in New York, running La Prairie. Yet in a city where wives were rewarded for staying in the background, they saw me coming.

Even before I arrived, people were talking about the fact that I wore bright, feminine clothes, had flaming red hair, was not born with money, had a business that required me to spend the week in New York and away from the Secretary-designate, and had friends with names like Trump who were often mentioned in society columns.

As far as I can tell, the problems came from the fact that I was the CEO of La Prairie. And the modus operandi of a CEO in New York is a lot different from the M.O. of a Washington wife. Because of all the political currents, there are certain things that just aren't "normal" in Washington that are perfectly normal and even ordinary in New York. New York is a more assertive, independent town, one with many power centers. Washington, on the other hand, is more conservative and has only one power center—*the* power center of the federal government. It was like oil and water.

Well, finally, the press could have some fun. So much fun, that before I even got to town a feature article about me appeared in *The Washington Post*. Written by a woman who had never talked to me or one single business colleague or family member, this article depicted me as a conspicuous consumer who didn't earn her keep, flew her name on charity mastheads without doing any of the work, and was nothing more than a social climber. "Social hurricane" was the exact phrase, picked up out of context from a *Women's Wear Daily* article that had been published about a month before.

To justify her argument, among other things this journalist said that I had showed up one night at the Kennedy Center wearing a huge leopard pin on my left nipple.

Well, in retrospect, this was the comment that more or less sealed my fate.

The item about the pin wasn't true. In a photo of me which appeared in that article, it's as clear as the nose on your face that the infamous brooch is pinned to the edge of my dress.

But perception is reality in Washington. That was one of the first lessons I learned there. No matter what the photograph showed, once that article came out, it seemed that no one in Washington wanted to talk about anything but my décolletage.

Now, plunging necklines were not my normal M.O. You would be hard-pressed to find too many photographs showing what Robert and I came to call "this bosom thing." But that's the way I was reported, and that's the way the press would continue to perceive me.

That's one unique thing about Washington. It's the only city in the world where you can go from a B cup to a C cup without surgery. There's not a lot of cleavage in a B cup, let's face it.

In retrospect, I can see that my problem in Washington was that I didn't fit any of the stereotypes. In my opinion, the expression "Children should be seen and not heard" pretty accurately sums up how Washington believes Washington wives should behave. I'd modify that just a little: "Washington wives should be seen only once in a very great while and never, ever heard."

You've seen the ideal models of the role: the women who sit in the front row in quiet blue or gray suits and demurely cast their eyes down while their husbands speak to committees.

Do you believe that's who these women really are? Of course not. It's just that in Washington there is an unwritten code that most wives of powerful men follow, regardless of their personal identity.

It goes something like this: "This is a man's town. The power is held by the men. They don't want anyone else taking the attention away from them. My job here is to fade into the woodwork." It's one of the ways those men *kept* their power.

And on the flip side of the coin were the few women power brokers, often from Congress, who were positive they had to be tough, acerbic, and combative to attract any attention. Known for their shrill one-liners, they helped to reinforce everyone else's conviction that if this was the alternative, it was far better to be a doormat.

I was neither here nor there. I didn't obey the rules because I didn't fit one stereotype or the other. Everything about who I am is an assertion of femininity—my look, my business, my ideals, my choices. And while I am feminine, I am *not* passive. I speak up. I grab attention and make waves.

The establishment just plain didn't know what to make of me. Since I didn't fit into one of the pre-existing categories, they had to invent some. What does it mean, they asked, to be both feminine and successful? This is what they came up with: *Excessive, conspicuous consumer. Glamour girl. Socialite. Tough.*

When men are called tough, it's intended as praise. When women are called tough, it means something else again.

Now let me say this. If having worked hard to have nice clothes and a beautiful home and wanting to dress well and have the best makes me a conspicuous consumer, then I guess I am. I was brought up to believe that this was a reward for working hard and being productive if you chose to have it. I have never done anything I'm ashamed of. I believe in honesty. I've exercised integrity in everything I've done, and I've worked hard. I believe I've *earned* whatever I have, and I've tried to share what I have with my loved ones and to give something back to the community.

But in Washington, no one asked and none of that counted.

Instead, the press went on a spree. It was as if half the columnists in Washington had just been looking for an excuse to unleash their most misogynistic impulses. Somehow, if a woman is successful in material ways, that fact automatically cancels out any other kinds of success she may have achieved—whether it's in loving and in being loved, in providing for those who need it, or in making a difference in her chosen field. Women, be forewarned: The idea that a woman can have it all is still threatening—to a lot of women, as well as to many men. No one doubts that a man can be handsome, can be a financially successful CEO, and can link himself to a beautiful woman all at the same time—and still be a legitimate and powerful influence in the community. But discover a woman with such good fortune who is direct about enjoying it, and she's suspect. She becomes fodder for the tabloids.

If the world can't believe that women have every bit as much right to a rich, full life, and every inch the capacity for greatness that men do, just how far have we come? Not very far, in my opinion. And every limiting label used to pin down individual women limits and pins down every one of us—no matter what our individual goals may be.

As my friend Marietta Tree, a former United Nations deputy ambassador, says, "What do I have to do *not* to be called a socialite?"

The infamous *Washington Post* article deserves high marks for imagination. It said I took my husband's private plane to Paris just to buy a Valentino sweater. In fact, my husband's plane—bought many years before he ever met me—had never once been to Europe, much less had it ever taken me there. That could have been verified by checking flight manifests, which, of course, this reporter didn't bother to do. That one was pure fiction.

The writer could claim that the unnamed source for this story was close to me, if you count living around the corner from my house in Houston as close. She and I had never exchanged more than one sentence, yet at that time she was the only person outside of New York and my circle of friends in Houston who had ever heard of me.

The story appeared on January 15, 1989, five days before the Bush administration was to take office, and instantly it ricocheted all over the country. It was picked up everywhere, and parts of it never went away. To this day, lines lifted from it still appear in magazines and newspapers. Clear out of the eighties and into the nineties reporters have somehow been amused to note that I worked as a switchboard operator to put myself through college and ended up being a cabinet wife (as if that were the end of the story, or even the point). So what? I sold shampoo out of cups, too. If I had done something illegal or immoral during college, *that* would have been worth reporting. People loved the fact that billionaire Sam Walton always drove old cars and pickup trucks—yet they make fun of the fact that I've been known to get a five-dollar manicure. Horatio Alger, roll over!

Although that one, largely fictitious, article seems to have the half-life of plutonium, at that time it didn't take more than about a minute for me to figure out that I had just become the official target for the Bush administration.

I was devastated. I was terribly worried about embarrassing the President, even though I received and was enormously grateful for the very encouraging notes he and Mrs. Bush sent me during this period, which always reiterated how proud they were of me and that they stood by me. I was just as concerned about embarrassing my husband, who had just come into his job as Secretary of Commerce.

After I got over being devastated, I became terrified and bewildered. I cowered in my office in New York and threw myself into my work. The strategy wasn't very effective. I endlessly questioned myself: "What have I done? Why is this happening? What am I supposed to do? How do I act? What's my proper role?" and even "Why don't they like me?" I was so upset that I actually missed the announcement that my husband's appointment had been confirmed.

Yes, these things mattered. My husband had come to do an important job, and I wanted to be able to support him in his role. And of course at the same time I wanted to be known as myself—who I was was not who they made me out to be. We all want people to like us.

I was learning some hard lessons. One is that labeling and pigeonholing is a way that those who have power make sure they keep it. If you can categorize someone—as a racial minority or as someone who fills only a very specific social role such as being a mother or a wife—you can keep that person out of the mainstream. Putting people into categories subliminally implies that they don't belong, that they don't have the interests of the greater group at heart—that, in fact, they aren't a *part* of the greater group.

The press coverage got worse and worse. They said I'd gotten dressed up in an evening gown and jewels to walk my dog Adam (which reminds me of the old Washington joke—if you want a friend, get a dog)—when in fact he needed to go for a walk after I was dressed and ready to go out for the evening. What was I supposed to do?

As I scanned the papers, I was shocked to notice that quite a bit of the bad press I got was from other *women*.

Is it possible that deep down, women are afraid that there is just so much success to go around, and therefore, if you have a lot, they will get less?

That fear is unfounded. Success is not a pie. Sometimes I wonder, though, whether this fear is born way back in grade school when girls miss out on the camaraderie of competitive sports, which teach that there's plenty of success to go around. Later as adults, men develop a tradition of networking, while women seem to be protective and territorial. Does it come from some ancient instinct to preserve our own individual nests? I don't know. But I do know that women, in particular, gave me a hard time, and some women continue to give each other a hard time.

Steeling myself, I went to Washington to be by Robert's side.

No matter what, *attention is power*. The senators who didn't want me to attend Robert's confirmation hearings knew that. I had my moment of disappointment and anger over that situation, but then I sat down and focused on the reality I was faced with.

"Georgette," my inner voice piped up, "things being what they are, what are you going to do to achieve your goals in this town? How are you going to become a team player without compromising who you are? You can't change your style and start in with the Peter Pan collars and the circle pins, because although there's nothing wrong with that, it isn't you. Not only that, but if you *did* do that, you'd just be playing into their hands. It would only give them a whole new line of attack."

What I did decide to do was make minor adjustments in my appearance. I didn't stop wearing jewelry or lengthen my skirts, but I did put away my most fanciful things and I left my shortest skirts and highest heels in the closet. I kept my bright lipsticks and nail polish and my hair style exactly as they were.

I found a middle ground. I could compromise and make adjustments to take the focus off something that was irrelevant to the real reasons Robert and I were spending four years in Washington. But I wasn't going to change who I was.

If you're not honest about who you are, then you have no chance. Ultimately people sniff out a fraud. In fact, I've come to believe that the reason I eventually overcame my initial stigma in Washington was that I didn't try to be someone I wasn't.

Who I am (and who I strive to be) is feminine, glamorous, proud to have achieved my dreams, and not shy about any of it. The fact that I had moved to a town that frowned on the idea that attention is power didn't mean I was going to change my identity. Following their code would cut me off from my Feminine Force.

When necessary, I could modify the part of myself that I presented publicly, if it made my husband's life easier. That was fine with me.

Almost immediately after my arrival, one press prediction bit the dust. That was the one that maintained that it would be old-guard, old-money Washington—the families with names like Bruce and Charles—who would be most repelled by my "flash." The *Post* muttered about the possibility of my "showing up uninvited on Evangeline Bruce's doorstep. In Washington," it went on, "it is Not Done."

Defying such knowing predictions, these were the very families that rallied around me. They weren't going to allow the Washington press to tell them whom they did or didn't like. I made great friends of them, and to this day I just adore them. These were women who clearly were in control of their Feminine Force. They weren't going to be dictated to. They weren't going to pigeonhole or label me.

Soon, among our other invitations, came one to a dinner party given by a local socialite. I knew the guest list included Ben Bradlee and Sally Quinn and other luminaries. Before that party I was in a quandary. What could I possibly wear into this lion's den that wasn't going to make me feel uncomfortable? Should I dress sedately? Or should I pile it on?

"Georgette," I finally said, "you are not going to play into their hands by wearing black. Don't let it get to you. Wear what *you* would feel most comfortable in." And so I marched right back to the closet and picked out my favorite orange and yellow metallic suit.

Instantly I felt better. I was ready for the fray.

I walked in the door, defiant, and the first person I saw was the hostess. I didn't know her very well, but I did know that she had to be about old enough to be my mother, and that she was what they call "front row couture." There she was, in all her glory, front and center among the Washington power elite, wearing a completely see-through blouse with no bra underneath. I was amazed. And then she stood up to give a speech, and as she spoke, I and everyone else in the room could see her nearly naked bosom.

"Georgette," I said to myself, "thank God you wore what you're comfortable in, because clearly it doesn't matter. Whatever you do, they're going to malign you and mock your appearance. (Remember, "glamorous" is a bad word in Washington.) Meanwhile, here is a woman who is going around town half naked and, because she's 'old Washington,' no one's going to say a word. That's the way they play the game here. You aren't going to gain anything by capitulating."

And so began the second phase of my Washington experience. Call it "So what do I do now?"

I knew I was part of a team. And that team was the Bush administration. I had my role to play in that sphere. I decided that there was an opportunity for personal growth and that it was a privilege to spend four years in a city with enormous opportunities I hadn't even known existed.

I was going to approach the experience as an education, as if I were getting a degree. I decided I would learn through observation. I made my first goal finding contacts and forming relationships within that network which would allow me to join that "men only" club of Washington power in my own way.

I started by observing the behavior of the members of the Washington power center that knew no way to name me but as "the wife of."

I asked myself an important question: "What can I offer this crowd that they need?"

The answer came quickly: My business contacts. My strengths that they had diminished and overlooked. It was the perfect way to turn a negative into a positive.

Then I asked myself what I cared about, what I would like to learn in this town, and the answer was clear. What I wanted to learn was what I could do to advance women in politics.

So I opened my home to organizations advancing women in politics and used myself as a catalyst to bring people together to support female candidates. I also opened my home to politicians from both sides of the aisle by inviting them to my dinner table. Through trial and error I was happy to discover that in small groups, conversation could be held on a more intimate and substantive level than is normally achieved on the Washington social circuit, which basically consists of cocktail receptions with throngs of lobbyists.

After that, I made sure my groups were always much smaller dinners, designed to get a dialogue going on issues that were in the news. That way, views were exchanged that could be discussed off the record and in an informal atmosphere. Either Robert or I would pose a question based on current events, and we'd go around the table and listen to everyone's response. This was a great way to get a lively conversation going, and the results were as enlightening as they were entertaining. It's become a tradition in our home.

These gatherings were also a great way for me to demonstrate who I really was. Without much fanfare, I was able to introduce some business leaders and entrepreneurs into the political scene, give them some political exposure, and involve them in the process.

As it turned out, there was a delicious irony in the media circus that made me so miserable when I first came to Washington. It made people really curious to meet me. As I met more and more interesting people there, I discovered that the perception of me as "colorful" actually paved the way for me to show them the real me. Talk about turning a negative into a positive!

My methods weren't always conventional. There were times they even surprised Robert.

I invited the Speaker of the House, Thomas Foley, to our first dinner party, along with the late Lee Atwater, who was then chairman of the Republican National Committee. It had either slipped my mind or I simply hadn't focused on the fact that there had been an extremely heated exchange in the press between these two men. They had never had a private or personal conversation, but the confrontation in the press was loaded with innuendo that bordered on name-calling. My party was the first time they'd met face to face. In fact, they shook hands, talked, and began to communicate. The situation between them cooled down. Little did I know what I was getting into at the outset—but that small party of mine defused what had been a pretty ugly quarrel.

On another occasion I invited Lou Dobbs, the celebrated business reporter on television, to dinner. To my delight, he accepted. When Robert saw the guest list, he asked, "How do you know Lou Dobbs?"

I answered, "I *don't* know Lou Dobbs."

"You mean you're inviting someone to dinner that *we don't even know??!*"

And I said, "Yes."

"But you can't *do* that!" he said.

And I said, "Honey, I just did. And not only did I do it, but he and his wife are coming."

Robert couldn't *believe* I'd invited someone to dinner that we didn't know. But this was Washington, and we and the Dobbses knew of each other, and I knew it would not only be interesting but useful for some of the political types in Washington to meet an opinionmaker in the business area. And it would be interesting and useful for *him* to meet some of the policymakers.

At first, I did just what Washington wives were supposed to do: I stayed in the background and served coffee. I became an observer. I paid attention. But I didn't see this as some kind of empty "Washington hostess" role. I saw it as something of value. The economy grows through the business sector, in my opinion, and not through the public sector, and I saw that something useful could come of bringing these two sectors together in an intimate setting where they could really talk and exchange ideas. I designed my dinner parties to accomplish exactly that.

I enjoyed every minute of it. Personally, I think there are few greater pleasures than sharing a good meal at a table surrounded by lively, passionate people with plenty to talk about.

And people began to notice what I had to offer. Gradually, it became apparent that I was someone who respected convention, someone who was respectful of the way things were done in this town—someone, in short, that the "old boys' club" could be comfortable with. Soon, I was gratified to see how some of the people I admired from afar had begun to view me with new respect. They began to accept me on my own terms. I was pleased to see them begin to accept the possibility that even though a woman had her own identity aside from "wife of," it didn't mean she was a wild card.

In the end, that "glamour girl" perception that made me such a curiosity actually *helped* me—and helped to further some positive causes that I passionately cared about. Now, did I feel "labeled" and "confined"?

Not in the least.

I felt powerful, I felt feminine, and I felt grateful and elated to have finally found a way in Washington to both support my country and my husband and my own inner voice. I had really tapped the power within me in a whole new way. Where it really mattered, the vise Washington had clamped on me just melted away. Instead of feeling victimized and boxed in by outside forces, I felt that I had tapped my inner power and figured out how to create the result I wanted for the greatest good of all concerned. I was refreshed, exhilarated, and ready for the next step. And I got my chance to take the next step and the one after that and the one after that: A to B to C to D.

And I didn't stop once I had achieved my first goal and became respected on my own terms. Now that I'd achieved step A, it was time to move on.

It was time to test the waters beyond my own doorstep. I realized there were some modest ways in which I could assert my individuality that might help. When invitations were sent out to Secretary and Mrs. Mosbacher, not only did Robert's office respond for him, but my office responded for me separately. I naturally assumed that I was invited by myself if he couldn't go. Now, I know that's not the way these invitations were intended. I knew they wanted the Secretary of Commerce and not me. But I decided that when they invited me they took the chance that he wouldn't be able to attend and were prepared for that possibility. So I accepted on my own behalf. I did this often. I went to several state dinners at the White House by myself this way. I called up first to make sure it was all right for me to come on my own, and the answer came back the same every time: "Of course, Georgette, you're always welcome." I wound up being seated next to

Kevin Costner and Chuck Norris that way—not too shabby as dinner partners. I also went by myself to a dinner for the Queen of Denmark at the Danish embassy, where I was seated next to His Royal Highness the Prince!

By the time I started doing this, enough had been written about me that people had a pretty good idea that I cut my own path, so while my acceptance was unusual, it wasn't unexpected. This was another way in which all the negative publicity about me worked in my favor.

I figured out my role as I went along. When Lee Atwater died in 1991, Robert was out of the country and couldn't go to the funeral. If Robert had been at home I would have gone along with him, but as it stood I flew down to Columbia, South Carolina, with Secretary of Defense Dick Cheney and attended the service in Robert's place. Lee and Sally Atwater were friends, and as a friend I also wanted to be there for Sally. During the church services, the cabinet members in attendance were asked to stand and pay tribute to Atwater.

It was one of those uncomfortable but important moments. I didn't know whether I should stand or not, because I wasn't a cabinet member, I was only the wife of one. But I had come to represent Robert. So I thought about it for a moment, and then resolved that I wanted this man's family and colleagues to know that even if Robert wasn't there, he was represented. Who cared what anyone else thought? So I stood along with all the others. Senator Strom Thurmond went around and acknowledged each secretary who was standing.

When he came to me he paused for a moment.

Clearly, he didn't know what to say next or how to say it. And clearly, I felt, he was assessing the appropriateness of my standing.

"Uh-oh," I thought to myself. "Here it comes."

But then he finally acknowledged that I was present to represent my husband, paused, and went on.

I was as relieved that my judgment had been accepted by the boys' club as I was that I had been able to be there on that solemn day for my husband.

In time I became known and respected as a fund-raiser, for my business experience, and as an advocate for women. I am particularly proud of my role raising campaign funds for Lynn Martin's senatorial bid in Illinois. I made a contribution, and both men and women noticed. One of the reasons I was able to raise money was curiosity about me and my feminine "aura." I used that curiosity, but the impression that lasted was of a party player—and someone who made a contribution.

In fact, near the end of the Republican administration, I had the great honor of being appointed to a presidential commission. In Washington, for women, the traditional plum among presidential appointments is a trusteeship of the Kennedy Center. It's a high-profile, ten-year post with unmatchable social perks, and if that's what interests you, it's perfection. In fact, when I came to Washington, the press gleefully pointed fingers at me for supposedly being snubbed by the Kennedy Center's "inner circle."

The incident they described never happened, but that wasn't the club I wanted to join in any event. I was much more interested in an appointment that was linked with my personal, substantive goals in life—which were and continue to be business-oriented. So it was my great privilege and pleasure to be appointed to the Advisory Committee on Trade and International Negotiations—or ACTIN. ACTIN is a committee that not only would offer me exciting opportunities to learn, it was one I thought I could make a real contribution to.

When I accepted that appointment, a lot of people, both women and men, were shocked.

"Why didn't you go on the Kennedy Center board?" they asked me—assuming that I could have had the appointment of my choice. And when I replied that I wanted to be on ACTIN, they were even more perplexed, because not only was the committee basically controlled by men but it didn't have any social cachet either.

"What do women know about trade policy?" I could hear them asking themselves—despite the fact that our chief trade negotiator at the time, Carla Hills, was a woman—and extremely effective at her job. And despite the fact that as CEO of La Prairie, I had opened up markets all over the world. In fact, our products were sold in over fifty countries.

So I just ignored them. I thought of Baba showing up at the steel pipe factory, and I didn't spend any time dwelling on any of the social ramifications of this or that appointment. I was just doing what I wanted to do.

However, during those years I continued to stumble on plenty of evidence that the old double standard was still alive and well in the nation's capital.

At the going-away lunch held by "cabinet spouses" for Barbara Bush, the cabinet wives came. And if the Secretaries themselves were women, they came—but their husbands stayed home.

Then there was a White House correspondents' dinner at a big hotel. I was the only woman at the Group W Broadcasting table. When a Congressman from a very large and influential political family came over to greet us, he shook everyone's hand but mine. When this total stranger came to me, he grabbed my shoulders and gave me a touchy-feely massage.

"A handshake would be more appropriate," I quietly pointed out.

There was no response from this particular public servant. Without saying a word, he quickly went on to the next guest.

And why did I have to report and document everything about my personal financial situation—including every personal gift I received—because of my husband's appointment? I still don't know the answer. When I was informed that I was going to have to take the time and go to the expense of documenting all my ongoing financial affairs—even though I wasn't the one holding an office—I was told that it was because I was considered to be one and the same with my husband. I pointed out that I had signed a legal document with him that said I was financially sole and separate. How can I be sole and separate and be one and the same at the same time? The answer to this was that the government's definition "superseded" my legal agreement. Which is not to say that it *changed* it.

Yes, I learned a lot about double standards during those four years. In April of 1990, the second year of the Bush administration, I was commuting from Washington to my office in New York. I was running La Prairie, and in discharging my professional responsibilities, I had written a letter to the FDA concerning import policies. Instantly, this routine event surfaced in the headlines: "Mosbacher's Wife Asks to Talk to FDA Head," *The Washington Post* trumpeted. Not "CEO of La Prairie asks to talk to FDA head."

It wasn't just that the *Post* was trying to imply some political impropriety—although clearly it was. By calling me "wife of," the press was totally dismissing my position as a legitimate businesswoman with legitimate business concerns.

In my private life, I love being called Robert's wife. There's nothing that makes me feel prouder or better. But calling a woman "wife of" (or "daughter of," or "sister of") in a public, professional context implies that she has no individuality or power of her own. It implies she is only powerful by association with a man, and that as a footnote to his life she's governed by all the rules he is. In this instance the headline implied that Robert was the one who set my agenda and made certain decisions for me. Well, some decisions in my life *are* based upon my role as Robert's wife. I came to Washington because of him, not because of me. That's part of who I am, and that's fine. But that's not all of who I am. And it's certainly not who I am professionally. Calling me a CEO in that context would have implied that I make my own decisions and set my own agenda. It would have acknowledged that I have some power of my own. It would have implied *acceptance* of that power.

Resenting the story, I'd already started to defend and explain myself when I realized it was just a one-day affair that would blow over. I could get through a brief storm like that. I realized that what I was called didn't distinguish who I was, no matter what the implications were. (Sticks and stones can break your bones, but words can never hurt you.) I realized that I was conducting myself properly, and doing my job properly. I reminded myself of that, and then I was fine.

So many women have to move in both worlds—public and private. And sometimes who you are in private and who you are in public collide. Don't misunderstand me—the fact that I had to ride that high-spirited horse called public opinion does not mean that I didn't get a great deal out of my Washington experience.

I love some of those old-boy traditions in Washington. There's the Alfalfa Club. It meets once a year. As far as I can tell, everyone belongs—the President, the Vice President, the Cabinet secretaries, the captains of industry. They all get dressed up in their tuxedos once a year for a big evening of pomp and circumstance. I say, let them have a good time. I think it's fabulous, and I, for one, wouldn't mind seeing more clubs just for women.

Things haven't changed a lot in Washington since I was there—even though the "Year of the Woman" has come and gone. That was 1992—the very year the media pitted Hillary Rodham Clinton, the First Lady-hopeful, against Barbara Bush, the First Lady-incumbent, while all America watched. Both women were pigeonholed. What were the issues? Whether or not Hillary took her husband's last name. Whether a lawyer could possibly be a good wife and mother. Which woman baked the best chocolate chip cookies.

Hillary Rodham Clinton had a career that wasn't traditional. Barbara Bush had one that was. Why did the press try to make us choose one over the other? Why did they try to suggest that one was more noble than the other? Both women should be admired for who they are. Both are to be commended for their individual choices. They are also to be applauded for the fact that they made those choices themselves, without allowing the press to define them. They defied the stereotypes that society likes to force on women—particularly on politicians or political wives, for whom the broadest mass approval is essential if they are to stay in the running.

When all is said and done, is it possible for us to yank all those stones and stumps out of our way when we're blazing our individual trails? Should we, as women, believe that the work has already been done because our senatorial representation has gone from two percent to six percent—when we number over fifty percent of the national population? Because Hillary Clinton has an office in the West Wing of the White House instead of the East?

Whether you're a businessperson trying to get your femininity recognized, or a woman trying to get recognition for your business sense, is it realistic to think you can carve out a niche that will accommodate both? And is it worth the bother?

I say it is. It's still a struggle, but it *is* possible to be feminine and excel in the old boys' club at the same time. Other women have done it: Anne Armstrong did it when she was appointed to be Ambassador to the Court of St. James's. Elizabeth Dole did it as Secretary of Transportation, and Ann McLaughlin did it as Secretary of Labor. It can be done, and sometimes it can be done just by showing up and doing the job.

One day in 1991, I received a very interesting phone call. Lou Gerstner was on the line. At that time Lou, now the CEO of IBM, was the CEO of RJR Nabisco. Although I now know he's a lovely guy, and that his wife is very attractive, smart, and outspoken—my kind of woman—at that point I'd never met him. Nevertheless I was intrigued by the call, because I thought he might be one of the best managers in the country.

Lou called to tell me that he was chairing a major political fund-raiser for President Bush. The goal for the event was two million dollars, which is a formidable amount. And then Lou asked me for my help in achieving that goal. I imagine I was on his "B" list: He'd never met me, but he knew I was a good fund-raiser, and knew I'd been very successful raising money for Lynn Martin's senatorial bid in Illinois. Perhaps someone had suggested me to him.

I told him that I'd help. By then I knew that raising money was the best contribution that I personally could make to the political process, and I knew that I wanted to continue to be politically involved. We all have our different talents, and fund-raising is one of mine.

Lou asked me if I'd be willing to put four tables together for the event. That would be forty people at a thousand dollars apiece. I realized that this would be a major undertaking, but I said I would try my best and would commit to doing it. That forty-thousand-dollar commitment made me co-chair. I could have been vice-chair and delivered twenty people, but that just wasn't enough. I wanted to be number one. I decided I would try to deliver more than four tables. I was going to go the limit and deliver as many tables as I could.

I had less than six weeks to deliver.

I very methodically made my list, set aside time, and I started calling. It doesn't matter how much lead time you have to accomplish a task like this. Either you do it or you don't.

As I set to work, I was conscious of the fact that I had an opportunity to prove women could raise money just as effectively as men, on a large scale.

By that point, I'd developed a very long A list, a very long B list, and a very long C list. As I called, I was able to prompt some of the people on my lists to put together their own tables for me. The people I inspired weren't always active Republicans; some were people who wanted to be active in politics but didn't quite know how to go about it. I simply used my intuition to pick those I thought would be the most predisposed to the process, and let them know how important the cause was.

I called everyone. Anyone I could think of that I'd ever met, people I didn't even know well. I told myself I didn't care what they said to me. I just kept calling.

I reached forty thousand dollars and I still had plenty of names to go.

"Georgette," I said to myself, "you're going to continue until you have exhausted every opportunity, every potential."

So I kept going. I wanted to see how far I could push the envelope. *How much money can you raise, Georgette, next to the big boys?*

There were people who told me no. And there were "no's" that turned into "yes's."

In fact, right before the lunch finally took place, I ran into a contributor who told me, "Georgette, I'm sending you a thousand dollars just so I don't have to get another message that you called. It's worth it to me for that and that alone."

When it comes to accomplishing your goals, there is nothing like tenacity. When you practice tenacity, if you don't wear them down one way, you'll wear them down another. I made calls, I sent faxes. And God forbid you committed to me and didn't get your money in. I'd go over to your office and collect it myself. First I'd call, and then I'd send a messenger. I learned that little trick fund-raising for charities.

Did I let embarrassment hold me back?

One man I contacted was what I call a political junkie. He always wanted to go to all the big political events, but he never, ever put his hand in his pocket when it came to supporting the party.

Predictably, this gentleman told me that he would like to give, but legally he couldn't, because he was on a government committee that posed a conflict of interest.

"So what committee are you on that you can't give?" I asked him. He told me.

"Somehow that doesn't sound right."

"Oh yes," he answered, "I checked."

I told him I'd get back to him. And of course, when I checked, I found out he wasn't on that committee at all. In fact, there *wasn't* any such committee.

So I called back and told him I'd be right over for his check.

He gave it to me. He had to.

To me, it was a matter of honor. If the man had had the guts to say to me, "I don't want to give," I would have left him in peace. But to say how much he wanted to but that he couldn't—well, I was going to hold him to his statement.

That's what I call using your Feminine Force!

*   *   *

When the dust had finally settled, I had raised $120,000. That's one hundred twenty people.

Then I got another phone call from Lou Gerstner.

"Georgette," Lou said, "you were the second-largest fund-raiser for this event. It's quite an achievement, and I hope you'll honor us by sitting on the dais with the other top four fund-raisers and the President and the First Lady."

What an incredible sense of accomplishment! Not only had I far surpassed my original goal, but I was also able to prove to my own satisfaction that as a fund-raiser I was the equal of the titans of industry—men who surely had far more sophisticated and elaborate Rolodexes than I did. But what I was probably most proud of was that I'd shown them a woman could deliver.

And to think it was all because I did something simple like talk myself through fear and embarrassment. Needless to say, it was a far cry from the days when Senator "X" had asked my husband if I would stay home and watch his confirmation hearing on TV.

As I looked down from the dais over this sea of prestigious, accomplished people, Lou Gerstner stood up and began to talk about what had been raised at the lunch and the importance of this fund-raising effort. And then, to my surprise, he began to talk about me. As I listened, Lou quoted something I'd said about raising the money.

The comment I'd made was that not only had I raised $120,000, but half of that money had come from new givers—people who had just become involved in the political process. This was just as exciting to me as raising the money—getting new people involved.

"And that's like a new customer," I'd said. "If you're going to grow, you have to have new customers."

As he told this story to everyone, I remember thinking, "Well, I guess they're not looking at me just because I'm another pretty face." And then Gerstner introduced the President. The President got up and paid tribute to several of those present for their efforts. And once again I heard my own name followed by some very kind and complimentary words.

Now, I was pinching myself.

"Georgette," I said to myself, "here you are in New York City, sitting on this dais, and the President of the United States is paying you a compliment in front of the captains of industry, the leaders of the community. You've come a long way, Georgette. I mean, it's hard to believe that a girl from Highland, Indiana, could be sitting up here with the President of the United States, and not only that but he's thanking *her* for something!"

There's nothing as rewarding as positive attention, and believe me, you especially appreciate it when you've seen the other side of the coin, as I had.

Afterward, a Republican senator whom I'd met countless times before—yet who never seemed to be able to remember my name—came up to me.

"Georgette," he said, shaking my hand, "I'd so like you to work on my reelection campaign. Would you consider it?"

As he turned away, I smiled to myself.

Chapter 18

Know Whom to Ask and When to Ask

"Formulate and stamp indelibly on your mind a mental picture of yourself succeeding. Hold this picture tenaciously. Never permit it to fade. Your mind will seek to develop this picture."

—NORMAN VINCENT PEALE

It was 1991 when the unthinkable happened: the German conglomerate Beiersdorf approached me and made a serious offer to purchase La Prairie from my investors and me.

And the offer was a good one—too good for us to responsibly ignore.

I looked at the offer. I thought about the offer. It made good business sense. It also terrified me.

It was time to ask myself some tough questions about who I really was. I had poured everything I had into La Prairie, and I'd been more than pleased to do so—I'd always gotten back far more than I gave. What you create always becomes a part of you, and La Prairie had become part of me. Not only had I evolved and had the company evolved under my management, but the basics of the business were still a major thrill. The truth was, I *loved* running a business. I got so much fulfillment out of this company that after three and a half years it was hard for me to tell where the business ended and Georgette began.

I even asked myself if I'd cease to exist without La Prairie!

Then my inner voice kicked in.

"Georgette," it said. "This is a business, and you ran the business well. But the key to business is knowing when to hold and when to sell. If you examine this offer for what it is, you will see that it's not only an outstanding deal for all involved, it will also allow you to reach one of your lifelong goals—to have enough money put away to maintain yourself and your family for the rest of your life. And there are other goals out there. Life will go on."

Once I'd heard that voice, I went forward and negotiated the deal. I had to work through some fear and uncertainty. I had to disengage my sense of self-worth from what I'd worked to acquire and build, but I knew the bottom line. The business was not *me*. The business was strictly business, and it made good business sense to sell. And so the deed was done. La Prairie went on without me—and I had gained the financial independence I'd always wanted.

But personal care was still my line of work. I loved the business and wanted to stay in it, but it wasn't at all clear that the world needed another cosmetics line. Cosmetics is a *very* competitive industry, dominated by multinational companies with multimillion-dollar budgets. How could I possibly compete with them? During the La Prairie years, I had tried to acquire Maybelline, one of the oldest and biggest mass-market brands around. In fact, I'd been tracking Maybelline even before I bought La Prairie, and had approached them before the La Prairie deal came together. The company had everything I was looking for—a strong trademark and good distribution. It was also owned by a pharmaceutical company, as La Prairie was. I finally had a real chance at acquiring it *after* I'd bought La Prairie, when the parent company, Shering–Plough, put the division up for sale.

For a time, I was the front-runner in the acquisition. If I had succeeded, it would have been a real case of the little fish eating the big fish. I reasoned that with the high-end recognition of La Prairie and the mass-market power of Maybelline, we could put together a fantastic international cosmetics company with niches at both ends of the spectrum.

My La Prairie experience had made me much more confident about going after a big acquisition like that one, and I went after it passionately.

At the last minute, my lead investor fell out, and there was no one to replace this investment firm. Acquisition just wasn't their strong suit. I had come close: the people who ultimately bought Maybelline told me that at one point they thought I'd had the deal tied down. They also confirmed my judgment about the potential there—they made a fantastic return on their investment, and they made their numbers in the same period of time I'd projected.

I learned one valuable lesson from the experience—always keep a second lead investor on a parallel track. That way, if your lead investor falls out you can bring the second one quickly up to speed and into the deal. Remember it may not always be possible to leave the dance with the one who brought you.

EXAGGERATE THE FLAWS

Opportunities to buy established companies with strong potential are rare, however, so when I sold La Prairie I was on the horns of a dilemma. I wanted to stay in the personal care business, but how was I going to do it? How could a single entrepreneur without deep corporate pockets compete with the corporate giants?

First, I accepted the reality of the situation. I had to acknowledge that there was no way I could compete with the majors' budgets. But I was confident I *could* compete with a better product. Even with a barebones start, and an overhead budget that would have been a drop in the bucket for a Revlon or a Noxell, if the product was good enough, I could do it.

A fast and targeted response to the consumer was something big corporations often have a hard time pulling off. To my mind, this is because they are dominated by the kinds of hierarchical structures that make them less flexible than small, entrepreneurial outfits. So I was going to take the "flaw" in my own set-up—the small size of an upstart company—and make it work *for* me. I would develop new products and get them on the market in about half the time it would take one of the giants. I was also going to get out there and listen to the customer—zero in on what women wanted *right then* that they weren't getting from the established cosmetics lines. With a product women would welcome, I'd have a fighting chance to make my business succeed.

COLD CALLS II: THE LONG SHOT

Raising capital for my new venture was no different from raising capital to buy La Prairie, with a few exceptions. I had more confidence in this go-round. I'd been married for several years and was not only feeling more settled, but still as happy as any newlywed. I was financially secure. I didn't feel I had to *prove* that I knew something about the business. But I *was* facing the challenge of starting a company from scratch and convincing potential investors that I could make my ideas work. This is what is known as raising pure venture capital. Venture capital is the toughest kind of money to raise, because you have nothing to raise it on but an idea.

So I wrote up a careful business plan that laid out my vision, and how I would make the venture I envisioned a reality. I plotted a three-year budget, listing expenses for research and development, manufacturing costs, staff salaries, and promotional and overhead expenses. My goal was to show how I could make my idea a reality, and how I could make that reality turn a profit.

Then I made those three lists I told you about—the A list, the B list, and the C list: the hot prospects, the maybes, and the long shots. I sent my plan out to every name on all three lists. Then I made my follow-up calls. But really, it didn't matter which list I was working on—A, B, or C. Each time I picked up my phone I calculated my odds, and the odds were always long. Even for the A list: in the end they're all long shots. But somehow I've always been one to believe that long shots pay off. Believing in long shots is the story of my life.

As it happened, when I made my calls I got far more interest than I had even hoped. Two investors were seriously interested. One was a famous entrepreneur on my C list, and the other was an investor group. I happened to make the cold call to that prominent entrepreneur on my husband's birthday.

"Yes, I'm very interested," said this gentleman, with whom I'd only had casual contact (he was on my C list). "Can you be in L.A. tomorrow morning at eleven to discuss the details?"

Eleven the next morning! I was planning a big party for Robert that night and I had intended to spend the rest of the time I'd carved out of my schedule in Houston, focusing all my attention on *him*.

I knew I had the presentation down cold. So somehow I hosted the party, found an early flight, got up at the crack of dawn, prayed the flight would be on time, sped to the meeting straight from the airport, sat down, and launched into my pitch.

But I didn't have to finish it. Before I could, this entrepreneur had committed himself verbally.

Why? He told me he'd happened to walk through Bloomingdale's in New York while I did an in-store appearance for La Prairie, and was impressed by my dedication to that venture. He told me he hadn't been able to believe his eyes, a "socialite" hand-selling a product. According to him, I didn't have to be doing that. The discovery that I was not a sheltered woman who preferred comfort to work, but a CEO determined to personally connect with her customers and willing to get out there and do it, had intrigued him. He'd even quizzed a mutual friend about me—long before I ever approached him. He was impressed with my dedication and that's why he was interested in making a commitment.

And then he gave me the commitment. A *full* commitment that made the whole deal possible.

The moral of the story? Always go that extra yard, no matter how improbable the result, and no matter how inconvenient doing so may seem at the time. You never know how or when it will pay off.

HOLDING A TIGER BY THE TAIL
AND LOVING ALMOST EVERY MINUTE OF IT

Some mornings I wake up at six-thirty, after five and a half hours of sleep, and ask myself, *Why am I doing this?* I could go to couture showings. I could have lunches with the girls. I could shop in the afternoon, and then go home and watch old movies on the Nostalgia Channel.

Once, my sister Lyn and I were walking down Madison Avenue window shopping, after dropping some samples off with Jennifer Balbier, our company color consultant. We'd just made a deadline that had kept us running at breakneck speed for two weeks. It was a beautiful fall day, and it felt great to be outdoors. Lyn had spotted a pretty scarf in a window that she wanted, and after she bought it I suggested we have an espresso at a café next door before we went back to the office. We settled at a table and looked out across the sunny street, and when I turned back to Lyn I sighed and said, "Wouldn't it be great just to do this sort of thing all the time?"

Lyn is the one who likes to tell this story, because she had the punch line. "Sure, Georgette," she said. "You'd love it for about three days, and then you'd get that look in your eye again, and if you couldn't go off and do some kind of work you'd freak out!"

I have to admit she's right. Occasionally wondering "Why am I *doing* this" is only a minor consequence of doing what I do. It's a given that if you start your own business, you're going to be (1) in control of your destiny, and (2) real busy.

BUILDING EXCLUSIVES

When I set out to design the line Exclusives by Georgette Mosbacher, I was interested in filling a need that other companies hadn't filled.

First, I went back and drew on all of my experience working the floors of department stores for La Prairie—doing makeovers and running what amounted to little seminars for the women who wanted advice on changing their look. I met scores of women around the world when I was representing La Prairie. I reviewed what I'd seen then, and what I'd heard them telling me—not just in their direct comments but in their reactions to their makeovers, in their questions about available products, and their requests for some that *weren't* available.

I approached all this with a completely clean slate, doing my best to abandon any notions that seemed preconceived. I had no idea exactly what product I would offer. What I wanted to do was A: identify a need or state the problem, and B: solve it.

I reviewed what I knew and then organized a couple of focus groups—small groups of women from different walks of life whose job was to voice what they wanted and respond to new product ideas.

These women wanted it all—and I believe we deserve it all. They wanted personal care products that really performed. They wanted products that not only made them look good but feel good, products that were simple to use and preorganized, offered great quality, and were a great financial value. I saw that the system I created had to be new and had to address all those wants. It had to be a product for the nineties.

And it is. Exclusives combines the latest skin-care technology with a complete, flexible color system at a moderate price. It contains no animal byproducts, and no animal testing was used. It's also dermatologist- and ophthalmologist-tested, and fragrance-free.

One of the main things I wanted to do was create a color line that would take all the guesswork out of coordinating lip color, eye color, and blush—and make it easy for women to wear a whole range of tones. Many women think they simply can't wear a certain color, but I set out to prove that wasn't true. I'm a great fan of red, and I think every woman can look fabulous in red lipstick—*and* in pink lipstick and coral and nude. I set out to prove that—by providing coordinated colors and adjusting each palette to flatter a woman's individual skin tone.

Each kit includes two shades of foundation, a tinted moisturizer with an SPF of 12, powder, four full-size blushers in red, pink, coral, and nude, four coordinating eye shadow duos, four full-size coordinating lipsticks, lip liner pencil, eyeliner, eyebrow powder, mascara, concealer, brushes, and applicators.

Whew! Not only that, but it all comes in two preorganized portfolios. All the products snap out of the portfolios and into a compact, so you never have to dig around in the bottom of your purse for your lipstick.

Marketing and distribution had to be as relevant and respectful of women's needs today as the product line was.

One of the big marketing successes of the nineties resulted from the spread of cable television. I had become intrigued by direct response marketing and by a relatively new form of promotion and distribution called an "infomercial." Clearly, a lot of consumers thought these sources offered convenient ways to purchase quality products they couldn't always purchase at department stores. And I knew from my own experience that it could be frustrating to shop at department stores. Sure, there are times I *like* to go shopping, but there are plenty of times I need to be doing something else. I'd shopped for everything from mattresses to office furniture by telephone and through catalogues, and I liked the convenience. Direct response marketing seemed to provide a very attractive alternative for my potential customers.

These ideas seemed to click, and they became the heart of my business plan, along with the numbers and a descriptive list of the principals and the set-up. The business plan helped to sell my investor, and the investor put up enough for me to make a go of it.

MAKING IT GO

If you visited the offices of Exclusives, you wouldn't find a big steel-and-glass building or even a suite in a small one. The offices of Exclusives by Georgette Mosbacher are a floor-through in a town house on New York's East Side. Three rooms of modest proportions. The central room doubles as office and reception area, with what we think of as a workshop on one side, and my office on the other. The small size of the space doesn't merely reflect a pragmatic attitude toward overhead costs: it also reflects the close working relationship of the women who run the company.

HIRING STAFF

Some small businesses can be started as a one-person operation, but I knew I wasn't going to be able to accomplish what I wanted to do on my own. I needed to hire staff, and I figured out how to do that by asking myself, "Now that I've got a good idea of what's involved here, what skills do I need to bring to the table that I can't bring myself?"

There is no more perfect example of the need to identify your own strengths and weaknesses. You can turn a weakness into a strength simply by hiring people whose strong areas offset your weakest ones. You run a major risk when you assume that you alone have all the answers: You don't, and that's okay. You don't have to be afraid to admit there are certain things you either don't like to do or aren't any good at. You reach a goal by covering all your bases, and you cover all your bases by hiring good people.

If you know your most important personal responsibilities—and personal strengths—are developing the idea, overseeing the final shape of the product, and selling that final product, you are going to need someone who has expertise in the manufacturing methods your product will call for. In my case, I needed someone who could design an attractive package that would function according to my specifications, and to engineer the package mold.

Other kinds of skilled help were required. I needed someone to provide legal assistance with tasks such as registering trademarks. I needed the services of chemists to formulate products, and the services of labs that could test them. I also wanted and needed to assemble an executive-level team who would share my vision and my commitment to making Exclusives work.

In a start-up business, it would have been a mistake to hire staff and rent or purchase space to meet every one of these demands. A true entrepreneur keeps fixed overhead as minimal as possible. I wanted to use consultants wherever I could. That way, when any particular stage of the business was completed, I wouldn't have to carry unnecessary overhead. The lower your overhead, the lower your risk, and the faster you turn a profit.

As my husband's father once told him, "It's not the knives and forks that break you." That's some of the best business advice I know. In other words, in a small business your financial health does not depend on whether or not you get your paper clips for seventy-nine cents a box or ninety-nine cents a box, or whether you get lunch at a sidewalk café or a steak house. However, if you commit to pay rent on a suite of offices in a fancy high-rise instead of the simple three-room office on the second floor, or put the expensive art director on staff instead of hiring her on a project-by-project basis, you may place your enterprise in jeopardy.

STAFFING THE COMPANY

Starting a business requires one set of skills. Running one requires another. The goal of management is to get the job done and get it done properly, based on the goals or business plan of your organization. And a large part of your ability to achieve those goals depends on the ability of the people working for you to achieve theirs. Choosing the right people for the job is obviously one of the most important decisions you'll ever make in business. I choose people who show they are responsible for themselves. Quality being equal, I hire based on energy, enthusiasm, and a positive attitude. Consciously surrounding yourself with positive, can-do people who clearly care about themselves and don't understand any part of the word "no" will have a direct impact on your success.

This is where the ability to delegate responsibility to others is crucial. I don't find it easy to do it, because I like to be in control, and when you're a control-oriented person like I am, it can be awfully hard to let go.

Of course, to delegate, you need to believe that the person you're delegating to can do the job. It's an issue of comfort and trust. If you've got to look over someone's shoulder every five minutes, it's easy to conclude that you might as well do it yourself—at least that way it will get done right.

It is one thing to say "I can delegate that" and quite another to find people who are ready, willing, and able to take on the responsibility you've delegated. The real trick is to find someone who fills the bill.

And it is a universal truth of management that if you do find that someone, *you should do everything you can to make her happy.*

When you're running the business, you can implement policies that reflect your own convictions about the best ways people work together. You can use what you know about your own Feminine Force to empower others. Even at La Prairie, where we used a standard organizational chart, I encouraged entrepreneurial units out in the field. Part of the reason we stayed competitive was that field managers had the range to make a lot of moves without all decisions having to come back to me. It was my belief that if I pushed that decision making *out*, and encouraged entrepreneurial thinking and entrepreneurial units within the larger unit, the company would develop much quicker reflexes.

It worked at La Prairie, and I knew it would work for Exclusives. I also knew that women empowered this way would get a strong taste of their own Feminine Force as they were pushed beyond their previous limits.

MANAGEMENT AND MENTORING

The classic good manager is a person with the skills of a strategic chess player. When a crisis comes along, she's the one who takes that budget and figures out what moves to make. She makes things come out the way she wants them to come out. A good manager is someone who has a knack for motivating others to execute very specific plans and achieve goals.

Whether or not you have the knack for managing professionally is something you can only learn by doing. But managing people so that you get the results you need is something you and most women already do every day.

The principles of Feminine Force that can empower your staff are the same principles employed by a good mentor. Mentoring a particularly promising employee can be one of the greatest satisfactions in your career. A good mentor is one who leads her people up to the mark, then empowers them to go beyond the farthest limits of what they imagined achieving. When you empower someone in this fashion, she may more than fulfill your expectations. She may flourish in ways you didn't dream of. The joy of it is that you never know who that surprising, enriching person in your life is going to be. Sometimes that golden employee is someone who came to your attention through her glow-in-the-dark resume. But often it's the person with no experience that you hire on instinct just because she has so much energy and basic smarts.

The person who has surprised me this way in my life is my sister Lyn, who is now vice president of Exclusives. I never knew Lyn too well when I was growing up. She was five years younger than I was—a big gap when you're eleven and she's six or you're seventeen and she's twelve. Lyn was the baby in our family, the one we always told to "go out and play." And she did.

And when I was young adult, I hardly saw Lyn at all. She was still back home in junior high school when I was in college. But when I was negotiating the La Prairie deal, I found that Lyn was the person I wanted to confide in. To my surprise and delight, I discovered that my sister was a great sounding board, and I sure needed one. Although there are plenty of times when showing your vulnerability and asking for help is the right move to make, the midst of deal making isn't one of those times. All you can show then is your strength. Maybe it had something to do with the fact that Lyn used to win all the marbles games in the neighborhood when she was kid, but as it turned out, she has sure instincts about tough aspects of negotiating. She has common sense, strength, and her own version of street smarts, and she became my best sounding board.

Lyn remembers how, as I gave her the blow-by-blows of those negotiations, I would sometimes get so exasperated that I cried. She laughs when she tells the story about the day I told her my investors didn't want to deal with a woman, and I didn't care!

"I want this deal," I told her, "and whatever it takes I'm gonna do it. If they want a gorilla in there, I'll give them a gorilla. If they want a man, I'll give them a man!" I didn't take it personally. I just kept my focus on the end result.

What impressed Lyn was how I didn't seem to care that the seller had a problem dealing with a woman. It meant something to her that I didn't let that stop me.

Meanwhile, I wasn't the only one who was getting an idea of Lyn's true potential. Her husband Vlad, an All-American basketball player turned real-estate lawyer and developer, had decided it was time for Lyn to come to work in his office.

Soon, Vlad was asking Lyn her opinion on important business decisions. No one had ever asked Lyn her opinion before. Her whole life, all people had told her was "Go out and play." Vlad saw this, and he was an excellent teacher. So good, in fact, that soon the Pygmalion story started to play out in Lyn and Vlad's marriage. As Lyn blossomed far beyond Vlad's expectations, her strength and curiosity began to unnerve him a little. Vlad was comfortable in his life the way it was, but Lyn was just beginning to see a different horizon. She wanted to see, learn, and do more.

Two months after the La Prairie deal was finalized, I decided to give Lyn a chance at a job of her own. She wasn't earning a salary working for Vlad, and she had certainly proved herself capable of holding down a position.

I called Lyn up as I'd done so often, but this time I made a simple statement that surprised her:

"I need you."

Lyn didn't miss a beat. "Okay, what can I do?"

I told her I wanted her to help me with the business. Would she meet with me in New York?

When she got to our offices I said, "Lyn, here's how you can help me. There's no training department in this company."

And again, without batting an eyelash, Lyn said, "Okay, I'll try training."

In the beginning she just did whatever was needed. She went on the road. She went into stores to work behind the counter, selling. She made visits to retailers with our account executives. She taught sales people how to use the products. As she traveled and worked, commuting from the Midwest to wherever her job took her, Lyn reported back to me and discovered her greatest talents, one being training others. She gained an understanding of how a cosmetics company worked overall. She also discovered what she *didn't* like to do. She didn't care for putting the La Prairie product on other people. Fine: I was good at that, and I needed her to handle the in-store arrangements for the field trips I'd be taking to demonstrate our line. So Lyn worked with the store to make sure they had enough inventory in place, enough beauty advisers, and extra staff to handle the traffic. She worked on preparing the counter for my personal appearances. She also worked with the store's public relations department to set up press interviews.

Although her new employment background was sales, public relations was one area where Lyn excelled. Coordinating projects was another strong suit. Soon she was handling all my in-store sales appearances and taking care of all the promotional gifts.

She'd come back with a lot of questions. "Georgette, what do you think of this idea?" or "Georgette, how do I keep all this stuff straight?"

And we'd work out a solution.

A lot of what I was able to teach her were things I'd learned through my work experience. But Lyn had skills that complemented mine. She's got a lot of common sense, and an innate ability to pull the different pieces of a project together—two great qualities for a manager to have. I felt very lucky to have her in my court.

Her attributes didn't merely *allow* me to delegate important aspects of the job to her, they *inspired* me to do that.

Lyn didn't realize how important and powerful her skills were until I began to rely on them. Then she wanted to prove she could do the job. At first, she rationalized her successes by saying that she was only helping *me*.

"No one had ever really asked anything important of me or really relied on me until Georgette did," Lyn says. "My whole life everybody always took care of me—even my mother jokes that she didn't know if I was ever going to talk. Because I was always the baby, all I had to do was grunt and point for everyone to say, 'What do you want? What do you want?' "

There were moments when Lyn stumbled as she tried to find her place at La Prairie. But as frightening as an adventure like that can be for someone new to a corporate environment, she couldn't help but seize the opportunity. She was finding that she just *loved* working. So she kept at it, even while her loving but protective husband was gently reminding her she could step back at any time.

She's a terrific example of the importance of listening to your own inner voice, even when some of the people closest to you get cold feet on your behalf.

Lyn calls me her "channel." What she means is that by concentrating on and empathizing with my needs, she could steer around her own fears. She could access the deep power of her own Feminine Force. It led to the day she woke up and realized her own strength, talent, and power.

Though we'd gone our separate ways for a while, our family is very close, and Lyn would have done anything for me when I called and asked for her help. She is as giving as she is loyal. But suddenly, Lyn didn't just want *me* to be a success. She wanted to succeed for her own sake. What allowed her to set personal goals for herself was her new faith in her ability to reach them. Lyn became a true testimonial for the power of Feminine Force. Once she had exercised it and gotten a feel for her own abilities, she acquired a positive appetite for carving her own niche in the world.

I chose to mentor a family member, but I'd try it with any woman who showed the initiative, curiosity, and loyalty that Lyn has. Those are the three basic qualities every manager values.

These days, Lyn is well beyond middle management. Now she's actually involved in the creation of the product, and works with our lawyers on product specifications.

Her story is another example of the power of Feminine Force.

CONCRETE LEADERSHIP

Empowering your managers doesn't mean that you're going to end up with an operation that will run along smoothly without you. Your leadership is crucial—and never more so than during the start-up period of an organization. I can't assume that my managers are always focused on our broadest responsibilities, as I constantly am. When you're immersed in the myriad details of the day-to-day operation, it can be all too easy to lose sight of the big picture.

In the summer of 1992, the inevitable moment came when pressures began to peak as we approached the culmination of a year's work, and success or failure came down to how well we would be able to sell our product through television advertising.

One day I was talking to Lyn and to the company chief operating officer. It was one of our daily status meetings. After weeks of rising to the occasion, these two smart, can-do women had hit the wall. Logistical roadblocks that could very well have prevented us from making our deadlines were suddenly getting the best of them. The skin foundation submission hadn't shown up for approval from the chemist on the promised date, and Customs was being uncooperative about releasing a prototype for our great red sunglasses. We needed them instantly to take advantage of a national magazine shoot. Timing was crucial.

Neither woman seemed able to execute according to timetable. As the three of us spoke together I got more and more annoyed, and ended up a little short with them both.

After they left, I thought about what I could do to improve the situation.

I asked myself, "What is it? These women are both intelligent and capable. Why aren't things moving the way they should be?"

I thought hard for a few minutes. Then I picked up the phone and called them back in.

"Okay," I began. "Sit down. I'm going to give you both a crash course in how to empower other people to get done what you want done. All I've been hearing for weeks is 'Well, we don't have the foundation submission because they said it would be another week before they could get it to us.' Or, 'The sunglasses were supposed to be here on Monday, but now the sunglass man says they're stuck in Customs.'

"You know what? You just don't *accept* answers like that. You say to yourself, I *need* that prototype today, and how do I resolve this situation in order to get what *I* want? You have to focus on the accomplishment of your own task. That has to be what makes your world go around—not your supplier's limitations. Your bottom line always has to center on your needs as a manager, because your ability to accomplish your task at this company is tied to other people's ability to accomplish theirs.

"So, what you have to do is to figure out how to motivate those people to be creative and to get it done."

That was when I noticed I wasn't only lighting a fire under my staff. I was also reminding *myself* of the basics. It became very clear that instead of accepting "no," all three of us had to focus, ask ourselves what the specific problem was, and come up with a solution.

When the specific problem is that the sunglasses prototype is in Customs but needs to be at a photo shoot, the next question should not have been "How do I tell Georgette about this problem?" but "How do I get those glasses out of Customs?"

If Lyn and my COO simply sat there and waited for Customs to do its job, they'd be giving all their power over to someone else—someone who had absolutely no stake in their success. If they continued to depend on the mercy of the Customs Department, they weren't going to have the prototype in time to make our first important advertising deadline.

Once they had asked the question that clarified the problem, the next step was to review all their options and think creatively about a solution. If our roadblock was a customs broker who wasn't doing his job, it was time for our COO and Lyn to ask themselves how to get that prototype out of Customs without his help.

One approach would be for someone from Exclusives to go down to Customs. Did that mean these women physically had to go down to the

Customs building themselves, or could they send a secretary or the company driver? Would any of these options be an effective solution—as well as a good use of valuable staff time?

A second approach would be to play their trump card—the broker's fee. My executive might choose to call the broker and tell him that if they didn't have those sunglasses today, they would no longer work with him. They'd find another way to get the job done.

Either of these approaches would have been viable, and I let the two of them know that. But I also pointed out that however they decided to handle this problem, they couldn't decide to handle it or any other management problem by allowing other people to stop them in their tracks. Managers have to keep moving and keep others moving. When you find yourself dependent on others to move forward, you've either got to find a way to get around the person who has become a roadblock or *get her* to shift her own weight.

WORKING A PROBLEM

This is one aspect of what I call "working a problem." No one returns your phone call, but you need a price quote on goods in order to figure the cost of your product and meet your deadline. Or, the pipe in your sink is gushing and the plumber won't come. Once you reach a dead end using the usual methods, how do you get what you want? When getting what you need depends on circumstances you can't always control, what do you do?

You go through the problem step by step to find non-obvious solutions. You solve that problem before *not* solving it creates three more new problems. The bottom line is that if that water pipe in the bathroom continues to leak, the floor may cave in. If the work doesn't get done, if you miss a manufacturing deadline because you don't have the numbers, you will lose money and you may have to lay an employee off. These outcomes will be a lot less convenient than taking care of the smaller problem right now. I call it the stitch-in-time rule: If you don't work the problem now, it's going to end up working *you*.

So how did my people "work the problem"? They considered hiring another customs broker to do the job, but realized that this would only create more red tape and delay because the package was already registered in the name of the man they were dealing with. The only way to go was to play the hand they'd already been dealt. So they called the uncooperative broker and explained to him firmly and clearly that if he was not at the office with the prototype at twelve noon, they would no longer be able to do business with him because he was not reliable, and they would find someone else to fill his place.

By twelve noon the boxes had shown up.

They didn't know it, but I'd dealt with this broker on one previous occasion and sized him up the same way. I'd had a conversation with him in which I told him what information I needed, and that I needed it by fax by the close of business that same day. I told him I just didn't work any other way.

The truth is, I *do* work in other ways—it just depends on who I'm working *with*. I'd realized during the course of our conversation that our company had been getting excuses from him for some time. I had very little to lose by giving him an ultimatum. If this was the way he worked, I had to replace him in any event. I long ago concluded that some people are only motivated by a threat, and I had to be realistic about it. It's sometimes necessary to play hardball if you're dealing with someone like that—even though hardball might not be the management style you prefer.

I'm going to make a brief but necessary digression here, on the meaning of the word "tough" when used to describe a woman manager. It's not always intended as flattery.

Women are called difficult and tough when (1) we negotiate the best deal, (2) we are perfectionists in doing our job, (3) we are willing to work harder and longer than men are willing to, and (4) when we question anything—*anything*—that someone else is doing, particularly if that someone is a man.

God forbid you do any of these things. You will be called difficult or tough. God forbid you raise your voice. You will be called hysterical. But men who work *their* responsibilities *the same way* will simply be called hard-driving managers who excel.

Get used to it. There's nothing you can do about it but ignore it. It happens to us all. There is not one successful woman around who has never been attacked in this way, so learn to anticipate it along with your success. Yes, it is a personal attack based on a stereotype and a double standard. But this is precisely why you cannot defend yourself against it. Objecting is a losing battle and waste of time that only perpetuates the "stereotype" in the eyes of your attackers.

If you can't simply ignore it when it comes, talk yourself through it. Sometimes I just have it out with myself in the mirror: I give my attacker a piece of my mind and rail against the unfairness of the criticism. But I do it only for myself.

But back to the story. In dealing with that broker, I used the most direct approach:

"If I don't have the information by five o'clock, we can't do business any more." Simple as that.

But, it wouldn't have done my managers much good if I had simply told them how I had dealt with this guy. Telling them exactly which route to take would not have been empowering. It wouldn't have been the kind of learning process that results in a better and more confident manager. Obeying orders is not a tenet of Feminine Force. To empower them, I had to clarify the problem and their responsibility. I had learned something, too. I had been reminded that motivation requires clarity and directness. It was *my* job to keep us focused on the big picture—the job we'd all been hired to do.

ASKING FOR HELP

As straight and clear and even tough as I was being, I was also showing my vulnerability—and my managers' power—in this situation. I was asking them for help.

Never hesitate to show your own staff that you need help. They need to be reminded how important they are to the process. In life and in business, we rely on each other to be responsible for individual tasks that benefit everyone. People sometimes forget how much interdependence there really is in a successful business. Learn the art of asking for help to empower and motivate others, and you will have learned a very powerful management strategy.

Though playing a little hardball was the tack to take with our customs broker, showing vulnerability by asking for help can achieve goals in situations where a show of force, even if you have the upper hand, could keep that goal at arm's length.

I worked with several actors and personalities in my days at Brut Productions and at Fabergé. I'll never forget one star and Brut spokesperson who had a particularly tough agent and manager. Her contract required her to work no more than a certain number of days to promote the product, but I wanted her to come in earlier because I wanted to spend a couple of days getting to know her. I believed that if we became aware of each other's concerns and sensibilities, we'd be able to develop a rapport that would inevitably show up on-screen.

However, I needed to think carefully about the best way to pull this off. As everyone who's dealt with agents and managers knows, they are capable of refusing proposals like the one I was going to make for no other reason than to ensure their clients that they're on their toes and earning their keep. It's an ancient and more or less honorable technique that most agents have resorted to at one time or another. I already knew from our difficult contract negotiations that this agent and this manager were entirely capable of drawing yet another line in the dust over this issue.

So I had a little talk with my inner voice.

"Now," I said to myself, "if there's this difficult agent and this difficult manager who want to be sure the world understands at all times the importance of their client, they're going to tell me she can only work so many days, she can only be in for so many hours. How do I get around that? My guess is this won't be the client's doing, but I can't speak directly to her. So to accomplish this goal, I need to help them to achieve theirs."

So I set up a conference call with the men involved. I started out by telling them how impressed I was with their client.

And then immediately I said, "And I need your help with something."

When you find the right way to tell someone "I need your help," what they'll hear is "You're the only one who can do this."

I continued: "Can you tell me what would make your client comfortable? Does she collect something? What's her favorite food? Her favorite hotel in town? Does she like to go to museums? Does she have a favorite designer? Could I arrange a special fitting for her? I want her to feel comfortable and special, so that she is totally, emotionally and physically, ready for this."

All of this was the truth. I wanted this spokesperson to know that we considered her an important part of our team.

The agent and manager both were delighted. I had acknowledged their power in the situation, and I had acknowledged the importance of their client at the same time.

Only *then* did I say, "You know, it's so important for her, for this project, that I'd like to get her in a couple of days early, so we could spend some quiet time together. I'd love to take her to a play, if there's one she wants to see. I'll take care of it all if we can get her in. If we could spend that little bit of time together, I just know it will show up on-screen. But I can't make it special for her, and spend this time with her, without your help and guidance."

My strategy was an unqualified success. These two men, who had been extremely tough in contract negotiations, eagerly promised to get their client into town two days early.

Until this conversation, I had been at the mercy of these two people. Nonetheless, the success of my business was to some degree dependent on them. This meant I had to sit myself down and ask, how do I get what I want?

My first inclination in this situation was to say, "Darn it! She's going to make money from this, and if it's successful, she earns more money. Why can't these two guys understand that? Why do I need to put myself through all this?"

But I caught myself. I said, "Georgette, stop! That's counterproductive. All that matters is the reality of the situation. It is what it is. So deal with that, quit thinking about how it *should* be. That's the only way you can make it all turn out the way you want it to be."

"Georgette, get real!" is something I say to myself pretty frequently. It is of paramount importance that we accept reality for what it is. You cannot achieve any goal until you do that. That's how I got my star to spend time with me at Brut and how my Exclusives staff got our prototype out of Customs. Reality is the only place you can deal from. If you're still worrying about the way things *should* be, you haven't even approached the starting line.

WHOM DO YOU ASK? WHEN DO YOU ASK?

1. *Find an expert.* There is no point in asking someone for help who doesn't know anything more about a subject than you do—unless you think he or she will be a good source of leads. This sounds obvious, but uninformed advice can be a distraction. The most innocuous suggestion, if it turns out to be irrelevant, will delay you when the job at hand is to get to a solution.

2. *Keep in mind that even experts sometimes have their own agendas—and they may not coincide with yours.* It's impossible to find an entirely objective expert; no human being is entirely objective. Come as close as you can, but always keep in mind that even experts have biases that may not serve all your interests. If it's really important, get a second opinion. If it's critical, get a third.

3. *Be careful how you ask for help.* To ask for help in the most effective way possible, put yourself in the shoes of the person you're turning to. In the case of the manager and agent, I understood their client was very important to them, and they wanted to take good care of her. I needed to show that I supported their goals, so I asked for help in a way that showed I wanted to make her feel special, too. I did not ask for help for myself. Although my ultimate goal was to feel comfortable with her, I put myself into their frame of reference, and stressed the importance of making their client feel comfortable with *me.* What they wanted was a step toward what I wanted. My success depended on their client's success—and that was where our mutual interests lay.

4. *Before you ask for help, figure out what the other person needs.* This is strategic. It's the key to negotiating, and the surest way to a win-win situation. It's a shrewd move whether you're fund-raising or asking for an ordinary favor. Focus clearly on that, and you're halfway home.

Knowing how to ask for help will serve you in any situation that requires cooperation. Don't forget when you negotiate successfully with your kids or your husband, your dry cleaner or your auto mechanic, you're using the same basic skills you use in business.

5. *NEVER lie.* Never try to get what you want by flattering anyone untruthfully. It will get you into hot water eventually, even if you're a

great actress and your target doesn't see through you right away. Insincere flattery doesn't do anybody's soul any good—certainly not yours. I absolutely believe, however, that in nearly any situation, if you look hard enough, you're going to find something about the person you're dealing with that rates a compliment. Our business and our daily lives depend upon the cooperative effort of a lot of people. What you know as a woman about motivation and empowerment can be used as tools to help *your* team thrive.

La Prairie was and Exclusives by Georgette Mosbacher is almost one hundred percent staffed by women. If two applicants are equally qualified, I usually hire the woman. My experience concurs with Linda Wachner's. I find women are able to build consensus, accomplish tasks, and roll with the punches more easily than men seem to, particularly in an entrepreneurial situation.

Product development just flew at Exclusives. In my opinion, it was because the women who worked there had less concern for internal politics and jockeying than men do, so we were able to get things done faster. When we had a status meeting to discuss our progress at Exclusives, we all knew instantly whether we loved a product or whether it didn't work. None of us had to corner and convince a whole phalanx of corporate vice presidents before we got to the table, as we would have had to do in any of the larger cosmetics firms. Consensus, when appropriate, was much more immediately available to us.

I don't think any of this is an oversimplification. As women and as entrepreneurs, we're just not as tied into the same sorts of traditional business models that men are. At Exclusives, each and every one of us is committed to each other's success. If each of us is successful, we are collectively successful.

Running a small business sometimes feels like sailing a very small boat on a very big ocean. It can feel very risky at times. But all of life is a risk and adventure, and taking charge of your own destiny strikes me as one of the best risks you can take. You might enjoy the same safe and comfortable harbor in corporate America for fifteen years when one day the bottom drops out from under you, your position is eliminated, and you find yourself living by your wits. Life just isn't seamless. The choice of what kind of risk to take or adventure to have is the only choice that's yours to make.

To tell the truth, right now I'm scared for my product. Even after all the focus groups and all the research and all the homework and all the listening to my inner voice, I still wonder if I was right. I wonder if what I think I saw and heard was right. And I worry whether what I've created will hit the mark. I've used all my wits and all my heart to try to create a quality product that's simple to use and that women can buy at a very attractive price.

Ultimately, though, it's up to the consumer to decide whether the Exclusives line works for her, and despite all the early evidence of success, I feel very vulnerable. When you start on a new venture, you're likely to feel that vulnerability too. Soon I'll have marketing data that will give me some grounding in reality, but until then, I'm crossing my fingers and listening to my inner voice to make my vision a reality.

Chapter 19

To Reverse Expectations Is to Be Powerful

"No one can make you feel inferior without your consent."

—ELEANOR ROOSEVELT

Some women enter the business world with an attitude best summed up in the expression "I don't do windows." Some have gone so far as to refuse to learn how to type, even if the opportunity has presented itself.

But in business, you must be careful not to be known for what you *don't* do. You want to be known for what you *do* accomplish. If you are in an entry-level position, for goodness sake, don't get a reputation as the one who took her stand refusing to make coffee. That's one of the little things that are part of the real world of business. If your job description includes making coffee or anything like that, make the fastest and *best* cup of coffee around, deliver it to your supervisor by hand, and take that moment as a golden opportunity to demonstrate who you really are and what you're capable of. Mention the new idea you had, or the new resource you heard about. Then quickly make your exit. I guarantee you that the suggestion is what will stick in her mind, while the cup of coffee simply drains away. If you make the coffee your last priority, she may be so annoyed by the time she gets it she won't even be able to hear what you have to say.

Sure, those "little things" are things women usually end up doing just because we're women. That's true throughout the culture. If your husband holds a public office, society still seems to expect you to prominently display your domestic side. Hillary Rodham Clinton made a point of doing that during the course of the Clinton campaign. And then she got on with her real business, from an office in the West Wing of the White House.

Did anyone ever ask Denis Thatcher for his chocolate chip cookie recipe? Of course not.

When those "little things" have to be done, the world—being what it is right now—will continue to expect women to do them. Accepting that is accepting reality. That's where you have to start.

On the day when women reach critical numbers in top management, all this will, I hope, change. (As we go to press, we number only three percent at top management levels and ten percent on corporate boards.) But the way I see it, if you don't make a mark in the world *the way it is right now*, you won't have the opportunity to empower the next generation with Feminine Force. Maybe in that next generation, the world will see that those caring little things like hostessing or remembering a client's birthday or taking notes at the board meeting are as important to the process as crunching numbers, making deals, or delegating tasks.

The truth is, proper attention to details is not some minor matter in the business world. It's what makes you competitive. It speaks of quality, seriousness, commitment, and professionalism. It will show up in your product. It will show up in the quality of the relationships you have with your suppliers and partners. In the end, it can mean the difference between failure and success.

As a CEO I'm *still* serving men that cup of coffee. It tends to throw them off guard, which is fine by me. I call it reverse power. Men these days are afraid to ask for a cup of coffee because they're afraid you'll refuse to serve it. So why wait to be asked? When people come to my office for meetings I ask them, "How do you like your coffee?" Then I walk out, make a fresh pot, and serve it to them. They're positively dumbfounded. I've been doing this to my lawyer for years, and it still throws him.

"Ron," I'll say, "I know you like it with lots of milk and two sugars."

Before I can finish the sentence he's jumping up and saying, "Oh, no, I'll get it."

Make no mistake about it. This is power. *To reverse expectations is to be powerful*. It tells people, in a positive way, that they don't know what to expect from you. Sometimes I help people off and on with their coats in the office. I walk business guests to the elevator. I press the button, I hold the door open. But making coffee is the best reversal of power of all. I love doing it and I do it often.

Does my approach to power work?

One year into the Bush administration, *Spy* magazine did a survey intended to "evaluate the relative might of some very influential people" in Washington. One of the tests was to see whose calls got returned the fastest. So the *Spy* reporters disguised themselves and made calls to half a dozen movers and shakers in town. They pretended to be assistants to Ben Bradlee, Chief Justice William Rehnquist, Oliver North, Daniel Patrick Moynihan, Hollywood agent Mike Ovitz (the only out-of-towner)—and *me*.

So which one of us got our phone calls returned the fastest?

I did.

This was during a period when negative press coverage had me staying out of the way in New York. In a sense, I got the last laugh. Without even trying to.

I feel comfortable about who I am, and practicing reverse power shows other people how I feel about myself. I don't make my stand at the coffee machine. I make my stand at closings. I don't have time to make a big deal out of symbolic issues. That isn't what makes me equal. What makes me equal is that the person I'm dealing with comes to *my* office for the meeting.

When Feminine Force and influence matches masculine force and influence in the business arena, maybe everyone will be doing those important little chores that women now do. But for the moment, there's only one way to get where you want to go, and that's by being the best at the game being played on the street today.

I think again of the M.B.A. candidates at Indiana University who were annoyed because the recruiters insisted they wear a dark suit and white blouse to their interviews. Their first impulse was to rebel against wearing a "uniform" in order to be taken seriously. They were right to believe that their academic credentials, and how they conducted the interview, were the real issues in that situation. Their only mistake lay in focusing on the way things *should* be, instead of the way things are. A man would also be told to wear a dark suit to an interview. So what's the big deal? You do what you have to do to get the job—that's the goal you should focus on.

In a recent *Glamour* magazine article, a panel of experts, including employers and headhunters, rated four different interview looks: a dark, conservative suit, a lighter suit with a subtle split skirt, a cardigan over a sweater, and pants with a turtleneck and blazer. Most of the panel went for the dark conservative suit, and most of those who didn't choose it first, chose it second. Make reality your starting place. Do what it takes to get your foot in the door. Once you're inside you can go back to your own good sense about style. And once you've moved up to doing the hiring yourself, you can ignore those dress codes and hire that bright young woman wearing the red sweater.

Once you're inside, you're going to face a lot more complicated questions.

Acquiring power on the job is like being accepted into a new club. When you're a woman working with men, joining the club can be a little more difficult than it is for your male counterpart. That's not fair, but sometimes it's reality. The first thing a corporation wants to know about an employee is whether he's a team player, and most men started learning the art of teamwork back when they were in Little League. This isn't just a figure of speech. What sports a man played, where he went to school, what clubs he's joined, and what his political affiliations are, are all evidence of a man's team affiliations. That's the sort of stuff that lies at the heart of the old boys' network. You're not part of any old boys' network, but that doesn't mean you can't learn their rules, and that's all that's important. You don't have to play by all of them, but you have to know what they are.

Figuring out the rules of the game in your particular organization is simply a matter of *paying attention*. That sounds obvious, but too many people just don't pay attention—and it's a real recipe for disaster. There aren't any shortcuts to this that I know of. Find out what the rules are in your corporation—the stated ones first of all. As for the hidden rules, the best way to discover those is to pay attention to who is succeeding in your corporate environment, and who's not, and draw your lessons from them.

Yes, you've got to be your own woman. Yes, your ultimate success may well depend on *breaking* some of the rules. But every successful person who breaks the rules *knows exactly which rules he or she is breaking*.

The bottom line is whether the people you work with can trust you to play the essential role you were hired to play.

How do you acquire power? Be the one who makes the extra effort to come up with ideas and solve problems. Always work the extra hour it takes to do the job well. Work the extra two or three hours when you need to. Don't be the one who's known for "not doing windows" or not typing or not sharpening pencils. Don't be the one who's always out the door at five o'clock.

The way to get ahead is to do more than is expected of you. Always.

These days, of course, the hard truth is that most corporations demand more of their employees than anyone could accomplish in a forty-hour work week—even though they're only paying you for a forty-hour work week. Right now there are probably many of you who are thinking, well, I'm already putting in fifty or sixty hours a week. Are you telling me I should do *more*?

Answer: Only if you love it. Only if it's getting you where you want to be. Once you start to arrive, once you become successful enough to gain a little clout, you can demand the help and support you need to make your burden bearable. If you've made yourself indispensable in the meantime, you'll get it.

Always do more than is required of you, but not to the point of self-abuse. We all want to be perceived as "doers" in life, but many women end up wearing themselves out and getting taken advantage of. Maybe it's because we've been trained from childhood to be all things to all people.

Some of us have only ourselves to blame for biting off far more than we can chew. But there are also many executives out there whose management style tends to drive their employees to the edge of burnout and beyond. Those executives usually don't recognize that the problem begins with *them*. Given the pressure on American corporations to compete in the world market, this is going to remain a problem. As long as it does, you're going to have to monitor your own "do it" button in order to stay healthy and productive.

THE PART OF "NO" YOU DO
NEED TO UNDERSTAND

Stop the World, I Want to Get Off is not just the name of a musical, it's a phrase many women find themselves muttering—or wailing, as the case may be—every day. There are so many demands made upon us and many of us haven't learned how to say "No," or "Wait a minute," or "Look, I had something else in mind here," or "I have a more important priority this week." Or maybe just plain "I don't want to."

In the business world, the one thing everyone understands is the importance of setting priorities. If it's your boss who's loading you with tasks that all have to be done today, sitting down with him and going over your list of priorities in a rational manner is the first move you should make. If he starts the morning by asking for a new report by five P.M., when the last thing he told you as he was leaving the night before was that he wanted the budget figures finished by four, don't just swallow hard and kid yourself that you're going to be able to polish off two major projects in one day, if it's just not possible. Ask him which one takes priority. Ask him if you can delegate a task or a piece of a task to someone else. When you can delegate, delegate.

This is a part of "no" that's really a "yes": Yes, I want to do the thing that has to be done today, and I need your help determining which thing that is. Being able to set priorities is one of the more highly valued skills in management. You may be in the unenviable position of having a supervisor who's not good at setting priorities. If that's the case, help out by regularly clarifying with him or her what *your* priorities are supposed to be.

If you attempt to do two jobs at once and get neither one done, then you've delivered *two* "no's"—a situation that's likely to frustrate not just your boss, but you as well.

Women in management positions may find themselves handling situations they hired their staff to do. This is another instance when clarifying the priorities can get the results you want. Reminding your managers and employees of how those sunglasses fit into the big picture is a way of reminding them of their priorities.

Those of us who, despite our worst intentions, do occasionally find the courage to say "no" are proud to report that the world doesn't end as a result of using the N-word. Try it next time someone wants you to do something that represents a big detour in your personal route from point A to point B. When you say "no," you'll be amazed how many things people can do for themselves, just because they don't have you to do it for them.

It's probably perfectly clear at this point, but I will confess right here that I'm a workaholic. There's a lot made of the notion that a workaholic misses out on the rest of life, and when I suggest that you do more than you're asked to do in the workplace, I'm not trying to suggest that you become a workaholic, too. There's a difference between being a willing team player and letting yourself be taken advantage of. Your own inner voice will tell you when you've crossed that line. As for me, I don't think I miss anything in life by working as I do. It's my education, my means of growth, my vocation. My work rewards me in more ways than I can count, and it does the same thing for all of us who love what we do. Even when I'm stressed out and fighting to cope, I still don't think of work as being onerous. It's exciting and it's a challenge. Even being at the end of my rope is a part of the high for me—and I know exactly what the end of a rope looks like.

At the 1992 Republican Convention in Houston, I gave a few press interviews. One journalist who approached me mentioned that as she left the press room for our appointment, someone in the office said, "Oh, Georgette Mosbacher. She only came to this convention to promote her new products."

I looked straight at this woman, and then nodded at the brand-new canvas tote bag, blazoned with a corporate logo and full of all kinds of corporate giveaways, that stood at her feet.

"Where did you get that bag?" I asked her.

"Oh," she said. "Someone was giving them out at a party."

"Okay," I answered. "So why is it that a Fortune 500 company can give an expensive promotional party complete with gifts at a national political convention, and no one gives it a second thought—but people feel perfectly justified in taking a shot at me over the same issue? As it happens," I went on, "my product isn't out of research and development yet. I don't have samples to give out. But if the line were ready, you'd better believe that people would be walking out of here with samples of it."

The journalist sat back in her chair. "Of course," she said. "You're absolutely right."

A male CEO giving a corporate party at a political event would be seen as smart for taking advantage of the opportunity to promote his business interests. Yet I was labeled an opportunist on that score—when I hadn't even done the deed. But I was a woman. My company was small and new. My product happened to be cosmetics. Somehow all this meant that I wasn't as *serious* as the man with the big company that sells chocolate chip cookies. I wasn't as *solid* as the man who runs the fast-food chain.

The truth is, any executive who hosted a corporate party and *didn't* take advantage of the opportunity would probably be regarded as someone who didn't know his job.

Again and again, life isn't fair. Just as you, a woman, may be asked to take on all those little things—and sometimes more than anyone could handle—when you *do* take the bigger step, when you *do* go that extra mile, when you *do* start to become visible, you may find yourself labeled an opportunist, a social climber, a super-feline. Those are the breaks.

All these things will change someday, but in the meantime, there are rules you must play by. There are also rules you can break, and you may discover it's in your best interest to break more than one of them. But you need to know just what rules you're breaking. Beyond maintaining your integrity, which is always uppermost, you need to calculate your risks.

THE REAL-WORLD CODE OF ETHICS

I believe it's important to be realistic about what happens when men and women are together. There are differences between men and women, there will always be differences between them, and for the most part, I would prefer to celebrate those differences than to make them a point of contention or to pretend they're not there.

Again, I happen to be a woman who *likes* having doors opened and chairs pulled out for me. I *like* a man to stand up when I enter the room, and I don't see any conflict in liking to be treated as a woman and wanting to be taken seriously for my business acumen. I set up my own criteria and definition of equality, of what's important to me. My choices may not be the same as yours, but each of us has to make judgment calls about what kinds of behavior seem appropriate to us.

We've come a long way from etiquette books of the 1950s to Judith Martin's "Miss Manners," but like Miss Martin, I believe good manners still have to do with making the other person feel good about him- or herself. Good manners have little to do with questions of equality. Equality lies in what we accomplish in the real world; it doesn't lie in whether the man does or does not open the door for you.

Nor does equality mean that harmless flirtation has to go the way of the dodo bird. It's okay to have a flirtatious personality in the workplace, so long as it's not getting in the way of your real job. If you find it's working against you, maybe you'd better take another look at your priorities. By the same token, if you find that getting angry over every perceived slight and sexual innuendo is getting in your way, maybe you need to consider the possibility that you're being thin-skinned.

I've stated my philosophy about achieving goals: Do whatever it takes to get what you want, as long as it isn't illegal or immoral. Taking advantage of the natural fireworks that go off between men and women is neither illegal nor immoral. I draw my own line on where flirtation stops and harassment begins. I'll let a man flirt with me, but I won't let him pinch my derriere.

The difference between the former and the latter is the difference between operating within acceptable limits and going beyond them. They are the same boundaries that lie between sexuality in its positive form and sexual harassment. The primary issue in sexual harassment is power. The man who uses his superior strength and size to overcome you is taking advantage of his physical power. That's assault. The supervisor who humiliates or pressures you for sexual favors is taking advantage of his professional power. That's sexual harassment.

If it does *not* revolve around a power play, if it's not deliberately offensive or humiliating, good-natured banter between individuals of the opposite sex is not sexual harassment. If all those sparks between the sexes completely disappear from the workplace, my guess is that the office will turn into a rather boring place to be.

Unfortunately, sexual harassment and abuse do occur in the workplace, and it's a tragedy for women in more ways than one. It's a disgrace that it still occurs, and any woman with a legitimate case of harassment should do whatever she can to nail the man who's guilty of it. But we're walking a fine line right now. When you accept advice from anybody on this score, you need to understand what that person's or that group's agenda is. Don't let yourself be Joan of Arc for anyone whose agenda isn't yours. Don't be used by men *or* women in this situation.

If you're having to deal with a situation that's borderline harassment, you might choose simply to keep your accoster at bay long enough to find another job. Or you might keep a little black book of your own in which you make a note each time you have to fend off an advance. It might start with your saying to the offender, "Look, I want to know just what's at stake here. Are you telling me that if I go out with you, I'll get that new assignment or that promotion? I'm here to do a good job and to move forward in my career, and I need to know what it's going to take to advance."

Chances are, once you confront a bully—and that's just what a man using his power in this way is—he'll back off. If he doesn't, you may be able to take things a step further without resorting to a lawsuit if there's a woman on the management team you feel you can speak to, or someone you trust in the personnel department. Take that black book with you. Make it clear that you like your job and want to stay with the company, but that you cannot do your job under the present circumstances. A corporation that values both your work and your discretion may see that it's to their advantage to move you into a position that's more comfortable for you.

Whether you hold the line, bail out, or bring suit, you must base your decision on your own sense of self-esteem and your own priorities. I resent any women's group that tries to make us feel guilty about making our own choices in these matters—so long as we're willing to accept the consequences of those choices.

I believe that if you live by Feminine Force, you always accept the consequences of your own actions. Making choices and taking the consequences for them is what liberation is all about. Real liberation is being able to make a decision that's best for you, without having a load of guilt piled on because you didn't make that decision somebody else's way.

Learn to draw a fine line between the kind of flirting that's simply fun, and behavior that threatens your sense of self and your ability to do your job. The line stops at the edge of your comfort zone. The line also stops at your colleagues' comfort zone: If your behavior consistently distracts your co-workers from the job at hand, you're breaking an important business rule.

Short of that, there is absolutely nothing wrong with dressing like a woman and acting like a woman in the workplace.

THE OFFICE ROMANCE

What happens if a professional relationship with a man in your office turns into a genuine romance?

There are consequences.

I was already involved with George Barrie when I moved from being one of several film production administrators at Brut Productions into Fabergé, and eventually into a position as head of a licensing division. As I moved from employee to employee-and-significant-other and eventually to employee-and-wife, the change in my personal status definitely had an impact on my ability to achieve my professional goals. So here is the answer to a very loudly unasked question: Does being romantically involved with the boss give a female manager an inside edge?

Short answer: It's a double-edged sword.

Long answer: In my experience, being romantically involved with the boss means you have to be even *more* careful politically and even *better* at what you do if you want to survive with your career and your reputation intact.

I'm not against flirting, even when it gets serious. Who knows? The handsome man in the next office may be your next husband. Strong couples have shared values and interests, so if you're committed to your field, why wouldn't you attract and be attracted to someone else with similar values and goals? A romantic alliance of this type is only natural.

But it's going to make life a lot more complicated if you get involved in an office romance. Quite apart from my own personal experience, I have mixed feelings about getting romantically involved with the boss.

It really tests your ability to determine and maintain your sense of equality and independence. Your job could be at stake if you call it wrong. It's something you need to think hard about, but it's not cut and dried. You live in the real world, and not a textbook example of it. Anyone who tells you this *is* a cut-and-dried issue is either dreaming or was never lucky enough—or unlucky enough—to fall for the guy over in the marketing department.

There's a price to be paid—make no mistake about that. No matter who you get involved with or who you flirt with, people are going to know. And in most instances it will make achieving your professional goals more difficult. If you find yourself in this situation, be realistic about the consequences, accept them, make your choice based on them, and plan accordingly.

A rare few corporations actually see such alliances as beneficial, and may even subtly encourage them. In smaller, more entrepreneurial firms, a romantic alliance with the boss definitely *can* boost your career. In my experience, however, most companies—especially the big corporations—frown upon office relationships and marriages, and may even ask one partner to leave.

The office romance is a situation in which you must become hyper-aware of the rules, especially the unspoken ones, of your particular organization. The question you want to ask yourself continually is, "Am I making other people uncomfortable?" If you're going to flirt, pick your times and places carefully. A little banter at the water cooler is fine. Flirting at the board meeting is definitely *not* fine. The water cooler and places like it are marginal areas, unimportant to the business at large. A corporate board room, on the other hand, is clearly at the apex of corporate culture. When your personal life and your professional life mix or threaten to mix, the message you want to give to others is of extreme decorum and respect for the institution and its rules. To bring your romance into the board room is not only breaking the rules, it's flouting them. While it's true that it's almost impossible to keep people from guessing that something's afoot when you start dating a superior or co-worker, you don't want every corporate V.P. in the country to know what you're up to if you can help it. If it's possible to disguise your relationship at work, do so. Just as you don't want to be known as the one who refused to make coffee instead of the one who dashes off those perfect market analyses in record time, you don't want to be known as the marketing manager who's going out with the COO instead of the marketing manager whose before-tax profits are the fastest-growing in the company.

If your romantic interest is a superior, it is inevitable that people will try to undermine your professional success by saying that you earned your promotion or success in private. I hate to say it again, but your best and perhaps only recourse is to work harder, toe the line more assiduously, and be more enthusiastic about your job than the next person. There's nothing you can do about the kinds of envy you're going to be confronted with except to be irreproachable in every aspect of your work. Some people will notice, and will not only stick up for you when you're being gossiped about, but will become your advocates in situations that count. You can't do anything about the gossip, and you'll have to accept it.

Have confidence. Just don't get so cocky that you start making dumb mistakes.

Many companies have stories about the secretary who got involved with her boss and suddenly started showing up at high-level meetings. Side-stepping corporate channels in this way benefits no one. It will eventually get your boss into trouble, and that's going to get you into trouble. There's breaking the rules, and then there's *breaking the rules*. Pay attention to your company's conventions and hierarchies. If you're breaking some rules in your corporation, make sure of two things:

One, that your contribution to the business at hand is up to the mark of others at your level of advancement. You must be very honest about this: fooling yourself will hurt no one but you.

And two, don't start throwing your weight around. Don't play a bigger role in the company before you've obtained the title or promotion appropriate to that role. People may grumble about your new position, but your contribution to the business will be officially sanctioned, and it will be a whole lot easier for people to deal with you. Staying within the bounds of your job description shows that you still respect the rules that the whole team plays by.

When I was involved with George Barrie at Fabergé, I absolutely toed the line. I made sure I didn't walk into his office when other people were in it. I was also very careful not to exert myself outside of my clearly defined territory—territory defined by my job description. That doesn't mean I didn't advance my career goals with him whenever I could. Sure, other people were well aware that I had a personal relationship with G.B. and assumed I got favored status because of it. I understood that, but I was not going to allow jealousy or pettiness to rule my life. If you're getting attention from the boss, use it to your best advantage. If you can get your projects approved and get promoted faster because you're getting attention from the boss, go for it. Again, as long as you behave in a way that's appropriate and respectful of the institution you're working for, jealousy is the other guy's problem.

People sometimes did say things to my face like "You just got that project approved because you're involved with the boss." I ignored the accusation, but I also worked the long hours it took to ensure my projects would succeed. I came in earlier in the morning and left later at night than the next person.

All my advice about getting involved with the boss can be summed up in three sentences.

If he's married, he's out of bounds.

If he's not, go for it.

Just manage it well.

If a real chance at happiness presents himself in the office upstairs, don't let that chance slip away. Do whatever it takes, so long as it's not immoral, to make your dream a reality. Just understand what the reality of the situation is to begin with, and be ready to accept the consequences of your actions—because there will be consequences. If you're a responsible, caring, and practical human being who understands that your future is in your own hands, and if you're very, very sure that this relationship is your heart's desire, then go after it. With your eyes wide open.

CASTING YOUR NET

A short time after *Backlash* was published, I read an article about it in *Forbes* written by staff writer Gretchen Morgenson. Morgenson shared my views exactly: "The women Faludi describes react to backlash stimuli like so many marionettes on strings. To the millions of spirited, accomplished females in this country, this is deeply insulting. Only mindless bimbos can be maneuvered the way women in Faludi's world seem to be. How many women do you know who would retreat, sob-

bing, into the kitchen because of something they read in a magazine?"*
The piece so perfectly expressed my own thinking that I wrote a letter
to the editor about it, which was published in a later issue. Soon after,
I needed some help on a speech and decided Gretchen Morgenson was
just the person to help me. So I called her cold. We made a date to get
together, and instantly hit it off. Now we're friends. We not only exchange ideas, but information and advice about business, too.

My friendship with Gretchen Morgenson doesn't simply enrich my
personal life. My relationship with her and with other women in business, politics, and the media can't be separated from my career and
vocational interests. Paying attention to details and keeping your eye
on the ball at work should never keep you from making the broader
contacts you'll want and need to accomplish your most important
goals.

There is nothing to prevent you from calling people cold when you
share a common interest. I lunch regularly with friends in many fields.
I met Sonya Friedman of the CNN show *Sonya Live* when I was doing
the show, and we seemed to have so much in common that we began to
have lunch regularly. Sherry Baker, the CEO of Swakorsky Jewelry, is
another woman I admire greatly and try to keep in touch with regularly. I met Pat Harrison of the National Women's Economic Alliance
when she was hosting the inaugural salute to women business owners
soon after I came to Washington in 1988, and she has since become not
only an important and enlightening business contact, but a dear friend.

At a time when I was struggling with the "Georgette Factor" in
Washington, Pat was a blessing. She appreciated my straightforward-
ness. She saw right through the press whirlwind, and appreciated my
pride in my working-class background and my passion for enjoying all
kinds of people. Our friendship developed fast partly because we had
a lot in common and partly because Washington is, as Pat puts it, so
intense. I now sit on the board of governors of the National Women's
Economic Alliance, which acts as a resource and helps to place qualified women on corporate boards. An alliance with a professional
woman who sees the world the way you do is invaluably rich.

I enjoy keeping in touch with the women—and the men—for whom
I have high regard, and I depend on those alliances. When I need a

* *K*, March 16, 1992, pp. 152–53.

contact, a recommendation, or even a piece of advice, it's great to be able to call one of them up. These contacts help me expand my horizons and learn more about the world. Some of the things I've learned from them have helped shape my own personal goals.

The recommendations I get from these sources are sterling, the advice is golden, and I reciprocate in spades. The friends I make this way know that if they are ever looking for a consultant, employee, or reliable vendor they can always call me, too. The exchange is useful, supportive, and stimulating. It's also fun. Seeing what other women are up to and the challenges they've met in their own lives can be genuinely inspiring. It's one of the more powerful ways you can build your own Feminine Force.

Women need to network more. We're used to nurturing children and husbands. We need to nurture *each other* more.

Sure, you can network with women you meet through business, mutual friends, churches and synagogues, organizations and advocacy groups. But you can also seek people out whom you haven't yet met but would like to make part of your life. That's what networking is really all about. Maybe there's someone featured in the office newsletter you'd like to meet. Maybe the principal of your son's school is an activist in an area you'd like to be involved in. It doesn't matter that you've spoken no more than two words to him or never laid eyes on her at all. If you read about someone in your community or in your field who interests you, and you feel you have something to offer that person in return, by all means get on the phone and call him or her.

Asking for advice or help is an ideal calling card. People just love to be of service to others. It helps us all to feel we're making a difference, and when someone seeks us out for counsel, it's a wonderfully affirming form of acknowledgment. Simply asking for advice also respects the other person's professional or personal constraints. If she can offer actual help on top of the advice, she will, without feeling pressured.

Networking helps you in a lot of ways; you end up with a friend, you end up with a business contact, you end up with a resource. It's a wonderful way to build your power base, and to help other women build theirs.

Don't ignore volunteer and charity boards as powerful sources of contacts, either. That's often where women meet the CEOs of the companies they become associated with. What you accomplish working in the "non-profit sector" can tell a businesswoman or man an awful lot about how well you'd function on a corporate board. Julia Walsh serves on the board of Pitney Bowes as a direct result of working with the chairman of Pitney Bowes on a charity event.

As Jennifer Balbier says, "Use every contact, even if you don't think it will work out. If you're looking for a job or starting a new business, no matter how bad you feel, now is not the time to stick your head in the sand. You've got to call everyone and network yourself to death!"

In fact, networking is how Jennifer met me. She had known another consultant in her field for a number of years, but she had never worked with her. She knew her only casually, but when it was time to develop the color line at La Prairie, this woman recommended Jennifer for the job, and I was immediately impressed. That casual contact led to a strong business relationship between Jennifer and me that continues to this day.

Too many women neglect to network. Too many of us won't take the initiative in getting to know particular people in our fields who interest us. Get to know women you admire in your field (men, too). If you admire someone, call her up and ask for her advice and help. Even the busiest person will often give you a few minutes of professional advice by appointment or by letter, and you end up not only with the advice but also with a new business contact.

If you're feeling really intrepid, why not invite that person to dinner? Have someone who knows her make an introduction for you. Or, write a letter of admiration for what she's accomplished. I've done it with great success.

There are techniques for doing this. Several years ago I became interested in getting to know Linda Wachner, because aside from Katharine Graham of *The Washington Post*, who was born to the role, Wachner was the only woman CEO of a Fortune 500 company. Wachner's company is Warnaco, the clothing conglomerate known for its lingerie line. As it happened, the head of a major New York department store was coming to dinner at our house. I suspected this was a contact Wachner would be interested in making—or in strengthening, if they'd already met. So I called her up and invited her over. She graciously accepted. Linda was very comfortable: she and the department store magnate had lots to discuss. And on the basis of that evening, Linda and I began a new friendship.

I know of a screenwriter who hosts a cash bar cocktail hour every month or so at a New York professional club. All she does is get people together, some of whom she doesn't know very well, but they're always happy to be invited—and delighted that someone is taking the initiative. Many friendships have been made and creative partnerships formed at those parties.

Social life is social life—the rules aren't a whole lot different wherever you live. As long as you share a context with the person you're interested in, the same rules are going to apply in your living room as apply in any penthouse, club, or corporate dining room in America. Make a point of reaching out to the people in your community with whom you share a common interest. You will benefit, and you'll brighten your guests' lives, too.

As more and more women have entered the corporate and political arena and kicked in the "glass ceiling" so much has been made of, too many of us have decided to play at the man's game instead of playing the man's game the woman's way.

Linda Wachner has said, "If women keep focused on facts, they have the edge over men: their flexibility. As men grow older, they grow more rigid. As women grow older, they become more flexible. Young women are frightened; they don't have the clear role definition that men have from childhood. But women are able to roll more with the punches, and because of their greater flexibility, they can breathe fresh air into a stodgy environment. If they took advantage of that, they'd get a lot further."

I agree with her. There are women who want so desperately to be accepted in the corporate men's club that they get caught up in the same ego politics. They work, dress, and act like men, figuring that if they do, they'll be taken seriously.

I advise against that route. Don't hide under a man's clothing. Rely on your innate abilities and trust your instincts. The way I see it, in the workplace as well as anywhere else, the advantages of being powerful and feminine at the same time are far too great to give up!

Chapter 20

What About Love?

"What do we live for, if it is not to make life less diffi-cult for each other?"

—George Eliot

I always figured that there would be plenty of time to have kids. I have more than one friend who pushed the envelope right up to the age of forty-five to give birth to the child she loves more than anything in the world. So I calculated that I'd be able to do the same thing. A woman whose husband gives her a mirror with lettering that reads WHAT PART OF NO DON'T I UNDERSTAND? is a woman who figures she can wait until the last minute.

I figured wrong.

There was really no way I could have known that I would develop a benign tumor on my right ovary, one that grew so fast that a hysterectomy was the only medically advisable option available to me.

To be honest, even at the point when the die was cast (and I can count the years since this event occurred on one hand), I had made no specific plans to become a mother. Since Robert already had four grown children, I received no pressure from that quarter. And I hadn't pushed for it, either. Before we married, Robert told me that if it ever became important for me to have my own family, he would support me. Since I grew up as what therapists call a "parentified" child, in many ways I felt I'd already tasted that experience in my own way. But becoming a mother myself was a potential I always nurtured in a very special place in the back of my mind.

Yes, throughout my thirties I consciously and quite happily put my professional life first. And the truth of the matter is that I wasn't really ready to raise a child. I spent many of those years working through my troubled second marriage and its aftermath. Having already raised three kids while my single mother struggled to put dinner on the table, I knew exactly what kind of commitment was involved. I wasn't really ready for that even when I married Robert.

I didn't see how I could take proper care of a baby when I was traveling between two or three cities a week by air (sometimes more). Some choices you make in life aren't win-win situations. Sometimes you *can't* have your cake and eat it, too.

That surgery was a rude awakening. I'd lost the dream I was nurturing deep inside. Before I'd stopped to fully examine that choice or make it, it had been made for me. I felt robbed. As I stared that fact in the face, I finally felt the pain. Because I don't believe in sugar-coating the truth, I acknowledged quite consciously that I did want to have a child of my own. And that I would have to live with the consequences of my actions, with the pain of saying to myself, "Georgette, you'll never have that in your life now. You don't regret what you've accomplished, but the truth is, you put off making this choice too long. You let the clock run out."

I'm not one for regret, and now that it's all said and done, I don't look back. There's nothing I can do about it, so there's no point. You go on with your life, and you fulfill it in other ways.

And luckily—no, make that providentially—there is no limit to the number of ways you can fill your life with love.

I don't have children, but I have the best husband in the world, and he has children. And my strong connections with the family I was born into continue to endure and grow. The bonds I developed as a "parentified" oldest child haven't loosened.

Melody has three boys now, and George has one. And one of Melody's boys has baby boys of his own! And the traditions and the values that were handed down to me and my siblings continue to be handed down to the next generation. My nephews not only have a deep respect for their elders in the family, but they effortlessly express their affection for them.

Every Christmas, when I see my two little great-nephews toddle up to their great-great-grandmother and great-grandmother, I get a special sense of what being a family is all about. I see those women take turns holding and kissing them. I also witness moments after the older boys have misbehaved, when those women give them little scoldings and tell them they're disappointed in them. With that scolding, they always reassure the boys that they know they'll do better next time. Watching them, I get a feeling of déjà vu. When I was very young, I didn't always appreciate the fact that even as my mother criticized us in ways that pulled no punches, it was always constructive. Mother believed in sternly and clearly reprimanding us when we deserved it, but at the same time she always made it crystal clear that we could accomplish goals and master skills just by working and trying harder. She might have criticized us, but she never lost an opportunity to build up our self-esteem. Although we could always be better, we were always *good* to begin with.

Seeing my mother and *her* mother nurturing their great-grandchildren and great-great-grandchildren this way gives me a renewed appreciation for the way those women raised us. It gives me an extraordinary feeling of love and pride and wonder all together. And it's a joy seeing my brother and sister with their kids. It was a joy to watch my brother George read *The Little Prince* to his son Shaun when Shaun was small. It was a joy when one of my sister Melody's three sons grew up enough to say, "We may not be rich, but we're rich in love."

What I feel for my family is rich and rewarding. It doesn't matter that my nephews aren't my biological children. No one can ever convince me that this love is a lesser love because those children are not my own. No, it's not the same, but as far as I can see, it's a question of apples and oranges, not of lesser and greater.

Being at the center of a traditional nuclear family is a great vehicle for love—one of the best—but it's not a prerequisite for experiencing love in all its abundance and all its joy.

THE TWO-CAREER MARRIAGE

I'm often asked whether having a demanding career interferes with love.

I don't know anyone who's an expert on love. If anyone offers a degree program, I want to know about it. Maybe we're all experts. Maybe life as a woman makes you an expert. But then again, maybe life is one big continuing education course. I don't know about you, but I sure feel that I'm taking one.

When it comes to balancing love and careers, not many of the women I know feel like experts. Almost every successful career woman I know struggles with issues of balance. Creating our own identity and blazing our own trails takes time, heart, and space. It takes focus. It takes resolve, it takes guts, and it takes practice. Is there any space left over for love?

You already know the answer. Women (and some men, too) *innately* know the answer.

You bet there is.

It's true that when your path is already narrower than is comfortable, it's a challenge not to guard your flanks. It's a challenge not to sink into the feeling that among all your professional and family and personal obligations, there's just not enough of you to go around.

I don't have any pat answers about any of this. All I know is that you've got to start by being honest—with yourself and with those you love. If you've got a career and you want to have children, you're going to have to make those tough decisions about how long you're going to stay at home after your babies are born, what kind of child care you're going to get when the time comes, and all the rest. You're going to have to work it all out with your husband. There aren't any shortcuts that I know of. All I know is that you're going to have to be honest about what's important to each of you. If you love each other and are honest about the things that *are* important and the things that really are *not*, you'll be able to make the kinds of compromises you can live with.

We can fight hard to achieve the things we want and need in our careers, but if we don't fight for love, what are we doing any of it *for*?

It's true that when I'm asked how Robert feels about the fact that I have a demanding career, my first impulse is usually defensive. Almost invariably, my first impulse is to say what does it matter what Robert thinks? My professional life has nothing to do with him.

But that's not honest. Robert's feelings *do* matter to me: I love him.

Both of us believe that love means sharing every part of our lives. It's just that in our lives, sharing everything doesn't mean spending twenty-four hours a day in consort. Or even in the same city. That's one of the basic assumptions we started out with. We accept that we're not going to be together all the time. And we believe that we can be loving and intimate partners anyway.

In all honesty, my professional life isn't an issue that either of us ever put on the table. It was always a given. I was already working on acquiring my first company when Robert and I met. If he hadn't felt good about my professional life, I wouldn't have changed who I was just to please him. I couldn't be who I am without that feeling of independence. If Robert *had* objected, his feeling would have manifested itself in our marriage somehow, and then we would have had to deal with that feeling. Both of us would have to bring all of our tolerance, forgiveness, patience, thoughtfulness, and consideration to that issue. When you define love, it usually comes down to issues of character. If you don't aspire to give all of those things to your loved one in the first place (and none of us gets an A+ across the board, except maybe for effort), you'll find it very difficult to be loved and to love.

Somehow, my husband had to either resign himself to my professional life, or feel good about it. And, by the way, I have the same two choices when it comes to him.

The truth is, what we've chosen is probably a little of both.

At a certain point in our relationship, I just chose to assume that Robert accepts my work, and that from his point of view I am that much more interesting for it.

I certainly *feel* more interesting for it. My work suits me. It's a challenge to me, it keeps me vibrant, it keeps me alive, and it makes me independent. Quite honestly, I think that the notion that he is not totally responsible for you is very attractive to a man. It keeps the romance going.

Robert says, "It amazes me that so many men come up to me and say, 'How do you feel about Georgette being off in New York and getting all that press?' I get back to wondering whether these are men who feel they are diminished if someone close to them is getting more recognition or money than they are. It kind of reminds me of that seventies pop psychology book, *I'm OK—You're OK*. But the trouble here is, what these guys are saying is 'If I'm okay, then you couldn't possibly be okay. And if you're okay, that means that I'm not.' "

This is a man who greatly appreciates Feminine Force. He is not the only one. Practice it and see whom *you* attract.

Then there are all those friends of mine who are always telling me, "Your husband's gotta come first. How do you do that? How does he live in one place and you in the other?"

And I say, "We make it work."

Making it work is actually very romantic. We look forward to seeing each other because when we do, we have a lot to tell each other. What I'm doing is as exciting to Robert as what he's doing is to me. We are always both learning from each other. It's a constant growing process. As the writer Barbara Amiel said in *Chatelaine* magazine, "Power is an aphrodisiac because it protects and offers a shield from the world. It envelops a woman and plays to her most basic instinct of vulnerability. . . . Power is sexy, not simply in its own right, but because it inspires self-confidence in its owner and a shiver of subservience on the part of those who approach it."

I don't know about that "shiver of subservience," but I agree that power is sexy, and I think that a powerful man who is also secure is going to see a powerful *woman* as sexy, too. It is just as great a challenge for a man to "catch" a powerful woman as it is for a woman to "catch" a powerful man. And once you've caught each other, life tends to get even more interesting.

There are women—and men, too—who prefer routine. They prefer to know exactly where they will be at every moment of every week, and they prefer to know that each week is identical to the one that came before. It's a lifestyle that has a very definite appeal. You always know what's expected of you, and how to be safe. And of course part of feeling loved is feeling safe. But the responsibilities of my life are the very things that excite me and make me feel most alive and turn life into an adventure.

That isn't to say that having professional commitments as Robert and I have doesn't impact on the romantic relationship. There are always scheduling conflicts and compromises. The limitations of our day-to-day realities do sometimes threaten to hem in love. And although both of us compromise to avoid this, I probably compromise more often than Robert does.

This, quite frankly, is because *both* of us are still working through what we believe the role of a wife should be—what parts of the traditional wifely role he can do without, and what parts he can't. What parts I can do, and what parts I can't.

When Robert has a business dinner at the house, I organize it. While I'm on the road developing my product, part of me is usually worrying about those arrangements. *And* whether he has enough shirts in the drawer, and whether they've been starched and folded the way he likes them, and whether his closet is organized.

Is all that part of love? Yes, the way I define it, it is.

Could I insist that Robert take responsibility for those things?

Yes, and he would probably still come to me and say, "What was I supposed to do again?" And I'd *still* be on the plane worrying about him when I should be doing my paperwork.

So I don't pigeonhole what it means to be a wife, either. I don't make hard-and-fast rules about it. It's a deal I've cut with myself, and I'm happy with it. Sure, there's a lot of rhetoric out there that offers a lot of compelling reasons that say Robert's the one who should be worrying about whether his socks have been washed, not me. And in theory, I more or less agree.

But there's theory, there is reality, and then there are my feelings. I know full well that part of loving a man like Robert—that is, a man of a certain generation, a man of stature who respects me and is interesting and exciting and who brings new dimensions to my life—lies in honoring and working with the traditional part of him. And for Robert, part of loving a woman like me—from a different generation and seriously committed to a career—lies in honoring and working with the *un*traditional part of *me*. These are just the prevailing winds of our relationship. We both have to work through them, and we're both intrigued with them, in no small part because there is also a very untraditional part of Robert and a very traditional part of me. And the process of figuring it all out just makes love that much more interesting.

Robert has come a long way in understanding that I can't always be there with him, even when it would be much more convenient and much more fun if I were. He knows he'll have to attend certain social events by himself, and he's handling that. He's even come to the point where he'll say it is "just fine" when I accept an invitation addressed to the two of us, and attend by myself when he can't go. He doesn't want to feel pressured to do something inconvenient, and I don't either.

He hasn't come to the point where he'll clean the house or worry about his socks, and I can live with that. But for the most part, he has gracefully accommodated himself to the complications of our social schedule. Some men might not. Some might like washing socks better than going solo to social events. It all depends on the man.

Robert has gone so far as to claim that when I went alone to dinner at the White House, the President actually preferred it.

"When I'd accuse the President of that," Robert says, "he'd just laugh and say, 'Darn right I prefer it that way.' "

Do I believe this? Of course not. But I'm grateful for that kind of acceptance. And I love Robert's pleasure in the joke.

There's another story Robert tells about a flight he took a few years back, when a good-looking stewardess came up to him and said, "Aren't you Secretary Mosbacher?"

"Yes I am," he said proudly, puffing right up and getting ready for a lovely conversation.

"Oh, then you must be Georgette's husband!" she cried.

The way Robert remembers it, he could hardly talk, he was so deflated.

A simple "That's right" is all he could manage. Yet Robert loves to tell this story, and it touches me that he tells it so proudly.

A lot of minor frictions in a marriage have nothing to do with the quality of love or the kind of respect you have for each other. Some are simply products of early conditioning. For instance, when my husband opens up the Sunday *New York Times*, he hands me the Arts and Leisure and Travel sections, and drops not only the Business but also the Week in Review sections in his own lap.

I had become CEO of my *second* company by the time I suddenly woke up one morning and said to myself, "Why? Why are those parts of the paper his?" And it was only then that I said to him, "Which one do you want first? I'll take the Week in Review and you take Business, or vice versa, but you can't have both sections on your lap this morning because you can't read both of them at the same time."

Now, despite the fact that he is conservative and tough-minded and Southern, Robert is also one of the more egalitarian men around. We try not to be terribly judgmental about other people's choices. I know that Robert's children have made a big impact on him this way. He has three daughters and a son, all have taken different paths, and he tries to be loving and supportive to each of them. I think the growth this has involved has also helped in his attitude toward me.

Nonetheless, like so many other men, Robert used to grumble when he came home and couldn't find *Forbes* and *Fortune*—magazines I happen to subscribe to in my name.

I'd tell him, "Guess what, they're on my dressing table."

And then he'd be cross because he had to go to my dressing table to get them!

One day I finally asked Robert point-blank, "Why don't you sub-scribe to these magazines at the office if you want them so badly?"

I got no response.

So I gathered up all those little subscription cards that are always falling on the floor and subscribed to the whole lot in Robert's name. Now they all go to his office with his name on them, and the ones that come home are mine.

Despite minor adjustments like these, the high value each of us places on our careers is part of the bedrock of our marriage. So is the fact that both of us are hard-driving. Although we're both very demon-strative and affectionate, we both like things the way we like them, and without any sugar coating. We don't always agree on how things should be. Robert is the nicest, sweetest guy in the world until you go too far with him. People make the mistake of seeing that charismatic, dynamic smile and charming personality and thinking he's easy. But Robert puts a high price on integrity. Don't cross that line with him. He's kind and he's fair, but don't cross him. Don't corner him. He's a formidable adversary, and that charm can turn to solid ice.

Me, I'm direct all the time. I don't say something unless I mean it. And when I say it, I *mean* it.

When our wills and personal styles clash, Robert describes it as "fussing with each other," and he adds, somewhat proudly I think, that when we fuss with each other the result can be real fireworks. But neither of us really minds, because directness and clarity are another value we share.

As Robert observes, "It's fun to tease and have fun, but when you're making a life together, you like to know where a person stands."

That doesn't mean he doesn't occasionally refer to my directness as "going into all sorts of gyrations." But deep down we're as loving and as supportive of each other's goals as we are hard-driving individually.

And one of the advantages of being a two-entrepreneur couple is that we often share work rhythms. Sure, each of us has to work fifteen or twenty days in a row. But after that, we can usually fit in one or two days of relaxation. Robert loves to sail, and we occasionally take a weekend and sail in the Bahamas. He even taught me how to sail, which is another way we expand each other's horizons.

If you ask him whether I was a good sailing student, he'll say, "Do you mean, did she listen?"

And the truth is that I listened for a while, and then I said, "I'm not going to be a great sailor, you go on ahead." And then I went on as a passenger and did my own thing.

I must admit that even when we're sneaking four days in the Bahamas between Christmas and New Year's, we still both suffer from a compulsion to call the office. Robert claims he actually manages to hide it better, because he's been practicing longer. The Bahamas present non-stop executives with a true challenge, because cellular phones don't work offshore there. You have to find a port to find a phone. That doesn't mean that we still don't take turns getting "freaked," as my husband so delicately puts it, about the fact that there's no way to call the office. One of us gets the other going, and then of course we have to go ashore and spend an hour or two sharing a phone back and forth.

This past vacation, we'd been on the boat about three days and we both had gotten desperate for a phone. We heard there was a phone on a small island close by. Many of the islands, of course, are deserted.

A squall came up as we headed in, and it started pouring rain just about the time we cast anchor. There was thunder and lightning. Both of us quickly got soaked through our parkas. Were we going to run for cover? No way! We were determined to FIND THAT PHONE. It was literally just a booth, standing more or less by itself. Now, at times like this we never fail to have the same argument when we reach a phone. That is, *whose* office are we going to call *first*? It has become almost a ritual. Robert's office has a more sophisticated system that is able to switch us forward to my office, so we called his first. I paced back and forth outside as I waited for him to complete his business. It was pouring rain, my clothes were clinging to my body, but all I could think of was getting my turn on the phone. It was the first time in my life I wasn't intimidated by thunder and lightning!

It was a slightly different story when we had to find a fax machine. In the islands, people often run their businesses out of their houses. When we located the one and only fax machine for miles around, it was in a private home. We were met at the door by a seven-year-old girl.

"Good afternoon, miss," my courtly husband said, "we'd like to send some faxes."

The child at the door just stared. We knew we didn't have the wrong place—we could actually see the machine back in a corner, with a list of fees posted on the wall.

"We'd very much like to use your fax machine," my husband repeated.

"Lady," the child said, staring at me and ignoring Robert, "I *like* that red lipstick! Where'd you get that red lipstick?"

I smiled at her, and she smiled back.

It was a triumphant moment. "Now, Robert!" I said. "*Whose* business is more important?"

That time, I got to use the fax machine first. And the little girl got herself a red lipstick.

Robert and I have arguments like these regularly, and although they're not *always* this lighthearted, the very fact that we have them demonstrates how deeply we understand each other.

On the rare quiet afternoon or evening when Robert sits down to watch a football game, he has no compulsion to call the office. He forgets it ever existed. He forgets *I* ever existed.

And you know what? I love it!

I sit him down, get him his beer, and then I have *four hours* all to myself.

Overtime? Even better. An extra half hour at least.

Sometimes, Robert is dismayed that I'll take a Saturday or Sunday afternoon as an opportunity to work, while he's watching a game. "You've got to slow down and smell the roses," he says.

"Oh yeah, I know," I'll say impatiently.

Robert says he knows it's not going to be easy, but he's going to teach me.

I'll keep you posted.

The truth is, *both* of our schedules are incredibly hectic, and scheduling is an ongoing chore in our lives. We both constantly entertain and travel for business as well as for personal reasons. And then there are speeches, conferences, policy dinners, not to mention our two large and beloved families. On top of all that, there's the commute. My company has to be based in New York because that's where the cosmetics industry is. And Robert's company has to be based in Houston, because that's where the oil business is.

At first, the two of us went through a period of telling each other that it wasn't *fair* that I had to be so far away in New York, and it wasn't *fair* that he had to be so far away in Houston—and we let ourselves get frustrated and unhappy over the time we spent apart. We'd take turns complaining that one of us wasn't sacrificing as much as the other for the sake of being together. But what's fair? We'd both made choices and commitments that made a two-career, two-city marriage a fact of life. Neither of us was prepared to say okay, your job is more important than my job, so I'll make the change and I'll make the sacrifices. And there is no way to make a perfectly equal division of time.

Once we acknowledged that "fairness" wasn't an issue, we accepted the reality for what it was and worked within it. We've come to respect the practical demands of the situation, and each other's responsibilities and commitments, and we find ways to make it all work without the marriage suffering, or the businesses suffering.

Now we calendar six months in advance, and we always include a vacation in there somewhere. We have a pact to spend uninterrupted time together, but we've found that actually writing in our books makes it a lot easier to say, "No, I can't do that, I've already got another appointment." We both know better than to wait for opportunities to come knocking. We know they won't.

In fact, Robert and I spend so much time scheduling that we've actually made it into an enjoyable ritual. Some people may go to brunch together on Sunday, but our version of spending a pleasant Sunday morning together is to bring our calendars to breakfast and go through our dates together.

I have a file in my briefcase that says "R.M." on it. During the course of the week, as invitations, speaking engagements, or other requests that can wait till the weekend come in, I throw them into that file. I also throw in little reminders and questions I've written to myself about scheduling. Robert has his own file, and over breakfast we spend time with those files and our calendars and go through it all together.

Sometimes we discover we're going to be in the same city at the same time for different reasons. We accept those invitations whenever possible! And one Sunday morning we even discovered that we'd each been asked to speak at the same convention and had both accepted the invitation, without even knowing the other one was going to be there! It turned out that we got to have dinner together.

We found this system through trial and error. You'll find your own system through your own process of trying out different methods that address your specific needs. The point is to accept this as an ongoing process, to face it as an ongoing challenge, and figure out how to turn ordinary chores into something special and pleasing for the two of you. It sounds corny, but the basic principle here is, acknowledge what's actually going on in your everyday lives, and then figure out ways to find pleasure in the details and small moments.

To keep love alive, you also have to be very clear about what you are going to do on your own, and what you are going to do together.

In the continuing education called marriage, I've found that when it is really important for your partner to be with you, you have to say so. And when it isn't crucial, you have to say that, too—even though you'd rather he was there. Be very careful about making clear distinctions between what is important and what is not, because the one thing you cannot afford to do in a two-career marriage is cry wolf. It's a fast way to lose your credibility. And if there's one thing I've learned about love, it is that your credibility has to be iron-clad. Your word is your bond, and it has to be as sacrosanct as your commitment.

When your partner says "I need you there," even when being there is worse than inconvenient, you must move heaven and earth to do it.

What if you live in two different cities the way we do? What we've learned is to share our experiences over the telephone. It's a form of continuing communication that lets us enjoy our separate experiences vicariously. The pleasant surprise is that in telling your stories, you end up enjoying the experience twice.

There are psychologists who say that you can't have true intimacy in a long-distance relationship. But based on my own experience, I have to disagree. You don't need proximity with your husband twenty-four hours a day, seven days a week, to have a strong, intimate relationship. I believe it's the quality and not the quantity of the time you spend together that counts. Because I am my own person with responsibilities and goals apart from my marital relationship, I deal with those responsibilities when we are not together. That means that when we are together, my focus is on "us" and on him specifically, and probably disproportionately. In fact, I think the time we spend apart helps our relationship because it allows me to give the relationship such an undivided focus when we are together.

I love my husband no matter where I am. Love doesn't require daily proximity to be nurtured. There can be intimacy in communication over the telephone. Sure, it's different from the intimacy you get when you're next to someone, holding him or touching him. It's also different from the intimacy that comes just from knowing he's in the same room. But Robert's still present with me no matter where I am. And to make him even more present, wherever I go—whether it's New York or a friend's house or a hotel room—I always carry a travel-sized picture of him in a little silver frame.

WHERE DOES YOUR MARRIAGE END AND YOU BEGIN?

It's an understatement to say that a big part of the world still hasn't caught up to the reality that a woman remains an individual even when she marries. That lag makes itself known in all sorts of ways—large and small—in your social life together.

It surprised me to discover that whether or not you take your husband's name is a topic that can still stir up articles in newspapers. To many of us that became a tame subject a long time ago. Evidently it remains an issue. The more we persist in dealing with such issues, however, the more quickly the rest of the world will catch up.

From a practical point of view, I think it's very difficult to take your husband's last name professionally, if you've already become known professionally under your original name. It's been done, of course: the perfect example of that is Roseanne Barr. She's become Roseanne Arnold quite effortlessly, almost without anyone really noticing or caring.

Roseanne had an easier time of it than some of us, because she had such a high profile that when she made the transition, it instantly ricocheted everywhere. She was able to let everyone know immediately, and her name change wasn't perceived as a big change. For those of us with a little less public exposure, it's not quite so easy. If you've made a name for yourself professionally, and recognition is important professionally, the logistics get more complicated. It's not just a simple matter of sending out change-of-address cards.

I use my husband's last name. When you take your first husband's name, and end up getting married three times, what else are you going to do? For those of us who have been divorced and remarried, this really may be the best alternative to an annoying and, in my opinion, rather unimportant problem. The truth is, if I had it to do all over again, I'd have kept my maiden name.

Unfortunately, while it may be necessary in business, society looks upon keeping your own last name with mixed emotions. It's traditional to take your husband's last name in this country, and traditions die hard. In most cases I think we should try to preserve our traditions. They're precious. This is a case where I think you can have it both ways. Some savvy women keep their professional name but use their husband's name whenever it's socially necessary, to appease tradition and make everyone else comfortable around them. Some of the most powerful and visible women I know use this ploy. I hear Carolyne Roehm introduced as Carolyne Roehm Kravis all the time. Barbara Taylor probably isn't a familiar name to you, but Barbara Taylor Bradford probably is.

Frankly, I never understood all the hoopla made over the fact that Mrs. Clinton chooses to go by Hillary Rodham Clinton—as if this were some new form of self-assertion. It's not. Women have been keeping their own names and adding their husband's in this fashion for generations.

Sometimes the name game does seem hard not to take personally. A writer I know is married to a wonderful man from a very traditional Mediterranean family. She has always gone by her maiden name. Nevertheless, after several years of marriage, whenever she receives a letter with her in-laws' return address on it, it invariably reads "Mrs. John Doe," and she gets very annoyed.

"You know, it's not 'Jane Smith Doe' or any version of a compromise," she says. "That would be fine with me. It's not even Mrs. Jane Doe. It's just my husband's name with a 'Mrs.' in front of it."

I advised my friend that one option was to send the letter back. If I had her concerns and feelings, I'd say, "There's no one of that name at this address!" But first I'd ask myself whether this issue was really worth having an argument about with his family, if they're really that rooted in that tradition. I doubt that it is. I still subscribe to the theory that sticks and stones can break your bones but names can never hurt you—or define who you are. If I were in this woman's shoes, I'd probably decide to think of "Mrs. John Doe" as my nickname. I mean, what else could it be? Let them call you King Kong. You know who you are.

There are other ways being an individual within a couple can have tricky social consequences. Robert may be glad that I'm willing to attend a social function without him when he can't go, but I'm not always sure that having a single woman show up when a couple was invited is something every hostess is prepared to deal with. As far as traditional protocol goes, some people just feel that having an extra woman at the table with an even number of seats skews the seating. So I don't force anyone to take me without Robert. If he can't attend with me, I always give the host or hostess a way out.

Robert and I actually have to coordinate our RSVP system between two offices. Given our busy schedules, things could easily fall through the cracks, and we could lose track of where each of us is supposed to be next week or next month. But we try to accustom our friends to the idea that anyone who invites us somewhere as a couple runs the risk of getting only one of us.

I'm not the only one to use this method. Just recently I invited a newspaper publisher and his wife, who uses her own name, to dinner. It was made very clear to me that her husband could only respond for himself. He could not confirm her acceptance for her; she had her own secretary who confirmed her schedule. I was glad to hear it. I never argue with Feminine Force.

But you can, I believe, take the issue of separate identities to an extreme. When I did *The Joan Rivers Show*, an author who is the wife of a very famous television personality was also a guest. She was adamant that there should be no mention of the fact that she was married to her famous husband on her book jacket. I don't really understand that. If there's a way that being married can help you succeed in your career, I say *use it to your advantage*. If there's something about being married to *you* that can help your husband achieve *his* goals, then he should use that fact to *his* advantage.

Isn't that one of the perks of marriage—the possibility that it may nurture us in all kinds of ways? Isn't that part of the give-and-take?

SELF-LOVE

Robert's political life includes a lot of handshaking, a lot of small talk. I think that's great for him. But attending all those receptions and cocktail parties isn't always something I want to do. While we've worked out our methods and he accepts the fact that sometimes I can't be there, there are times when I could be there but prefer *not* to be. Despite the accommodations we've learned to make, sometimes we still fuss over these things. But really, he doesn't always need me at those gatherings. And when you routinely work twelve-hour days, seven days a week, you value any half hour of regenerating time you can get for yourself.

One of the drawbacks of wanting and trying to do it all is that people come to expect it of you—and no matter what kind of effort you put in, you can get called on the carpet for the one thing you don't do. I realize that, and try to remind myself of it whenever I start to feel guilty about one of those things.

One day I went to one of those cocktail parties, walked around chatting and being attentive and being "on"—and discovered myself resenting it. Finally I said to myself, "Georgette, why are you doing this? You don't even know where Robert *is* in this room."

So I decided to go home. I found my husband and said, "Robert, I want to be supportive of you, but I'm beat and I just don't have anything left in me to give right now. You'll have to manage on your own."

And guess what?

He did manage, and he managed not to be at all unhappy about it.

This led me to the conclusion that, for a woman, uttering the word "no" can be one of the most powerful acts of self-love in the universe—this one, or any other. It's the same in your personal life as it is in your career.

So how do you bring yourself to do it?
It's like the old joke about the best way to get to Carnegie Hall.
Practice, practice, practice.

My sister Melody adores her three sons and her husband of twenty years. She's gone to the office and worked every day for most of her marriage, and she's still a great wife and a great mother. The fullness and productivity of her life are remarkable. Yet, like many women, she thinks it's totally unremarkable.

Most women don't realize how remarkable they are. We tend to tear ourselves down instead of patting ourselves on the back. We tend to sell ourselves short.

Again and again I come back to this question. Why is it that I can take time to stop and pay attention to my dog, but I can't take time to stop for myself? Why do you and I have to get to the point where we feel sick or frightened or depressed before we'll stop and take care of ourselves? Why can't all of us do that routinely, as a habit? Can't we be kind to ourselves and give ourselves the benefit of the doubt, just as we do for the people we love, the people we merely like—and even for strangers?

It's an old saw that you have to love yourself before you can truly love another person, and although the martyr in each of us may take exception, I believe there's real truth in it. The more you feel like a whole and worthy person, the greater your capacity for love. If you feel that the best kind of love between men and women is a gift exchanged by equals, you have to believe you have room to give such gifts, room for such generosity. You have to have enough self-love to understand how valuable the gift of your love is. If you take yourself for granted, then those around you are more likely to make the same mistake. Just as you understand that the love you need—and deserve to get—remains one of life's great treasures, you must not forget that the love you have to *give* is a gift beyond price.

The truth is, the only unconditional love you're likely to encounter in this life is what you get from your dog. Don't take me wrong: the joy I get from taking care of my dog Adam is beyond my wildest expectations. I never understood people who talked baby talk to their pets until I got one.

But people need something back, and it's more complicated than the simple kinds of care that pets so completely appreciate.

As far as I can tell, finding out that you can nurture yourself *and* nurture others—despite all the demands of your particular circumstances—is one of the biggest rewards of tapping your Feminine Force.

The giving and getting of genuine love is a true perpetual motion machine, because as love nourishes you and those you care about, it gains strength itself. A good marriage takes work, yes, but the love you put into it returns to you and replenishes itself—over and over and over.

When you say, "To heck with it. I can *so* do it. I can focus on my goals and work toward them *and* be generous with my love all at the same time," you tap capabilities and discover depths of character you may not have even known you had.

To discover them is to use your Feminine Force to the fullest.

The Force Is with You

"To assume that I am being discriminated against assumes that I am being victimized. And I am not a victim."

—BARBRA STREISAND

It was your average Monday afternoon during the years when I was CEO of La Prairie and Robert was Secretary of Commerce. I'd taken the shuttle from D.C. to New York early in the morning and gone straight to the office. At about four P.M. I decided it was time to go home and regroup for my dinner date that night.

Because my apartment was being renovated, home that month was a suite at the Barbizon Hotel. Lugging my briefcase—which always weighs about twenty pounds once I load it up with my file folders, my agenda, and my telephone—I breathed a sigh of relief as the Barbizon's elevator finally stopped at the twenty-sixth floor. That was where my small suite was located.

As I got out into the hallway with my purse already open and key in hand, I stepped aside so a well-dressed man wearing a parka and carrying a camera bag could get by me and into the elevator. I had already turned to put the key in my door, which was about three feet to the right, when I heard the elevator doors close.

And then I heard a male voice.

"Be quiet," the voice growled, "and get into that room."

I froze.

Whoever he was, he was standing so close to me I could feel his breath on my neck.

I will never forget those words, and how they chilled me to the bone.

It was then that my inner voice said to me, calmly, "Is this where you're going to die, Georgette?"

"No," it answered swiftly. I reached down and felt inside for that Force with a need I had never known. At this moment my very survival depended on it. This was my true hour of need. And my Feminine Force responded as intensely as I called it, focusing with a laser-like strength and concentration. First it calmed my mind, body, and emotions. And then it coached me to stay absolutely alert for an opening that would allow me to take control of the situation. I turned around. As I had suspected, the voice belonged to the man in the parka. You can always hear a pin drop in the tiny, intimate hallway of the twenty-sixth floor of the Barbizon Hotel. But at that moment it had never been quieter.

"Be quiet, and get into the room," the man repeated.

He was clearly agitated, and becoming even more agitated.

By now, my life was flashing before me. I thought of Robert. I thought of all the things I'd never taken the time to say to my mother. I tried to remember the last time I'd seen my grandmother. There was so much more I wanted to share with my family.

"This is no time to reminisce, kid," my inner voice cut in sharply. "Let's pay attention here."

Instinctively, I tried to buy some time. When it looks as if your time is up, what else do you do? So, trying to keep a lid on my terror, I turned and started fiddling with my key.

"It's stuck," I said to my assailant. "If you want to open the door, why don't you try it?"

Then I got out of his way. I knew the door would open the minute he turned the key, and when it did, I didn't want to make it easy for him to throw me inside my room.

Almost as soon as I'd finished that thought he was standing in the open doorway.

"Get in there," he said.

I stepped back again, trying to contain my fear and straining to think on my feet. Although I was terrified, I realized that everything around me had come into sharp focus. I was all eyes, all ears. My head felt absolutely clear. I stood, primed, trying to read the tiny noises from the elevator: did that rattle mean it would stop here? The noise died away. *Silence.*

I instinctively knew that my chances of survival were better out in the hallway than they were if I got cornered in my room.

"I'm not going in there with you," I said, listening very carefully to the inner coaching I was getting. I couldn't afford to lose either my cool or this connection to the voice inside. Somehow, I had to stay in complete control of my role in this scene—even if the other guy had a weapon.

"Let's understand each other," I went on. "I am not going in that room. But I *am* prepared to give you all my money and all my jewelry. Let's understand each other right now."

With that, he unzipped the camera case he was carrying, took out a large gun, and pointed it at me.

"Lady, I don't want to have to shoot you."

I flinched. The gun seemed enormous, but it didn't really come as a surprise.

"I don't want you to shoot me, either," I said, "but I'm not going anywhere with you. I'm going to give you what you came for, right here."

Just then, my assailant's body language seemed to change. He was the one holding the gun, but suddenly he seemed to slump a little. He seemed confused. Clearly, my refusal to obey his orders and the fact that I was not hysterical but calm and speaking clearly and rationally were not part of his game plan. So his initial plan had failed. And he had no Plan B. By staying in control of *myself*, I had somehow taken control of the situation. I had found the opening my Feminine Force had alerted me to. And now I was going to run with it.

"From here on, I am going to read this situation right," I coached myself. "I am going to buy time and think on my feet. I am not going to die."

As slowly and methodically as possible, I began to take off each individual piece of jewelry. As I did, I described it in detail, told him how much it was worth, and dropped it into my briefcase. I wanted the man with the gun to see that he was going to get something from me. I pointed out how easy these things would be to fence, as the rest of my brain tried to figure out my next step.

Basically, I had three options: I could wait for the elevator doors to open again. I could try to disarm the man and make for the stairs. Or I could rush for my room and get the door shut before he fired. Meanwhile, my eyes kept darting from door to closed door, hoping someone else here had heard, that another door would open. *Nothing.*

The elevator was a long shot. So were the odds I could safely lock myself in my room. My best shot would be to try to disarm him in some way, so I devised a plan using my twenty-pound bag.

By this time, I had finished describing my earrings, my ring, my wedding band, and my watch, and putting each of them into my briefcase. All that was left was to tell the man exactly how much cash I had in my wallet, and point out exactly where he would find it.

I did that, and my attacker still didn't move.

"Okay, kid," said my inner voice, "this is it. This is what you're going to do. He doesn't know how heavy this bag is. When he takes it, it should throw him a little off balance. That's the moment you shove him and make a run for it."

No sooner had I finished the thought than the elevator door opened. There were four people in it. I threw the bag at my assailant, who grabbed it as I dove for the elevator. He was turning toward the stairs as I hit the "close door" button.

The four men on the elevator simply froze. "I was mugged," I gasped. Suddenly I found myself shaking all over. "He had a gun. He's getting away!"

Not one of them said a word. The elevator stopped at their floor, and they made their exit—leaving me to ride back down to the lobby where I ran to the desk. I alerted hotel security, and called the police. I kept telling them to block the exits, because the mugger was headed down a stairwell.

Did they catch him? No. I'm sorry to say that they never did. But that wasn't the important thing. The important thing was that I'd escaped alive. Deeply shaken, but otherwise unhurt.

"Robert," I told my husband later, "God must have been on that elevator."

"Yes," Robert said. "And what's more, He was on time!"

I most certainly hope you never get mugged, and if we were able to go back and change the past, that afternoon in the Barbizon would be one of the first things I'd change. But the truth is, no matter how far you come, no matter how wise and joyful and powerful you become, life will always be ready to deal you the unexpected blow. Those confrontations won't necessarily be life-threatening. Whatever they turn out to be, the point is not that you've been dealt that blow. The point is how you handle it. The important thing is to learn that you can make it through, that you can survive, and that you can flourish—regardless.

God willing, you'll never find yourself at the wrong end of a gun. But at some point, and usually more than once in our lives, almost every one of us has to face the kinds of crises that bring real heartache with them. My family arrived at such a point about eight years ago, when it became apparent to us that my brother George had a serious problem with alcohol.

Many people realize a loved one has a problem with alcohol when that person becomes mean and violent. But that wasn't George. My brother always has been and always will be generous and kind. But gradually, the family noticed that we could no longer communicate with him.

It wasn't for want of trying. But over time, George gradually lost his ability to finish a thought. He was always late, he no longer seemed to take anything very seriously, and he couldn't commit to the simplest things. In fact, he seemed to be incapable of following through on anything. He seemed to be wandering.

George wasn't an alcoholic who went through a personality change when he drank. I always knew when G.B. started drinking, because one minute his eyes would be his own and the very next minute they'd be glazed over like an animal's. To me, G.B. went from being Dr. Jekyll to being Mr. Hyde.

But George was entirely different. We knew that he was getting harder and harder to communicate with. We knew that we missed him. We knew we simply weren't able to get through.

It's possible that I was so close to my brother that I was in denial of the situation. Mother was the one who finally suspected alcoholism as the cause. And by that time, George had been an alcoholic for many years.

Mother confronted George and that's when the trouble really started. Violent arguments erupted between the two of them. George denied he had an alcohol problem while Mother insisted he did. Two people who loved each other were suddenly at each other's throats, and their vicious cycle of accusations and denials gradually drew the rest of us in. Suddenly, we were all arguing with each other about what was going on with George and what to do about him.

We were all shocked. We never fight. We are a close and harmonious family. There was an ominous, tangible sense that something was very wrong. Our whole world was disoriented, out of kilter. The situation finally became so traumatic for me that I managed to rouse myself out of my hurt and confusion long enough to realize that action was required.

I consulted with my mother and my sisters. What we had to do was painful. We all agreed. Never has exercising Feminine Force been so difficult—or so necessary. I volunteered to take the lead.

I called George in Los Angeles.

He was sober at the time, so he answered and he listened.

The conversation we had that day was a brief one. But it will be branded in my memory for the rest of my life.

"George," I began, "I love you and I will always love you. But I can't talk to you any more. I have to let go of you. The pain of watching what you're doing to yourself is affecting my life and my well-being. It's affecting the well-being of the entire family. You know we all love you and now we simply cannot bear to stand back and watch you self-destruct. We've had to face some hard facts. We've realized we can't help you, because you don't want to help yourself. More than anything we want to help you, but the truth is, we can't. So what we have to do is save ourselves."

I drew a deep breath. *"I love you,"* I continued, *"but I can't go on like this. I will not speak to you again. I have to cut you out of my life. The rest of the family has made the same decision."*

This was probably the most painful day of my life. I choked back my tears to continue.

"If and when the day comes that you are prepared to say, 'I am an alcoholic, and I need help,' that is a phone call I will take, and the help will be there. Otherwise, do not call me again. Do not call the rest of the family again."

And then I hung up.

A year passed. I didn't speak to George. None of us spoke to George. There was a terrible emptiness in my life where my relationship with my brother had been. Gone was the accepting, gentle presence and voice I'd connected with in a phone call or in person for almost every day of my life. Gone was the brother who had accepted me when I'd shown up out of the blue to share his California apartment. Gone was the friend and companion who'd been at my side through the worst times with G.B. Although I didn't yet know it, the two of them had done a lot of drinking together. There was so much we were not able to share, including my marriage to Robert Mosbacher. I cannot even count the times I had to curb that reflex to pick up the phone and dial that number in California I knew almost as well as my own, or even to ask people who were in touch, "How's George doing?" I wondered what he was doing. Was he in trouble? Were things getting worse? What would become of him?

I tried to blot those questions out of my mind.

One year later, in April of 1985, the telephone rang at our house in Houston. At that time, Robert and I had been married for about a month.

"Hi," said the familiar voice. "This is George." There was the briefest pause. "I'm an alcoholic, and I need help.

"I watched a show last night on television about alcoholism," he continued. "They said, 'If you can answer yes to any of the following questions, you're probably an alcoholic.'

"I answered yes to all of them."

"George. Where are you?" I asked. He told me he was at home.

"Don't move. I'm going to call you right back."

I hung up and dialed Lyn's number. Lyn was still married to Vlad then.

First I told Lyn what had happened. And then Lyn handed the phone to my brother-in-law.

"Vlad, what is the best substance abuse treatment center in America for him to go to?" I asked.

Vlad told me that the best place he knew of was Hazelden, in Minnesota.

I said, "Vlad, I need help. I've got to get George in there."

Vlad called Hazelden and called me back. Then I called George, who was still sitting next to the phone, and told him I was arranging to fly him to a treatment center.

"The clinic is in Minnesota," I said. "Stay where you are. We're setting it all up and I'll get back to you."

He was nervous and frightened, but grateful and ready to go.

Vlad, Lyn, and I called Hazelden again for a conference. The Hazelden people asked us if George was ready to commit himself to the thirty-day treatment program, because that commitment was a prerequisite. And we were honestly able to say that he was. I was shaking. Then they told us that he was accepted, and that he should fly to Minnesota immediately.

Next I dialed the travel agency and bought George a ticket, and then set up for the Hazelden people to meet him at the other end.

I called my brother and told him he had a pre-paid ticket to Minnesota. Then I called a friend of mine in L.A. and asked him to please see George to the plane. Since his flight stopped in Chicago, where he had to change planes, Vlad, Lyn, and I decided Vlad would be there to make sure George got on that connecting flight to the clinic. Vlad saw George successfully off to Minnesota, and when he landed, someone from the clinic met my brother at the airline gate.

George's recovery was his own, but in every way, that effort was a team effort. Each member of our family had to agree to have a series of individual counseling sessions with Hazelden during the course of George's thirty-day program. As usual, we were all in different parts of the country. We were all prepared to travel to Minnesota. We would have done *anything* for George. But as it happened, that wasn't necessary and we were able to consult by telephone.

I can also still remember my own counseling sessions with Hazelden as if they'd happened yesterday. The experience was both terrifying and cathartic. The terror came as George's counselor told me some of the things that George had told him about his childhood and youth. I realized that many of my brother's tales of things we did and places we went were pure fantasy. After all, I had been there, too. It was completely sobering to actually confront the true depth of the abyss that alcoholism created in my brother's life. Even though I myself had been married to a man with an alcohol problem, I had not been able to recognize the same problem in my own brother. I had to face facts. We all did. And that's how the catharsis came.

During the sessions, George himself seemed to be disoriented. His account of what it was like to withdraw from alcohol dependency broke my heart. And every family member came away from the counseling sessions feeling the same way I did.

But at the same time, I was grateful that I had created the material resources that allowed me to give my brother the financial support he needed to heal. I was relieved that I had been able to tap that force to rally my family to make the terrifying and painful decision to cut off contact with George for that long year. Never have I felt Feminine Force so deeply.

George's thirty-day treatment program was successful. The man who emerged from that clinic was the brother I had always known. The wandering, evasive, angry stranger was gone for good. And, as of this writing, my brother has been a recovering alcoholic for eight precious years.

These days, George often tells the story of that flight he took to Minnesota with nothing in his pocket but a single hundred-dollar bill supplied by Vlad in Chicago when George realized he had left home without a cent in his pocket. When the flight attendant came around, my brother decided it was time for one last drink, but he couldn't get it because the flight attendant couldn't make change. When George realized he couldn't have the drink, he panicked. So he stood up and went from passenger to passenger down the whole length of the plane, looking for the change.

No one had it.

Terrified, he sat back down in his seat.

The fact that he was an alcoholic had finally sunk in one hundred percent. He was shaking. He was sweating. He had to completely face the fact he couldn't help himself. He would have done *anything* for that drink. He was truly desperate. He *was* an alcoholic. He was on his way to a place where he would have to confront that reality in every detail and throw himself upon the mercy of people who could help him help himself. That was the right place to be. He hadn't hit rock bottom yet, but he was sinking fast. It was time to fight his way back to the surface.

These days, my brother tells that story as a story of triumph. It was a moment of epiphany in his life. That's when he saw, with absolute clarity, exactly where he was and exactly where he had to go.

But I still can't hear or think of that story without being moved to tears all over again.

*　　*　　*

During George's month at Hazelden, when he was not allowed to see anyone beyond the four walls of the clinic, I sent him a needlepoint pillow with the Serenity Prayer on it.

"God, give us grace to accept with serenity the things that cannot be changed, courage to change the things which should be changed, and the wisdom to distinguish the one from the other," the brightly colored pillow said.

Hazelden didn't allow its patients to simply accept packages. All mail was always opened during group therapy to ensure no one slipped liquor or drugs inside. So when my package arrived, George opened it in front of his group—a very moving moment which he says he's never forgotten.

Reflecting on the ordeal of recovery eight years later, my brother says he endured it not just for himself, but for his son, Shaun. When George realized he was alcoholic, he also realized that he was just one step away from being on the street. Here he had a law degree and a wonderful education he'd achieved through academic scholarships, and he had almost thrown it all away. He realized that for all practical purposes, the only thing that kept him from ending up on skid row was the fact that he had a family who loved him and supported him. And if anything happened to him, what would happen to Shaun? George already knew what it was like to grow up without a father, and without financial resources. He had decided that for both their sakes, it was time to stare down his demons.

This experience brought home to me once again what strength of character my brother really has. Eight years later, he is not only a responsible, productive adult and a good parent. He is also a man who counsels other recovering alcoholics—other people who got into the same kind of trouble he did. I tell my mother how lucky she is. She has four children who are all decent, productive human beings. I tell her she must have done something right! And I thank her for imbuing the Feminine Force in me.

I'll never, ever forget the day that I told George "I won't speak to you again." This was my *brother*, someone I spoke to almost every single day. And nearly a year went by before I heard from him again.

That year put a strain on all the family. But we all pulled together.

And we've all *stayed* together. I see the various members of our clan on a regular basis, and talk to them all the time on the telephone. And once a year we have a big family reunion. We've gone on a cruise and to Las Vegas. We've gone to Disneyworld. We even dress up in the same outfits. Those reunions I count among my happiest experiences. Just as the people we love can give us the greatest pain, they give us the greatest joy.

Someday, I'll be the oldest, the matriarch of my family. I hope one day I'll be Great-great-aunt Georgette to my brother's and sisters' great-grandchildren.

And I'll continue to practice the principles of Feminine Force until the day I die. I know that if you do the same, you'll begin to experience more joy, success, and love in *your* life—just as I have. You will continually delight in your freedom to reinvent yourself, to grow, and to deal with all those surprises that inevitably lie around the corner.

Though disappointments will still hurt you—they hurt *me* just as deeply—they won't take you as far down as they once did. You'll rebound faster. You'll find, as I have, that you may still be wounded, but you won't be crippled. You may occasionally find that you've gotten detoured, but you'll know you'll never be lost.

As long as you never stop listening to your inner voice, you will never forget you're the hero of your own life. Not the victim or the beneficiary of someone else's. You have what it takes to get the results you want, step by step by step. And you'll have *earned* what you get.

If I could leave you with just one thought, it would be this one: Success isn't a dot at the end of a road map. It's more like a series of doors to open. There is always another one to get through, and the process of getting through that next door is at once more challenging *and* more rewarding than the process of getting through the last.

Naturally, I wouldn't want anyone ever to have to turn her back on her brother—however temporarily. But that ordeal taught me how deep and tight the bonds of love and loyalty really go. And I'd never wish a gun-point mugging on anyone, for any reason. But that experience turned out to be deeply life-affirming. It showed me a facet of Feminine Force I had assumed existed, but had never experienced. It showed me that my Feminine Force could actually keep me *alive*. It refocused my Feminine Force in an entirely new way. It showed me that refusing to be a victim wasn't just the most important step toward financial, emotional, and professional security, but that it could play a vital role in my very survival.

Not every day brings such wrenching drama, thank heaven. My Feminine Force gets its most consistent workout in the ordinary, day-to-day work of my life—keeping my business growing and thriving day after ordinary day.

Remember the phone booth on the corner? Remember how there was no one to call? These days, no matter how well I work that problem, once in a while I still want to dash out and pick up a phone.

The difference is, the phone I pick up these days isn't on the corner. It's on the edge of my desk or in my car.

And although there are now many, many supportive and caring people in my address book, the buck still stops with me. And that's the way I like it. As the cliché goes, I'm the CEO of my own life. And there's no higher authority, at least not in human form. Sure, life is filled with sharing and support. But no matter how loving, kind, and wonderful the person or persons you choose to share it with may be, if you leave the responsibility for your happiness, financial security, or well-being to any one of them, then YOU ARE NOT FREE!

That's why the first person I call on my call list today is *me*. I call on my inner strength, my Feminine Force, to get me through. I now know that whatever happens in life, I can handle it. I can realistically look for those happy endings, and I will usually find them.

As a matter of fact, now that I've found my Feminine Force I don't think I'll ever find myself on that corner again. When you practice Feminine Force, the challenge of your life no longer lies in wrestling with the bad things that come your way. The challenge lies in finding out exactly how *good* things can be. And sometimes the growth you experience is the sort you never expected. As you grow, you evolve, and your goals change accordingly. When I was young, my goal in life was simply to expand my horizons and move past my modest upbringing to help my family and make life easier. But I never dreamed what all of those things would turn out to be. My list of goals is still definitely "in progress." The doors I'm opening this year are doors I never would have dreamed I was going to open even a few years ago. Each door leads to the next one. The only way to get to the next door is to open the first one. And you have to walk up to that door all by yourself.

The doors *I* choose to open can still surprise my own husband—even after nearly ten years of marriage.

One evening, when we were attending a big cocktail reception in Washington, Art Buchwald walked up to Robert and me. He chatted a bit, asked how we were, then said, "I can't believe we keep missing each other. You two are never going to invite me to dinner again—I haven't been able to accept *one* of your invitations. I really feel bad about it. I hope you haven't given up on me!"

I replied, "Art, I don't give up! I just don't *hear* 'no.' You can say 'no' as many times as you want, and I'll keep inviting you!"

Everyone laughed. We chatted a bit more, then Art moved on, and my husband turned to me.

"Well," he said, "I'm almost afraid to ask, but how do you know Art Buchwald?"

I said, "I *don't*, honey. I've never met him before."

Robert froze. He was absolutely mortified. This was worse than Lou Dobbs!

"Well, it's true, I don't know him," I said reassuringly, "but, honey, he doesn't *know* that. I've invited him to dinner so many times, he probably doesn't *know* we don't know him!"

The doors *you* open may be different ones. Your journey is your own, but whatever new places your doors lead you to, one thing is certain. When you practice Feminine Force, you will be strong no matter what situation confronts you. You will find the strength you need to prevail, to prosper, to grow, to enjoy life, and to be happy.

Now reach out, open that door, and start creating the life you deserve!

I will never be able to thank my Grandmother Mary enough for those nights at the Baltimore & Ohio railroad, where, by example, I learned of the existence of the Feminine Force. Or Mother, for the way she used that same Force to stare down life's challenges, or Baba, for the way Feminine Force truly permeated every detail of every decision she ever made. If you had no such examples—and also if you did—it is my humble hope that this book will have offered you the incomparable life lessons that were passed down to me.

The late psychiatrist Carl Rogers once said, "Through accepting my own individuality, which I can't expect everyone else to recognize and pat me on the back for, I shape my goals and desires. I am not compelled to be simply a creature of others, molded by their experiences or shaped by their demands."

Accept your individuality, glory in it. No woman should accept any less. But whatever you do . . .

May the Force be with you!

Georgette Mosbacher's

Feminine Force Principles

1   I love being a woman.

2   I am totally responsible for myself—and know this is the one and only path to true happiness, success, and freedom.

3   Life isn't fair—so what?

4   I have the courage to take the first small step and I know it will illuminate the next one.

5   I start by accepting my reality. Then I *change* it.

6   I can buy my own crystal and china and feather my own nest—with or without a man.

7   When facing a challenge, I create solutions and ask, "What do I have to lose?" and "What's the worst thing that can happen?"

8   I do not tolerate abuse of any kind.

9   I don't depend on luck—I make my own.

10   I view the success of others as a symbol of what I can achieve.

11   I have many resources and all of them hold potential.

12   I'm proud of my ability to express affection.

13   My appearance is talking and I like what it is saying.

14   I keep some money in a place that's only known to me.

15   Fidelity, trust, and respect are honored in my marriage.

16   Sure, I do windows and I make coffee . . . I do whatever is necessary to get to the next step and succeed.

17   I know whom to ask, when to ask, and how to ask.

18   Having it all may mean having a few extra pounds.

19   Network, network, network!

20   Entrusting my financial security to anyone else is an unacceptable risk.

21   I always find a way to turn a negative into a positive.

22   I deserve to enjoy my life and have fun—and I don't feel guilty about it!!

23   I have the ability to be at ease in any situation.

24   I do not need to lean on others in order to create the life I choose for myself.

25   I expect to be treated like a lady.

26   I know how to give and receive compliments.

27   I have the confidence to say "Yes, now"—and I know how to say "no."

28   I can compromise . . . and still win.

29   I never hesitate to ask him to dance.

30   I value my self, not my position.

31   I am my own provider.

32   Any goal is a worthy goal.

33   When I look my personal best, I am powerful.

34   Manicures, pedicures, facials, hair care, exercise, make-up—I call these necessities, not luxuries. And I find a way to have them, even if I do it myself.

35   I always do a little more than is required.

36   I always work the problem.

37 Where I come from doesn't have to define me.

38 I believe this is a woman's world—and a man's world.

39 I take risks—calculated risks.

40 I do my homework.

41 I can talk my way through any "no."

42 I don't waste time thinking, "Am I doing it right?" I say, "Am I doing it?"

43 I make mistakes—so what?

44 Regardless of the difficulties in my life, I will *never* become a victim.

45 I know I can't be a *winner* and a *whiner* at the same time. And I'm a *winner*.

46 I never look back.

47 I may not always see it from where I'm standing, but I know there is always something better just around the corner.

48 I put one foot in front of the other until I get there.

49 I finish the job—then move on.

50 Self-pity is a poor excuse for not moving forward.

51 There is dignity in any work that I do.

52 When I move from A to B to C to D, I can achieve my goals.

53 I don't have to map out the rest of my life "right now."

54 There may be moments when I am scared. But I can't be stopped.

55 I achieve success by not accepting failure.

56 I will not love a man who doesn't cherish me.

57 I know how to interest a man.

58 I'm not afraid to show a man all of who I am.

59 I love having time alone.

60 I control the decisions about sex in my life—and I take responsibility for my body.

61 I deserve love and affection and I can have it.

62 I don't waste my valuable time fretting or fighting over the "small stuff."

63 I can have style without money. And I can have money if I choose to make that a goal.

64 I know hard work is always rewarded.

65 I pack my own parachute.

66 They can call me whatever they want—I know who I am.

67 I trust my instincts to do what is necessary to succeed in any situation.

68 Real guts are nothing more than making my inner voice stronger than the voice of my fear.

69 As God is my witness, I'll never be *helpless* again.

70 My expectations always exceed my circumstances.

71 I know that every day of my life is full of opportunity and possibilities.

72 The Force is with me.

Photo Credits

Michael Halsband: 18
Horst: 21, 34, 35
Warren Huber: 10
John Martini: 32
Mosbacher Collection: 2, 3, 4, 5, 6, 7, 8, 11, 12, 13, 14, 16, 22, 23, 25,
    26, 27, 29, 30, 31
Paul Schumach: 15
Michael D. Shutko: 9
© Star Black: 17
Stark's Studio: 1
© Jeanne Trudeau: 20
Shonna Valeska: 33
The Walt Disney Collection (© 1992): 19
Official White House Photo: 24, 28